Hymnal: According To The Use Of The Protestant Episcopal Church In The United States Of America

Episcopal Church

Nabu Public Domain Reprints:

You are holding a reproduction of an original work published before 1923 that is in the public domain in the United States of America, and possibly other countries. You may freely copy and distribute this work as no entity (individual or corporate) has a copyright on the body of the work. This book may contain prior copyright references, and library stamps (as most of these works were scanned from library copies). These have been scanned and retained as part of the historical artifact.

This book may have occasional imperfections such as missing or blurred pages, poor pictures, errant marks, etc. that were either part of the original artifact, or were introduced by the scanning process. We believe this work is culturally important, and despite the imperfections, have elected to bring it back into print as part of our continuing commitment to the preservation of printed works worldwide. We appreciate your understanding of the imperfections in the preservation process, and hope you enjoy this valuable book.

HYMNAL:

ACCORDING TO THE USE

OF THE

PROTESTANT EPISCOPAL CHURCH

IN THE

UNITED STATES OF AMERICA.

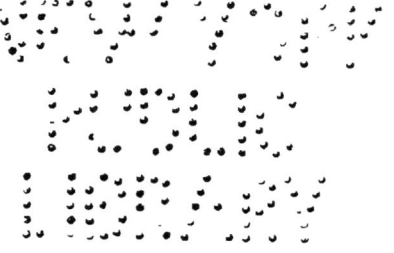

REVISED EDITION.

NEW YORK
E. P. DUTTON AND COMPANY
713 BROADWAY
1877

Entered according to Act of Congress, in the year 1874, by

THE TRUSTEES OF THE FUND FOR THE RELIEF OF WIDOWS AND ORPHANS
OF DECEASED CLERGYMEN, AND OF AGED, INFIRM, AND DISABLED
CLERGYMEN OF THE PROTESTANT EPISCOPAL CHURCH
IN THE UNITED STATES OF AMERICA,

In the Office of the Librarian of Congress, at Washington.

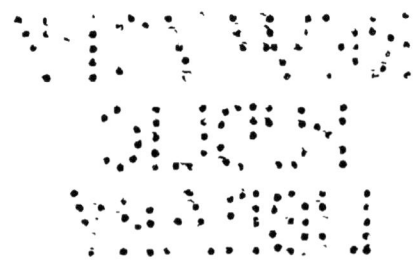

By the Bishops, the Clergy, and the Laity of the Protestant Episcopal Church in the United States of America, in General Convention, held in the year of our Lord one thousand eight hundred and seventy-four, it was

Resolved: That future Editions of the Hymnal shall be printed so as to conform to the revised Edition presented by the joint Committee on the Hymnal, and that no other Hymns be allowed in the public worship of the Church, except the Hymnal as thus revised, and such hymns and psalms as are now ordinarily bound up with the Book of Common Prayer: provided that any Congregation may continue to use the Editions of the Hymnal heretofore published, until further action of the Convention.

Certificate.

I do hereby certify that this edition of the Revised Hymnal, having been by me compared with and corrected by the Standard Book, as the General Convention has directed, is permitted to be published accordingly.

On behalf of the Trustees of the Fund for the Relief of Widows and Orphans of deceased Clergymen, and of aged, infirm, and disabled Clergymen.

LLOYD W. WELLS, *Sec'y of the Board of Trustees.*

General Convention of the Protestant Episcopal Church.

HOUSE OF BISHOPS.

BALTIMORE, MD., *October, 1871.*

Resolved: That this Hymnal shall not be bound up with the Book of Common Prayer, until order to that effect shall be taken by the General Convention.

NEW YORK, *October, 1874.*

Resolved: That this Hymnal now revised and adopted shall be free to be printed and published by all responsible publishers, who shall obtain a license to that effect from the Trustees of the Fund for the Relief of Widows and Orphans of deceased Clergymen, and of aged, infirm, and disabled Clergymen, and who shall assure to such Trustees a payment, to be applied for the uses of said fund, equivalent to ten per cent. upon the retail selling price: and that the copyright of the Revised Hymnal shall vest in said Trustees, subject, however, to the farther order of this Convention: Also that the Trustees be authorized to superintend the revision and publication of the revised editions of the Hymnal, with power to make the typographical and literary changes necessary to conform it to the Committee's Report made to this Convention.

From the Journal.

Attest:

HENRY C. POTTER, *Secretary of the House of Bishops.*

Concurred in by the House of Deputies.

Attest:

WILLIAM STEVENS PERRY, *Secretary.*

CANON 22 OF TITLE 1 OF THE DIGEST.

Of Church Music.

§ 1. The Selections of the Psalms in Metre, and Hymns, which are set forth by authority, and Anthems in the words of Holy Scripture, are allowed to be sung in all Congregations of this Church before and after Morning and Evening Prayer, and also before and after Sermons, at the discretion of the Minister, whose duty it shall be, by standing directions, or from time to time, to appoint such authorized Psalms, Hymns, or Anthems as are to be sung.

§ 2. It shall be the duty of every Minister of this Church, with such assistance as he may see fit to employ from persons skilled in music, to give order concerning the tunes to be sung at any time in his church; and especially, it shall be his duty to suppress all light and unseemly music, and all indecency and irreverence in the performance, by which vain and ungodly persons profane the service of the Sanctuary.

Adopted in General Convention, October 1874.

Attest:
HENRY C. POTTER, *Sec'y of the House of Bishops.*
WILLIAM STEVENS PERRY, *Sec'y of the House of Deputies,*
 General Convention of Protestant Episcopal Church.

TABLE OF SUBJECTS.

I. THE CHRISTIAN YEAR—   HYMN.
- Advent 1– 15
- Christmas 16– 27
- End of the Year 28– 29
- New Year 30– 31
- Circumcision 32– 33
- Epiphany 34– 47
- Ash Wednesday and Lent 48– 71
- Palm Sunday and Passion Week 72– 81
- Good Friday 82– 89
- Easter Even 90– 97
- Easter 98–112
- Ascension 113–124
- Whitsuntide 125–137
- Trinity Sunday 138–146
- The Lord's Day 147–169
- Ember Days 170–171
- Rogation Days 172–174
- Other Holy Days 175–182

II. THE COMMUNION OF SAINTS 183–189

III. THE CHURCH 190–202

IV. THE SACRAMENTS—
- The Lord's Supper 203–211
- Baptism 212–218

V. OFFICES OF THE CHURCH—
- Catechism 219–233
- Confirmation 234–246
- Holy Matrimony 247–248
- Visitation of the Sick 249–257
- Burial of the Dead 258–261

TABLE OF SUBJECTS.

	HYMN.
Burial of a Child	262–263
For Those at Sea	264–269
Ordination or Institution of Ministers	270–273
Consecration of Bishops	274
Laying of a Corner-Stone	275–276
Consecration of Churches and Chapels	277–282

VI.	MISSIONS AND CHARITIES	283–300

VII. SPECIAL SEASONS—

Thanksgiving and Harvest-Home	301–306
National Festivals	307–309
National Fasts	310–313
Family Worship	314–327
Morning	328–332
Evening	333–352
The Seven Hours	353–359

VIII.	THE HOLY SCRIPTURES	360–368
IX.	REDEMPTION	369–385

X. THE CHRISTIAN LIFE—

Repentance	386–389
Faith	390–398
Prayer	399–404
Praise	405–433
Self-consecration	434–435
Trust	436–446
Hope	447–453
Love	454–461
Joy	462–464
Humility	465–466
Peace	467–468
Courage	469–473
Action	474–479

XI.	THE JUDGMENT	480–484
XII.	HEAVEN	485–497
XIII.	MISCELLANEOUS	498–532

HYMNS.

I. THE CHRISTIAN YEAR.

ADVENT.

1 *"Behold, he cometh with clouds, and every*   [8s. 7s. 4.
eye shall see him."

LO, he comes, with clouds descending,
  Once for favour'd sinners slain;
Thousand thousand saints attending
  Swell the triumph of his train;
    Alleluia!
Christ, the Lord, returns to reign.

2 Every eye shall now behold him,
  Robed in dreadful majesty;
Those who set at nought and sold him,
  Pierced, and nail'd him to the tree,
    Deeply wailing,
Shall the true Messiah see.

3 Every island, sea, and mountain,
   Heaven and earth, shall flee away:
All who hate him must, confounded,
   Hear the trump proclaim the day;
     Come to judgment,
Come to judgment, come away.

4 Now redemption, long expected,
   See in solemn pomp appear:
All his saints, by men rejected,
   Now shall meet him in the air:
     Alleluia!
See the day of God appear.

5 Yea, Amen; let all adore thee,
   High on thine eternal throne:
Saviour, take the power and glory;
   Claim the kingdom for thine own.
     O come quickly!
Alleluia!   Come, Lord, come!

2   *"He cometh to judge the earth."*   [L. M.

THE Lord will come: the earth shall quake,
   The hills their fixèd seat forsake;
And, withering from the vault of night,
The stars withdraw their feeble light.

2 The Lord will come: but not the same
   As once in lowly form he came,
A silent Lamb to slaughter led,
The bruised, the suffering, and the dead.

3 The Lord will com'. a dreadful form,
With wreath of flame, and robe of storm,
On cherub wings, and wings of wind,
Anointed Judge of human-kind.

4 Can this be he who wont to stray
A pilgrim on the world's highway;
By power oppress'd, and mock'd by pride,
O God! is this the Crucified?

5 Go, tyrants, to the rocks complain;
Go, seek the mountain's cleft in vain;
But faith, victorious o'er the tomb,
Shall sing for joy, The Lord is come.

3 *"They shall perish, but thou shalt endure."* [L. M

THAT day of wrath, that dreadful day,
When heaven and earth shall pass away,
What power shall be the sinner's stay?
How shall he meet that dreadful day?

2 When, shrivelling like a parchèd scroll,
The flaming heavens together roll,
When louder yet, and yet more dread,
Swells the high trump that wakes the dead.

3 O! on that day, that wrathful day,
When man to judgment wakes from clay,
Be thou, O Christ, the sinner's stay,
Though heaven and earth shall pass away.

4 *"Blessed is he that cometh in the name of the Lord; Hosanna in the highest."* [L. M
with Chorus.

HOSANNA to the living Lord!
Hosanna to the incarnate Word!
To Christ, Creator, Saviour, King,
Let earth, let heaven, Hosanna sing.
    Hosanna, Lord! Hosanna in the highest!

2 Hosanna, Lord! thine angels cry;
Hosanna, Lord! thy saints reply;
Above, beneath us, and around,
The dead and living swell the sound;
    Hosanna, Lord! Hosanna in the highest!

3 O Saviour, with protecting care,
Return to this thy house of prayer:
Assembled in thy sacred name,
Where we thy parting promise claim:
    Hosanna, Lord! Hosanna in the highest!

4 But, chiefest, in our cleansèd breast,
Eternal! bid thy Spirit rest;
And make our secret soul to be
A temple pure, and worthy thee.
    Hosanna, Lord! Hosanna in the highest!

5 So in the last and dreadful day,
When earth and heaven shall melt away,
Thy flock, redeemed from sinful stain,
Shall swell the sound of praise again.
    Hosanna, Lord! Hosanna in the highest!

5   *"Behold the Bridegroom cometh."*   [7s. 6s.
Double.

REJOICE, rejoice, believers!
  And let your lights appear;
The evening is advancing,
  And darker night is near.
The Bridegroom is arising,
  And soon he will draw nigh;
Up! pray, and watch, and wrestle!
  At midnight comes the cry.

2 See that your lamps are burning,
  Replenish them with oil;
Look now for your salvation,
  The end of sin and toil.
The watchers on the mountain
  Proclaim the Bridegroom near,
Go meet him as he cometh,
  With alleluias clear.

3 O wise and holy virgins,
  Now raise your voices higher,
Till, in your jubilations
  Ye meet the angel choir.
The marriage-feast is waiting,
  The gates wide open stand;
Up, up, ye heirs of glory!
  The Bridegroom is at hand.

4 Our hope and expectation,
  O Jesus, now appear;
Arise, thou Sun so longed for,
  O'er this benighted sphere!

With hearts and hands uplifted,
We plead, O Lord, to see
The day of earth's redemption,
And ever be with thee!

6   *"The Lord said unto my Lord, Sit thou on my*   [SIX 8s
*right hand, until I make thine enemies thy
footstool."*

From the cx. Psalm.

THE Lord unto my Lord thus spake:
"Till I thy foes thy footstool make,
  Sit thou in state at my right hand:
Supreme in Sion thou shalt be,
And all thy proud opposers see
  Subjected to thy just command.

2 "Thee, in thy power's triumphant day,
The willing people shall obey;
  And, when thy rising beams they view,
Shall all (redeem'd from error's night)
Appear more numerous and bright
  Than crystal drops of morning dew."

3 The Lord hath sworn, nor sworn in vain,
That, like Melchizedek's, thy reign
  And priesthood shall no period see;
Anointed Prince! thou, bending low,
Shalt drink where darkest torrents flow,
  Then raise thy head in victory!

7 *"Thy kingdom come."*

THY kingdom come, O God,
　Thy reign, O Christ, begin;
Break with thine iron rod
　The tyrannies of sin.

2 Where is thy rule of peace,
　And purity, and love?
When shall all hatred cease,
　As in the realms above?

3 When comes the promised time
　That war shall be no more,
Oppression, lust, and crime
　Shall flee thy face before?

4 We pray thee, Lord, arise,
　And come in thy great might;
Revive our longing eyes,
　Which languish for thy sight.

5 Men scorn thy sacred name,
　And wolves devour thy fold;
By many deeds of shame
　We learn that love grows cold.

6 O'er heathen lands afar
　Thick darkness broodeth yet:
Arise, O morning Star,
　Arise, and never set.

8 *"Take ye heed; watch and pray; for ye know* [D. C. M.
   not when the time is."

Once more, O Lord, thy sign shall be
  Upon the heavens displayed,
And earth and its inhabitants
  Be terribly afraid:
For, not in weakness clad, thou com'st,
  Our woes, our sins to bear,
But girt with all thy Father's might,
  His judgment to declare.

2 The terrors of that awful day,
  O who can understand?
Or who abide, when thou in wrath
  Shall lift thy holy hand?
The earth shall quake, the sea shall roar,
  The sun in heaven grow pale;
But thou hast sworn, and wilt not change
  Thy faithful shall not fail.

3 Then grant us, Saviour, so to pass
  Our time in trembling here,
That when upon the clouds of heaven
  Thy glory shall appear,
Uplifting high our joyful heads,
  In triumph we may rise,
And enter, with thine angel train,
  Thy palace in the skies.

ADVENT.

9   *"He saith, Surely I come quickly: Amen.*   [Six 8s.
     Even so, come, Lord Jesus."

COME, quickly come, dread Judge of all;
   For, awful though thine advent be,
All shadows from the truth will fall,
   And falsehood die, in sight of thee:
Come, quickly come: for doubt and fear
Like clouds dissolve when thou art near.

2 Come quickly come, great King of all;
   Reign all around us, and within;
Let sin no more our souls enthral,
   Let pain and sorrow die with sin:
Come, quickly come: for thou alone
Canst make thy scattered people one.

3 Come, quickly come, true Life of all;
   The curse of death is on the ground;
On every home his shadows fall,
   On every heart his mark is found:
Come, quickly come: for grief and pain
Can never cloud thy glorious reign.

4 Come, quickly come, sure Light of all,
   For gloomy night broods o'er our way;
And fainting souls begin to fall
   With weary watching for the day:
Come, quickly come: for round thy throne
No eye is blind, no night is known.

10   *"Behold, I stand at the door and knock."*   [7s. 6s. Double.

O JESUS, thou art standing
   Outside the fast-closed door,
In lowly patience waiting
   To pass the threshold o'er:
We bear the name of Christians,
   His name and sign we bear:
O shame, thrice shame upon us,
   To keep him standing there.

2 O Jesus, thou art knocking:
   And lo! that hand is scarr'd,
And thorns thy brow encircle,
   And tears thy face have marr'd:
O love that passeth knowledge,
   So patiently to wait!
O sin that hath no equal,
   So fast to bar the gate!

3 O Jesus, thou art pleading
   In accents meek and low,
"I died for you, my children,
   And will ye treat me so?"
O Lord, with shame and sorrow
   We open now the door:
Dear Saviour, enter, enter,
   And leave us nevermore.

ADVENT.

11 "*Our God shall come, and shall not keep silence.*" [Six 8s.

From the l. Psalm.

THE Lord hath spoke, the mighty God
Hath sent his summons all abroad,
  From dawning light till day declines:
The listening earth his voice hath heard,
And he from Sion hath appeared,
  Where beauty in perfection shines.

2 Our God shall come, and keep no more
Misconstrued silence as before,
  But wasting flames before him send;
Around shall tempests fiercely rage,
Whilst he does heaven and earth engage
  His just tribunal to attend.

12 "*The voice of one crying in the wilderness, Prepare* [L. M.
ye the way of the Lord, make his paths straight."

ON Jordan's bank the Baptist's cry
Announces that the Lord is nigh;
Awake, and hearken, for he brings
Glad tidings of the King of kings.

2 Then cleansed be every breast from sin;
Make straight the way for God within;
Prepare we in our hearts a home,
Where such a mighty guest may come.

3 For thou art our salvation, Lord,
  Our refuge and our great reward;

THE CHRISTIAN YEAR.

  Without thy grace we waste away,
  Like flowers that wither and decay.

4 To heal the sick stretch out thine hand,
 And bid the fallen sinner stand;
 Shine forth, and let thy light restore
 Earth's own true loveliness once more.

5 All praise, Eternal Son, to thee,
 Whose advent doth thy people free;
 Whom with the Father we adore,
 And Holy Ghost for evermore.

13 *"The Redeemer shall come to Zion."* [SIX 8s.

O COME, O come, Emmanuel,
 And ransom captive Israel;
That mourns in lonely exile here,
Until the Son of God appear.
  Rejoice! Rejoice! Emmanuel
  Shall come to thee, O Israel!

2 O come, thou Rod of Jesse, free
 Thine own from Satan's tyranny;
 From depths of hell thy people save,
 And give them victory o'er the grave.
  Rejoice! Rejoice! Emmanuel
  Shall come to thee, O Israel.

3 O come, thou Day-Spring, come and cheer
 Our spirits by thine advent here;

Disperse the gloomy clouds of night,
And death's dark shadows put to flight.
    Rejoice! Rejoice! Emmanuel
    Shall come to thee, O Israel!

4 O come, thou Key of David, come,
And open wide our heavenly home;
Make safe the way that leads on high,
And close the path to misery.
    Rejoice! Rejoice! Emmanuel
    Shall come to thee, O Israel!

5 O come, O come, thou Lord of might;
Who to thy tribes, on Sinai's height,
In ancient times didst give the law,
In cloud, and majesty, and awe.
    Rejoice! Rejoice! Emmanuel
    Shall come to thee, O Israel!

THE ADVENT ANTHEMS.

14   *"The Desire of all nations shall come."*   [SIX 8s.

Dec. 16.—O Sapientia.

O WISDOM! spreading mightily
From out the mouth of God most high,
All nature sweetly ordering,
Within thy paths thy children bring.
    Draw near, O Christ, with us to dwell,
    In mercy save thine Israel.

Dec. 17.—O Adonai.

RULER of Israel, Lord of might,
 Who gavest the law from Sinai's height;
Once in the fiery bush revealed,
With outstretched arm thy chosen shield;
 Draw near, O Christ, with us to dwell,
 In mercy save thine Israel.

Dec. 18.—O Radix Jesse.

O ROOT of Jesse! Ensign thou!
 To whom all Gentile kings shall bow,
From depths of hell thy people save,
And give them victory o'er the grave.
 Draw near, O Christ, with us to dwell,
 In mercy save thine Israel.

Dec. 19.—O Clavis David.

O ISRAEL'S Sceptre! David's Key!
 Come thou, and set death's captives free,
Unlock the gate that bars their road,
And lead them to the throne of God.
 Draw near, O Christ, with us to dwell.
 In mercy save thine Israel.

Dec. 20.—O Oriens.

O DAY-SPRING and Eternal Light!
 Pierce through the gloom of error's night;
Predestined Sun of Righteousness!
Haste with thy rising beams to bless.
 Draw near, O Christ, with us to dwell,
 In mercy save thine Israel.

Dec. 22.—O Rex Gentium.

O KING! Desire of nations! come
Lead sons of earth to heaven's high home;
Thou chief and precious Corner-stone,
Binding the sever'd into one.
 Draw near, O Christ, with us to dwell,
 In mercy save thine Israel.

Dec. 23.—O Emmanuel.

O LAWGIVER! Emmanuel! King!
Thy praises we would ever sing;
The Gentiles' hope, the Saviour blest,
Take us to thine eternal rest.
 Draw near, O Christ, with us to dwell,
 In mercy save thine Israel

---

15   *"He hath sent me to bind up the broken-hearted,*   [C. M.
    to proclaim liberty to the captives."

HARK! the glad sound! the Saviour comes,
 The Saviour promised long:
Let every heart prepare a throne,
 And every voice a song.

2 On him the Spirit, largely pour'd,
 Exerts his sacred fire;
Wisdom and might, and zeal and love,
 His holy breast inspire.

3 He comes the prisoners to release
 In Satan's bondage held;

  The gates of brass before him burst,
   The iron fetters yield

4 He comes from thickest films of vice
  To clear the mental ray,
 And on the eyes oppress'd with night
  To pour celestial day.

5 He comes the broken heart to bind,
  The bleeding soul to cure:
 And with the treasures of his grace
  To enrich the humble poor.

6 Our glad Hosannas, Prince of Peace,
  Thy welcome shall proclaim;
 And heaven's eternal arches ring
  With thy belovèd name.

CHRISTMAS.

16 *"The Desire of all nations shall come."* [8s. 7s.

HAIL! thou long-expected Jesus,
 Born to set thy people free;
From our fears and sins release us;
 Let us find our rest in thee.

2 Israel's strength and consolation,
  Hope of all the earth thou art;
 Long desired of every nation,
  Joy of every waiting heart.

3 Born thy people to deliver,
    Born a child, yet God our King,
  Born to reign in us for ever,
    Now thy gracious kingdom bring.

4 By thine own eternal Spirit,
    Rule in all our hearts alone:
  By thine all-sufficient merit,
    Raise us to thy glorious throne.

17   *"Glory to God in the highest, and on earth peace,*   [7s.
         good-will toward men."

HARK! the herald angels sing
    Glory to the new-born King;
  Peace on earth, and mercy mild,
  God and sinners reconciled!

2 Joyful, all ye nations, rise,
  Join the triumph of the skies;
  With the angelic host proclaim,
  Christ is born in Bethlehem!

3 Christ, by highest heaven adored;
  Christ, the everlasting Lord;
  Late in time behold him come,
  Offspring of the Virgin's womb:

4 Veil'd in flesh the Godhead see;
  Hail the incarnate Deity,
  Pleased as Man with men to dwell;
  Jesus, our Emmanuel!

5 Risen with healing in his wings,
  Light and life to all he brings.
  Hail, the Sun of Righteousness!
  Hail, the heaven-born Prince of Peace!

18 *"Unto you is born this day in the city of David a* [C. M.
  Saviour, which is Christ the Lord."

WHILE shepherds watch'd their flocks by
    night,
  All seated on the ground,
The angel of the Lord came down,
  And glory shone around.

2 "Fear not," said he, for mighty dread
  Had seized their troubled mind;
"Glad tidings of great joy I bring
  To you, and all mankind.

3 "To you, in David's town, this day
  Is born of David's line,
The Saviour, who is Christ the Lord;
  And this shall be the sign.

4 "The heavenly Babe you there shall find,
  To human view display'd,
All meanly wrapt in swathing bands,
  And in a manger laid."

5 Thus spake the seraph; and forthwith
  Appeared a shining throng
Of angels, praising God, who thus
  Address'd their joyful song:

6 "All glory be to God on high,
  And to the earth be peace;
Good-will henceforth from heaven to men
  Begin, and never cease."

19   *"Let us now go even unto Bethlehem."*   [P. M.

O COME, all ye faithful,
  Joyful and triumphant;
O come ye, O come ye, to Bethlehem;
  Come and behold him
  Born, the King of angels:
    O come, let us adore him,
    O come, let us adore him,
O come, let us adore him, Christ the Lord.

2 God of God,
  Light of Light,
Lo! he abhors not the Virgin's womb;
  Very God,
  Begotten, not created:
    O come, let us adore him, &c.

3 Sing, choirs of angels,
  Sing in exultation,
Sing, all ye citizens of heaven above,
  Glory to God
  In the highest;
    O come, let us adore him, &c.

4 Yea, Lord, we greet thee,
   Born this happy morning;
Jesus, to thee be glory given;
   Word of the Father,
   Now in flesh appearing;
   O come, let us adore him,
   O come, let us adore him,
O come, let us adore him, Christ the Lord.

20 *"And suddenly there was with the angel a multi-* [8s. 7s.
   tude of the heavenly host, praising God."

HARK! what mean those holy voices
   Sweetly sounding through the skies?
Lo! the angelic host rejoices,
   Heavenly hallelujahs rise.

2 Listen to the wondrous story,
   Which they chant in hymns of joy—
"Glory in the highest, glory!
   Glory be to God most high!

3 "Peace on earth, good-will from heaven,
   Reaching far as man is found;
Souls redeemed and sins forgiven,
   Loud our golden harps shall sound.

4 "Christ is born; the great Anointed!
   Heaven and earth his praises sing!
O receive whom God appointed
   For your Prophet, Priest, and King!

5 "Hasten, mortals, to adore him;
　Learn his name to magnify,
Till in heaven ye sing before him,
　Glory be to God most high!"

21　*"Behold I bring you glad tidings of great joy."*　[SIX 10s.

CHRISTIANS, awake, salute the happy morn,
　Whereon the Saviour of mankind was born;
Rise to adore the mystery of love,
Which hosts of angels chanted from above;
With them the joyful tidings first begun
Of God incarnate and the Virgin's Son.

2 Then to the watchful shepherds it was told,
　Who heard the angelic herald's voice: "Behold,
I bring good tidings of a Saviour's birth
To you and all the nations upon earth:
This day hath God fulfill'd his promised word,
This day is born a Saviour, Christ the Lord."

3 He spake; and straightway the celestial choir
　In hymns of joy, unknown before, conspire:
The praises of redeeming love they sang,
And heaven's whole arch with alleluias rang:
God's highest glory was their anthem still,
Peace upon earth, and unto men good-will.

4 To Bethlehem straight the happy shepherds ran,
　To see the wonder God had wrought for man:

And found, with Joseph and the blessèd maid,
Her Son, the Saviour, in a manger laid;
Amazed the wondrous story they proclaim,
The earliest heralds of the Saviour's name.

5 Let us, like these good shepherds, then employ
Our grateful voices to proclaim the joy;
Trace we the Babe, who hath retrieved our loss,
From his poor manger to his bitter cross;
Treading his steps, assisted by his grace,
Till man's first heavenly state again takes place.

6 Then may we hope, the angelic thrones among,
To sing, redeemed, a glad triumphal song;
He, that was born upon this joyful day,
Around us all his glory shall display;
Saved by his love, incessant we shall sing
Eternal praise to heaven's Almighty King.

22 *"Behold a ladder set up on the earth, and the top* [D. C. M.
*of it reached to heaven; and behold the angels
of God ascending and descending on it."*

IT came upon the midnight clear,
   That glorious song of old,
From angels bending near the earth
   To touch their harps of gold;
Peace on the earth, good-will to men,
   From heaven's all-gracious King;
The world in solemn stillness lay
   To hear the angels sing.

2 Still through the cloven skies they come,
    With peaceful wings unfurl'd;
  And still their heavenly music floats
    O'er all the weary world:
  Above its sad and lowly plains
    They bend on hovering wing,
  And ever o'er its Babel sounds
    The blessed angels sing.

3 O ye beneath life's crushing load,
    Whose forms are bending low,
  Who toil along the climbing way
    With painful steps and slow!
  Look now, for glad and golden hours
    Come swiftly on the wing:
  O rest beside the weary road,
    And hear the angels sing.

4 For lo, the days are hastening on,
    By prophets seen of old,
  When with the ever-circling years
    Shall come the time foretold,
  When the new heaven and earth shall own
    The Prince of Peace their King,
  And the whole world send back the song
    Which now the angels sing.

23   *"Behold I bring you good tidings of great joy."*   [P. M.

Chorus.

SHOUT the glad tidings, exultingly sing;
   Jerusalem triumphs, Messiah is King!

1 Sion, the marvellous story be telling,
   The Son of the Highest, how lowly his birth!
The brightest archangel in glory excelling,
   He stoops to redeem thee, he reigns upon earth:

Chorus.

Shout the glad tidings, exultingly sing;
Jerusalem triumphs, Messiah is King!

2 Tell how he cometh; from nation to nation,
   The heart-cheering news let the earth echo round:
How free to the faithful he offers salvation,
   How his people with joy everlasting are crown'd:

Chorus.

Shout the glad tidings, exultingly sing
Jerusalem triumphs, Messiah is King!

3 Mortals, your homage be gratefully bringing,
   And sweet let the gladsome Hosanna arise;
Ye angels, the full Alleluia be singing;
   One chorus resound through the earth and the skies:

Chorus.

Shout the glad tidings, exultingly sing;
Jerusalem triumphs, Messiah is King!

24   *"We are come to worship him."*   [8s. 7s. 4

ANGELS, from the realms of glory,
  Wing your flight o'er all the earth;
Ye who sang creation's story,
  Now proclaim Messiah's birth:
    Come and worship,
  Worship Christ, the new-born King.

2 Shepherds in the field abiding,
  Watching o'er your flocks by night;
God with man is now residing,
  Yonder shines the infant-light:
    Come and worship,
  Worship Christ, the new-born King.

3 Sages, leave your contemplations;
  Brighter visions beam afar:
Seek the great Desire of nations,
  Ye have seen his natal star:
    Come and worship,
  Worship Christ, the new-born King.

4 Saints before the altar bending,
  Watching long in hope and fear,
Suddenly the Lord, descending,
  In his temple shall appear:
    Come and worship,
  Worship Christ, the new-born King.

25   *"Let us now go even unto Bethlehem."*   [6s. 5s. Double.

COME hither, ye faithful,
    Triumphantly sing!
Come, see in the manger
    The angels' dread King!
To Bethlehem hasten
    With joyful accord!
O come ye, come hither
    To worship the Lord!

2 True Son of the Father,
    He comes from the skies;
To be born of a Virgin
    He doth not despise.
        To Bethlehem hasten, &c.

3 Hark, hark to the angels!
    All singing in heaven,
"To God in the highest
    All glory be given!"
        To Bethlehem hasten, &c.

4 To thee, then, O Jesus,
    This day of thy birth,
Be glory and honour
    Through heaven and earth;
True Godhead incarnate!
    Omnipotent Word!
O come, let us hasten
    To worship the Lord!

26 *"The Word was made flesh and dwelt among us."* [C. M.

CALM on the listening ear of night
  Come heaven's melodious strains,
Where wild Judea stretches far
  Her silver-mantled plains.

2 Celestial choirs from courts above
  Shed sacred glories there;
And angels, with their sparkling lyres,
  Make music on the air.

3 The answering hills of Palestine
  Send back the glad reply;
And greet, from all their holy heights,
  The Day-Spring from on high.

4 O'er the blue depths of Galilee
  There comes a holier calm,
And Sharon waves, in solemn praise,
  Her silent groves of palm.

5 "Glory to God!" the sounding skies
  Loud with their anthems ring,
"Peace to the earth, good-will to men.
  From heaven's eternal King!"

6 Light on thy hills, Jerusalem!
  The Saviour now is born!
And bright on Bethlehem's joyous plains
  Breaks the first Christmas morn.

27 *"For unto us a Child is born, unto us a Son is given."* [C. M.

TO hail thy rising, Sun of life,
  The gathering nations come;
Joyous as when the reapers bear
  Their harvest treasures home.

2 For thou our burden hast removed;
  The oppressor's reign is broke;
Thy fiery conflict with the foe
  Has burst his cruel yoke.

3 To us the promised Child is born;
  To us the Son is given;
Him shall the tribes of earth obey,
  And all the hosts of heaven.

4 His name shall be the Prince of Peace,
  For evermore adored;
The Wonderful, the Counsellor,
  The mighty God and Lord.

5 His power increasing still shall spread,
  His reign no end shall know;
Justice shall guard his throne above,
  And peace abound below.

END OF THE YEAR.

28   *"The time is short."*   [D. S. M

A FEW more years shall roll,
   A few more seasons come,
And we shall be with those that rest
   Asleep within the tomb:
   Then, O my Lord, prepare
   My soul for that great day;
O wash me in thy precious blood,
   And take my sins away.

2 A few more suns shall set
   O'er these dark hills of time,
And we shall be where suns are not,
   A far serener clime:
   Then, O my Lord, prepare
   My soul for that blest day;
O wash me in thy precious blood,
   And take my sins away.

3 A few more storms shall beat
   On this wild rocky shore,
And we shall be where tempests cease,
   And surges swell no more:
   Then, O my Lord, prepare
   My soul for that calm day;
O wash me in thy precious blood,
   And take my sins away.

4 A few more struggles here,
 A few more partings o'er,
A few more toils, a few more tears,
 And we shall weep no more:
 Then, O my Lord, prepare
 My soul for that bright day;
O wash me in thy precious blood,
 And take my sins away.

5 'Tis but a little while
 And he shall come again,
Who died that we might live, who lives
 That we with him may reign:
 Then, O my Lord, prepare
 My soul for that glad day;
O wash me in thy precious blood,
 And take my sins away.

29 *"Lord, thou hast been our refuge from one generation to another."* [C. M.

O GOD, our help in ages past,
 Our hope for years to come,
Our shelter from the stormy blast,
 And our eternal home:

2 Under the shadow of thy throne
 Thy saints have dwelt secure;
Sufficient is thine arm alone,
 And our defence is sure.

3 Before the hills in order stood,
    Or earth received her frame,
  From everlasting thou art God,
    To endless years the same.

4 A thousand ages in thy sight
    Are like an evening gone;
  Short as the watch that ends the night
    Before the rising sun.

5 Time, like an ever-rolling stream,
    Bears all its sons away;
  They fly forgotten, as a dream
    Dies at the opening day.

6 O God, our help in ages past,
    Our hope for years to come,
  Be thou our guard while life shall last,
    And our eternal home.

NEW YEAR.

30   *"My times are in thy hand."*   [L. M

THE God of life, whose constant care
  With blessings crowns each opening year,
My scanty span doth still prolong,
And wakes anew mine annual song.

2 Thy children, panting to be gone,
  May bid the tide of time roll on,
  To land them on that happy shore
  Where years and death are known no more.

3 No more fatigue, no more distress,
　Nor sin, nor hell, shall reach that place;
　No groans, to mingle with the songs
　Resounding from immortal tongues:

4 No more alarms from ghostly foes;
　No cares to break the long repose;
　No midnight shade, no clouded sun,
　But sacred, high, eternal noon.

5 O long-expected year! begin;
　Dawn on this world of woe and sin;
　Fain would we leave this weary road,
　And sleep in death, to rest with God.

31 *'Lord, thou hast been our dwelling-place in all generations.'* [7s. DOUBLE.

WHILE with ceaseless course the sun
　　Hasted through the former year,
Many souls their race have run,
　　Never more to meet us here:
Fixed in an eternal state,
　　They have done with all below:
We a little longer wait,
　　But how little, none can know.

2 As the wingèd arrow flies
　　Speedily the mark to find;
As the lightning from the skies
　　Darts, and leaves no trace behind;

Swiftly thus our fleeting days
   Bear us down life's rapid stream;
Upward, Lord, our spirits raise;
   All below is but a dream.

3 Thanks for mercies past receive;
   Pardon of our sins renew;
Teach us henceforth how to live
   With eternity in view:
Bless thy word to young and old;
   Fill us with a Saviour's love;
And when life's short tale is told,
   May we dwell with thee above.

CIRCUMCISION.

32 *"And when eight days were accomplished for the*   [S. M
circumcising of the Child, his name was called
Jesus."

THE ancient law departs
   And all its terrors cease;
For Jesus makes with faithful hearts
   A covenant of peace.

2 The Light of light divine,
   True Brightness undefiled,
He bears for us the shame of sin,
   A holy, spotless Child.

3 To-day the Name is thine,
   At which we bend the knee;
They call thee Jesus, Child divine!
   Our Jesus deign to be.

33 *"None other name is given under heaven whereby we must be saved."* [7s.

JESUS! Name of wondrous love!
Name all other names above!
Unto which must every knee
Bow in deep humility.

2 Jesus! Name decreed of old:
To the maiden mother told,
Kneeling in her lowly cell,
By the angel Gabriel.

3 Jesus! Name of priceless worth
To the fallen sons of earth,
For the promise that it gave—
"Jesus shall his people save."

4 Jesus! Name of mercy mild,
Given to the holy Child,
When the cup of human woe
First he tasted here below.

5 Jesus! only Name that's given
Under all the mighty heaven,
Whereby man, to sin enslaved,
Bursts his fetters, and is saved.

6 Jesus! Name of wondrous love!
Human Name of God above;
Pleading only this we flee,
Helpless, O our God, to thee.

EPIPHANY.

34 *"All the earth shall be filled with his majesty."* [7s. 6s. Double.

HAIL to the Lord's Anointed,
 Great David's greater Son!
Hail, in the time appointed,
 His reign on earth begun!
He comes to break oppression,
 To set the captive free:
To take away transgression,
 And rule in equity.

2 He comes with succour speedy
 To those who suffer wrong,
To help the poor and needy,
 And bid the weak be strong;
To give them songs for sighing,
 Their darkness turn to light,
Whose souls, condemn'd and dying,
 Were precious in his sight

3 He shall descend like showers
 Upon the fruitful earth;
And love and joy, like flowers,
 Spring in his path to birth:
Before him, on the mountains,
 Shall peace, the herald, go;
And righteousness, in fountains,
 From hill to valley flow.

4 To him shall prayer unceasing,
   And daily vows ascend;
His kingdom still increasing,
   A kingdom without end:
The tide of time shall never
   His covenant remove;
His name shall stand for ever;
   That name to us is Love.

35 *"Great and marvellous are thy works, Lord God* [5s. 6s. 5s
Almighty; just and true are thy ways, thou
King of saints."

HOW wondrous and great
   Thy works, God of praise!
How just, King of saints,
   And true are thy ways!
O who shall not fear thee,
   And honour thy name?
Thou only art holy,
   Thou only supreme.

2 To nations long dark
   Thy light shall be shown;
Their worship and vows
   Shall come to thy throne:
Thy truth and thy judgments
   Shall spread all abroad,
Till earth's every people
   Confess thee their God.

EPIPHANY.

36 *"Arise, shine; for thy light is come and the glory of the Lord is risen upon thee."* [10s.

RISE, crown'd with light, imperial Salem, rise;
  Exalt thy towering head and lift thine eyes:
See heaven its sparkling portals wide display,
And break upon thee in a flood of day.

2 See a long race thy spacious courts adorn,
  See future sons, and daughters yet unborn,
  In crowding ranks on every side arise,
  Demanding life, impatient for the skies.

3 See barbarous nations at thy gates attend,
  Walk in thy light, and in thy temple bend:
  See thy bright altars throng'd with prostrate kings,
  While every land its joyous tribute brings.

4 The seas shall waste, the skies to smoke decay,
  Rocks fall to dust, and mountains melt away;
  But fix'd his word, his saving power remains;
  Thy realm shall last, thy own Messiah reigns.

37   *"We have seen his star in the East."*   [P. M.

BRIGHTEST and best of the sons of the morning,
  Dawn on our darkness, and lend us thine aid;
Star of the East, the horizon adorning,
  Guide where our infant Redeemer is laid.

2 Cold on his cradle the dew-drops are shining,
    Low lies his head with the beasts of the stall;
  Angels adore him in slumber reclining,
    Maker and Monarch and Saviour of all.

3 Say, shall we yield him, in costly devotion,
   Odours of Edom, and offerings divine,
  Gems of the mountain, and pearls of the ocean,
   Myrrh from the forest, and gold from the mine?

4 Vainly we offer each ample oblation,
   Vainly with gifts would his favour secure;
  Richer by far is the heart's adoration,
   Dearer to God are the prayers of the poor.

5 Brightest and best of the sons of the morning,
   Dawn on our darkness, and lend us thine aid:
  Star of the East, the horizon adorning,
   Guide where our infant Redeemer is laid.

38 *"The mountains shall bring peace, and the little* [C. M.
         hills righteousness unto the people."

From the lxxii. Psalm.

LO! hills and mountains shall bring forth
  The happy fruits of peace,
Which all the land shall own to be
  The work of righteousness;

2 While David's Son our needy race
   Shall rule with gentle sway;
  And from their humble neck shall take
   Oppressive yokes away.

3 In every heart thy awful fear
   Shall then be rooted fast,
  As long as sun and moon endure,
   Or time itself shall last.

EPIPHANY.

4 He shall descend like rain, that cheers
    The meadow's second birth;
  Or like warm showers, whose gentle drops
    Refresh the thirsty earth.

5 In his blest days the just and good
    Shall spring up all around:
  The happy land shall everywhere
    With endless peace abound.

6 His uncontroll'd dominion shall
    From sea to sea extend;
  Begin at proud Euphrates' stream,
    At nature's limits end.

7 To him the savage nations round
    Shall bow their servile heads;
  His vanquish'd foes shall lick the dust,
    Where he his conquest spreads.

8 The kings of Tarshish and the isles
    Shall costly presents bring;
  From spicy Sheba gifts shall come,
    And wealthy Saba's king.

9 To him shall every king on earth
    His humble homage pay;
  And differing nations gladly join
    To own his righteous sway.

10 For he shall set the needy free,
    When they for succour cry;
  Shall save the helpless and the poor
    And all their wants supply.

11 For him shall constant prayer be made,
    Through all his prosperous days:
  His just dominion shall afford
    A lasting theme of praise.

12 The memory of his glorious name
    Through endless years shall run;
  His spotless fame shall shine as bright
    And lasting as the sun.

13 In him the nations of the world
    Shall be completely bless'd,
  And his unbounded happiness
    By every tongue confess'd.

14 Then bless'd be God, the mighty Lord,
    The God whom Israel fears;
  Who only wondrous in his works,
    Beyond compare, appears.

15 Let earth be with his glory fill'd,
    For ever bless his name;
  Whilst to his praise the listening world
    Their glad assent proclaim.

39 *"A Light to lighten the Gentiles."* [8s. 7s

LIGHT of those whose dreary dwelling
    Borders on the shades of death,
  Jesus, now thyself revealing,
    Scatter every cloud beneath.

2 Still we wait for thine appearing;
   Life and joy thy beams impart,
Chasing all our doubts, and cheering
   Every meek and contrite heart.

3 Show thy power in every nation,
   O thou Prince of peace and love!
Give the knowledge of salvation,
   Fix our hearts on things above.

4 By thine all-sufficient merit,
   Every burden'd soul release:
By the presence of thy Spirit,
   Guide us into perfect peace.

40 *"The Lord reigneth."* [C. M.

JOY to the world! the Lord is come:
   Let earth receive her King;
Let every heart prepare him room,
   And heaven and nature sing.

2 Joy to the world! the Saviour reigns:
   Let men their songs employ;
While fields and floods, rocks, hills, and plains,
   Repeat the sounding joy.

3 No more let sins and sorrows grow,
   Nor thorns infest the ground;
He comes to make his blessings flow
   Far as the curse is found.

4 He rules the world with truth and grace,
    And makes the nations prove
The glories of his righteousness,
    And wonders of his love.

41 *"The mountain of the Lord's house shall be established in the top of the mountains."* [C. M

O'ER mountain-tops the mount of God
    In latter days shall rise,
Above the summits of the hills,
    And draw the wondering eyes.

2 To this the joyful nations round,
    All tribes and tongues, shall flow;
Up to the mount of God, they'll say,
    And to his house we'll go.

3 The beams that shine from Sion's hill
    Shall lighten every land;
The King who reigns in Salem's towers
    Shall all the world command.

4 Among the nations he shall judge;
    His judgments truth shall guide:
His sceptre shall protect the just,
    And crush the sinner's pride.

5 For peaceful implements shall men
    Exchange their swords and spears;
Nor shall they study war again
    Throughout those happy years.

6 Come, O ye house of Jacob! come
    To worship at his shrine;
  And, walking in the light of God,
    With holy graces shine.

42   *"The Lord God Omnipotent reigneth."*   [7s. Double

HARK! the song of jubilee,
    Loud as mighty thunders roar;
  Or the fulness of the sea,
    When it breaks upon the shore.
  Alleluia! for the Lord
    God omnipotent shall reign;
  Alleluia! let the word
    Echo round the earth and main.

2 Alleluia! hark! the sound,
    From the centre to the skies,
  Wakes above, beneath, around,
    All creation's harmonies:
  See Jehovah's banners furled;
    Sheathed his sword; he speaks,—'tis done,
  And the kingdoms of this world
    Are the kingdoms of his Son.

3 He shall reign from pole to pole
    With illimitable sway;
  He shall reign, when, like a scroll,
    Yonder heavens have pass'd away:
  Then the end; beneath his rod,
    Man's last enemy shall fall;
  Alleluia! Christ in God,
    God in Christ, is all in all.

43   *"Watchman! what of the night!"*   [7s. Double.

WATCHMAN! tell us of the night,
    What its signs of promise are.
Traveller! o'er yon mountain's height,
    See that glory-beaming star.
Watchman! does its beauteous ray
    Aught of joy or hope foretell?
Traveller! yes; it brings the day,
    Promised day of Israel.

2 Watchman! tell us of the night;
    Higher yet that star ascends.
Traveller! blessedness and light,
    Peace and truth, its course portends.
Watchman! will its beams alone
    Gild the spot that gave them birth?
Traveller! ages are its own;
    See, it bursts o'er all the earth.

3 Watchman! tell us of the night,
    For the morning seems to dawn.
Traveller! darkness takes its flight;
    Doubt and terror are withdrawn.
Watchman! let thy wanderings cease;
    Hie thee to thy quiet home.
Traveller! lo! the Prince of Peace,
    Lo! the Son of God is come.

EPIPHANY. 51

44 *"How beautiful upon the mountains are the feet* [S. M.
*of him that bringeth good tidings, that publisheth
peace."*

HOW beauteous are their feet,
  Who stand on Sion's hill;
Who bring salvation on their tongues,
  And words of peace reveal!

2 How charming is their voice:
  How sweet their tidings are!—
"Sion, behold thy Saviour-King,
  He reigns and triumphs here."

3 How happy are our ears
  That hear this joyful sound,
Which kings and prophets waited for,
  And sought, but never found!

4 How blessèd are our eyes
  That see this heavenly light!
Prophets and kings desired it long,
  But died without the sight.

5 The watchmen join their voice,
  And tuneful notes employ;
Jerusalem breaks forth in songs,
  And deserts learn the joy.

6 The Lord makes bare his arm
  Through all the earth abroad:
Let every nation now behold
  Their Saviour and their God.

45 *"When they saw the star they rejoiced with exceeding great joy."* [SIX 7s.

AS with gladness men of old
Did the guiding star behold;
As with joy they hailed its light,
Leading onward, beaming bright;
So, most gracious Lord, may we
Evermore be led to thee.

2 As with joyful steps they sped
To that lowly manger-bed;
There to bend the knee before
Him whom heaven and earth adore;
So may we with willing feet
Ever seek the mercy-seat.

3 As they offered gifts most rare
At that manger rude and bare;
So may we with holy joy,
Pure and free from sin's alloy,
All our costliest treasures bring,
Christ! to thee our heavenly King.

4 Holy Jesus! every day
Keep us in the narrow way;
And, when earthly things are past,
Bring our ransomed souls at last
Where they need no star to guide,
Where no clouds thy glory hide.

5 In the heavenly country bright,
   Need they no created light;
Thou its Light, its Joy, its Crown,
Thou its Sun which goes not down,
   There forever may we sing
   Alleluias to our King.

46   *"I am the bright and morning star."*   [L. M.

WHEN, marshall'd on the nightly plain,
   The glittering host bestud the sky,
One star alone of all the train
   Can fix the sinner's wandering eye.

2 Hark, hark! to God the chorus breaks,
   From every host, from every gem;
But one alone the Saviour speaks;
   It is the Star of Bethlehem.

3 It is my guide, my light, my all,
   It bids my dark forebodings cease;
And through the storm and danger's thrall,
   It leads me to the port of peace.

4 Then, safely moor'd, my perils o'er,
   I'll sing, first in night's diadem,
For ever and for evermore,
   The Star, the Star of Bethlehem!

47   *"We have seen his star in the East."*   [7s.

SONS of men, behold from far,
  Hail! the long-expected star;
Jacob's star that gilds the night,
Guides bewilder'd nature right.

2 Mild it shines on all beneath,
  Piercing through the shades of death;
Scattering error's wide-spread night,
Kindling darkness into light.

3 Nations all, remote and near,
  Haste to see your God appear:
Haste, for him your hearts prepare,
Meet him manifested there.

4 There behold the Day-Spring rise,
  Pouring light upon your eyes:
See it chase the shades away,
Shining to the perfect day.

5 Sing, ye morning stars, again,
  God descends on earth to reign,
Deigns for man his life to employ;
Shout, ye sons of God, for joy!

ASH WEDNESDAY AND LENT.

48 *"Rend your heart and not your garments, and turn unto the Lord your God."* [C. M.

ONCE more the solemn season calls
   A holy fast to keep;
And now within the temple walls
   Both priest and people weep.

2 But vain all outward sign of grief,
   And vain the form of prayer,
Unless the heart implore relief,
   And penitence be there.

3 We smite the breast, we weep in vain,
   In vain in ashes mourn,
Unless with penitential pain
   The smitten soul be torn.

4 In sorrow true now let us pray
   To our offended God,
From us to turn his wrath away,
   And stay the uplifted rod.

5 O God, our Judge and Father, deign
   To spare the bruisèd reed;
We pray for time to turn again,
   For grace to turn indeed.

6 Blest Three in One, to thee we bow;
   Vouchsafe us in thy love
To gather from these fasts below
   Immortal fruit above.

49 *"And Jesus was led by the Spirit into the wilderness,* [7s. *being forty days tempted of the devil. And in those days he did eat nothing."*

FORTY days and forty nights
  Thou wast fasting in the wild;
Forty days and forty nights
  Tempted, and yet undefiled.

2 Shall not we thy sorrow share,
  And from earthly joys abstain,
Fasting with unceasing prayer,
  Glad with thee to suffer pain?

3 And if Satan, vexing sore,
  Flesh or spirit should assail,
Thou, his Vanquisher before,
  Grant we may not faint or fail.

4 So shall we have peace divine;
  Holier gladness ours shall be;
Round us, too, shall angels shine,
  Such as minister'd to thee.

5 Keep, O keep us, Saviour dear,
  Ever constant by thy side;
That with thee we may appear
  At th' eternal Eastertide.

50 *"O Lord, rebuke me not in thine indignation, neither* [S. M. *chasten me in thy displeasure."*

From the vi. Psalm.

IN mercy, not in wrath,
  Rebuke me, gracious God!
Lest, if thy whole displeasure rise,
  I sink beneath thy rod.

2 Touch'd by thy quickening power,
   My load of guilt I feel;
 The wounds thy Spirit hath unclosed,
   O let that Spirit heal.

3 In trouble and in gloom,
   Must I for ever mourn?
 And wilt thou not at length, O God,
   In pitying love return?

4 O come, ere life expire,
   Send down thy power to save;
 For who shall sing thy name in death,
   Or praise thee in the grave?

5 Why should I doubt thy grace,
   Or yield to dread despair?
 Thou wilt fulfil thy promised word,
   And grant me all my prayer.

51 *"Put me not to rebuke, O Lord, in thine anger;* [C. M.
neither chasten me in thy heavy displeasure."

From the xxxviii. Psalm.

THY chastening wrath, O Lord, restrain,
   Though I deserve it all;
 Nor let on me the heavy storm
   Of thy displeasure fall.

2 My sins, which to a deluge swell,
   My sinking head o'erflow,
 And, for my feeble strength to bear,
   Too vast a burden grow.

3 But, Lord, before thy searching eyes
 All my desires appear;
The groanings of my burden'd soul
 Have reach'd thine open ear.

4 Forsake me not, O Lord, my God,
 Nor far from me depart:
Make haste to my relief, O thou
 Who my salvation art.

52 "*O Lord, thou hast searched me out, and known me.*" [L. M.

From the cxxxix. Psalm.

THOU, Lord, by strictest search hast known
 My rising up and lying down;
My secret thoughts are known to thee,
Known long before conceived by me.

2 From thy all-seeing Spirit, Lord,
What hiding-place does earth afford?
O where can I thy influence shun,
Or whither from thy presence run?

3 The veil of night is no disguise,
No screen from thy all-searching eyes;
Through midnight shades thou find'st thy way,
As in the blazing noon of day.

4 Search, try, O God, my thoughts and heart,
If mischief lurk in any part;
Correct me where I go astray,
And guide me in thy perfect way.

53 *"In that he himself hath suffered being tempted, he is able to succour them that are tempted."* [7s. DOUBLE.

SAVIOUR, when in dust to thee,
Low we bow th' adoring knee;
When, repentant, to the skies
Scarce we lift our streaming eyes;
O by all thy pains and woe,
Suffer'd once for man below,
Bending from thy throne on high,
Hear our solemn litany.

2 By thy birth and early years,
By thy human griefs and fears,
By thy fasting and distress
In the lonely wilderness,
By thy victory in the hour
Of the subtle tempter's power;
Jesus, look with pitying eye;
Hear our solemn litany.

3 By thy conflict with despair,
By thine agony of prayer,
By the purple robe of scorn,
By thy wounds, thy crown of thorn,
By thy cross, thy pangs, and cries,
By thy perfect sacrifice;
Jesus, look with pitying eye;
Hear our solemn litany.

4 By thy deep expiring groan,
By the seal'd sepulchral stone,

By thy triumph o'er the grave,
By thy power from death to save;
Mighty God, ascended Lord,
To thy throne in heaven restored,
Prince and Saviour, hear our cry,
Hear our solemn litany.

54 *"Turn ye! turn ye! for why will ye die."* [7s. DOUBLE

SINNERS! turn, why will ye die?
God, your Maker, asks you why:
God, who did your being give,
Made you with himself to live:
He the fatal cause demands,
Asks the work of his own hands:
Why, ye thankless creatures! why
Will ye cross his love, and die?

2 Sinners! turn, why will ye die?
God, your Saviour, asks you why:
He who did your souls retrieve,
Died himself that ye might live.
Will you let him die in vain?
Crucify your Lord again?
Why, ye ransomed sinners, why
Will ye slight his grace, and die?

3 Sinners! turn, why will ye die?
God, the Spirit, asks you why:
He who all your lives hath strove—
Woo'd you to embrace his love.

Will ye not his grace receive?
Will ye still refuse to live?
O, ye dying sinners, why,
Why will ye forever die?

55 *"I look for the Lord; my soul doth wait for him;* [S. M.
in his word is my trust."

From the cxxx. Psalm.

MY soul with patience waits
    For thee, the living Lord;
My hopes are on thy promise built,
    Thy never-failing word.

2 My longing eyes look out
    For thy enlivening ray,
More duly than the morning watch
    To spy the dawning day.

3 Let Israel trust in God,
    No bounds his mercy knows;
The plenteous source and spring from whence
    Eternal succour flows;

4 Whose friendly streams to us
    Supplies in want convey;
A healing spring, a spring to cleanse
    And wash our guilt away.

56 *"There is forgiveness with thee, that thou mayest be feared."* [C. M.

HOW oft, alas! this wretched heart
  Has wandered from the Lord!
How oft my roving thoughts depart,
  Forgetful of his word!

2 Yet sovereign mercy calls, "Return;"
  Dear Lord, and may I come?
My vile ingratitude I mourn;
  O take the wanderer home.

3 And canst thou, wilt thou yet forgive,
  And bid my crimes remove?
And shall a pardon'd rebel live
  To speak thy wondrous love?

4 Almighty grace, thy healing power,
  How glorious, how divine!
That can to life and bliss restore
  So vile a heart as mine.

5 Thy pardoning love, so free, so sweet,
  Dear Saviour, I adore:
O keep me at thy sacred feet,
  And let me rove no more.

57 *"My soul fleeth unto the Lord."* [L. M.

MY God, permit me not to be
  A stranger to myself and thee:
Amidst a thousand thoughts I rove,
Forgetful of my highest love.

2 Why should my passions mix with earth,
And thus debase my heavenly birth?
Why should I cleave to things below,
And all my purest joys forego?

3 Call me away from flesh and sense;
Thy grace, O Lord, can draw me thence:
I would obey the voice divine,
And all inferior joys resign.

58   *"Awake to righteousness, and sin not."*   [7s.

HASTEN, sinner! to be wise;
  Stay not for the morrow's sun:
Wisdom, if you still despise,
  Harder is it to be won.

2 Hasten, mercy to implore;
  Stay not for the morrow's sun;
Lest thy season should be o'er,
  Ere this evening's stage be run.

3 Hasten, sinner! now return;
  Stay not for the morrow's sun;
Lest thy lamp should cease to burn,
  Ere salvation's work is done.

4 Hasten, sinner! to be blest;
  Stay not for the morrow's sun;
Lest perdition thee arrest,
  Ere the morrow is begun.

59 *"See then that ye walk circumspectly, not as fools, but as wise, redeeming the time."* [7s

SINNER, rouse thee from thy sleep,
Wake, and o'er thy folly weep;
Raise thy spirit dark and dead,
Jesus waits his light to shed.

2 Wake from sleep, arise from death,
See the bright and living path:
Watchful tread that path; be wise,
Leave thy folly, seek the skies.

3 Leave thy folly, cease from crime,
From this hour redeem thy time;
Life secure without delay,
Evil is the mortal day.

4 Be not blind and foolish still;
Call'd of Jesus, learn his will:
Jesus calls from death and night,
Jesus waits to shed his light.

60 *"Have mercy upon me, O God, after thy great goodness."* [S. M.

From the li. Psalm.

HAVE mercy, Lord, on me,
As thou wert ever kind;
Let me, oppress'd with loads of guilt,
Thy wonted mercy find.

2 Wash off my foul offence,
    And cleanse me from my sin;
For I confess my crime, and see
    How great my guilt has been.

3 Against thee, Lord, alone,
    And only in thy sight,
Have I transgress'd; and, though condemn'd,
    Must own thy judgment right.

4 Blot out my crying sins,
    Nor me in anger view:
Create in me a heart that's clean,
    An upright mind renew.

5 Withdraw not thou thy help,
    Nor cast me from thy sight;
Nor let thy Holy Spirit take
    His everlasting flight.

6 The joy thy favour gives
    Let me, O Lord, regain;
And thy free Spirit's firm support
    My fainting soul sustain.

61 *" Strait is the gate, and narrow is the way, which* [C. M
    leadeth unto life."

AS o'er the past my memory strays,
    Why heaves the secret sigh?
'Tis that I mourn departed days,
    Still unprepared to die.

2 The world and worldly things beloved,
    My anxious thoughts employ'd;
And time unhallow'd, unimproved,
    Presents a fearful void.

3 Yet, holy Father, wild despair
    Chase from my labouring breast;
Thy grace it is which prompts the prayer,
    That grace can do the rest.

4 My life's brief remnant all be thine;
    And when thy sure decree
Bids me this fleeting breath resign,
    O speed my soul to thee.

62   *" Search me, O God, and know my heart."*   [L. M.

O THOU, to whose all-searching sight
    The darkness shineth as the light,
Search, prove my heart; it looks to thee,
O burst its bonds, and set it free.

2 Wash out its stains, remove its dross,
Bind my affections to the cross;
Hallow each thought; let all within
Be clean, as thou, my Lord, art clean.

3 If in this darksome wild I stray,
Be thou my light, be thou my way;
No foes, no violence I fear,
No harm, while thou, my God, art near.

4 When rising floods my soul o'erflow,
  When sinks my heart in waves of woe,
  Jesus, thy timely aid impart,
  And raise my head, and cheer my heart.

5 Saviour, where'er thy steps I see,
  Dauntless, untired, I follow thee;
  O let thy hand support me still,
  And lead me to thy holy hill.

63   *"My soul fleeth unto the Lord."*   [P. M.

LORD, in this thy mercy's day,
  Ere the time shall pass away,
On our knees we fall and pray.

2 Holy Jesus, grant us tears,
  Fill us with heart-searching fears,
  Ere the hour of doom appears.

3 Lord, on us thy Spirit pour,
  Kneeling lowly at thy door,
  Ere it close for evermore.

4 By thy night of agony,
  By thy supplicating cry,
  By thy willingness to die,

5 By thy tears of bitter woe
  For Jerusalem below,
  Let us not thy love forego.

6 Judge and Saviour of our race,
  When we see thee face to face,
  Grant us 'neath thy wings a place.

7 On thy love we rest alone,
  And that love will then be known
  By the pardoned round thy throne.

64 *"If we confess our sins, he is faithful and just to forgive us our sins."* [7s. 6s. Double.

MY sins, my sins, my Saviour!
  They take such hold on me,
I am not able to look up,
  Save only, Christ, to thee;
In thee is all forgiveness,
  In thee abundant grace,
My shadow and my sunshine
  The brightness of thy face.

2 My sins, my sins, my Saviour!
  How sad on thee they fall!
Seen through thy gentle patience,
  I tenfold feel them all;
I know they are forgiven,
  But still, their pain to me
Is all the grief and anguish
  They laid, my Lord, on thee.

3 My sins, my sins, my Saviour!
   Their guilt I never knew
 Till, with thee, in the desert
   I near thy Passion drew;
 Till, with thee, in the garden
   I heard thy pleading prayer,
 And saw the sweat-drops bloody
   That told thy sorrow there.

4 Therefore my songs, my Saviour,
   E'en in this time of woe,
 Shall tell of all thy goodness
   To suffering man below.
 Thy goodness and thy favour,
   Whose presence from above,
 Rejoice those hearts, my Saviour,
   That live in thee and love.

65 *"Lord, remember me."* [D. C. M.

O THOU, from whom all goodness flows,
   I lift my heart to thee;
 In all my sorrows, conflicts, woes,
   Dear Lord, remember me.
 When on my aching, burdened heart
   My sins lie heavily,
 Thy pardon grant, thy peace impart:
   In love, remember me.

2 When trials sore obstruct my way,
   And ills I cannot flee,
O let my strength be as my day:
   For good, remember me.
If worn with pain, disease, and grief,
   This feeble frame should be,
Grant patience, rest, and kind relief:
   Hear and remember me.

3 And oh, when in the hour of death
   I own thy just decree,
Be this the prayer of my last breath,
   Dear Lord, remember me.
To Father, Son, and Holy Ghost,
   The God whom we adore,
Be glory, as it was, is now,
   And shall be evermore.

66 *"Be not thou far from me, O Lord; thou art my succour, haste thee to help me."* [C. M.

O GRACIOUS God, in whom I live,
   My feeble efforts aid;
Help me to watch, and pray, and strive,
   Though trembling and afraid.

2 Increase my faith, increase my hope,
   When foes and fears prevail;
And bear my fainting spirit up,
   Or soon my strength will fail.

3 Whene'er temptations fright my heart,
    Or lure my feet aside,
My God, thy powerful aid impart,
    My guardian and my guide.

4 O keep me in thy heavenly way,
    And bid the tempter flee;
And let me never, never stray
    From happiness and thee.

67 *"In whom we have redemption through his blood, the*   [10s.
      forgiveness of sins."

WEARY of earth, and laden with my sin,
    I look at heaven and long to enter in,
But there no evil thing may find a home:
And yet I hear a voice that bids me "Come."

2 So vile I am, how dare I hope to stand
In the pure glory of that holy land?
Before the whiteness of that throne appear?
Yet there are hands stretch'd out to draw me near.

3 The while I fain would tread the heavenly way,
Evil is ever with me, day by day;
Yet on mine ears the gracious tidings fall,
"Repent, confess, thou shalt be loosed from all."

4 It is the voice of Jesus that I hear,
His are the hands stretched out to draw me near,
And his the blood that can for all atone,
And set me faultless there before the throne.

5 'Twas he who found me on the deathly wild,
And made me heir of heaven, the Father's child,
And day by day, whereby my soul may live,
Gives me his grace of pardon, and will give.

6 Yea, thou wilt answer for me, righteous Lord:
Thine all the merits, mine the great reward;
Thine the sharp thorns, and mine the golden crown,
Mine the life won, and thine the life laid down.

68 *"Whom resist, steadfast in the faith."* [6s. 5s. Double.

CHRISTIAN! dost thou see them
 On the holy ground,
How the powers of darkness
 Rage thy steps around?
Christian! up and smite them,
 Counting gain but loss;
In the strength that cometh
 By the holy cross.

2 Christian! dost thou feel them,
 How they work within,
Striving, tempting, luring,
 Goading into sin?
Christian! never tremble;
 Never be down-cast;
Gird thee for the battle,
 Watch and pray and fast.

3 Christian! dost thou hear them,
 How they speak thee fair?
"Always fast and vigil?
 Always watch and prayer?"
Christian! answer boldly:
 "While I breathe I pray!"
Peace shall follow battle,
 Night shall end in day.

4 "Well I know thy trouble,
 O my servant true;
Thou art very weary,
 I was weary too;
But that toil shall make thee
 Some day all mine own,
And the end of sorrow
 Shall be near my throne."

69 *"A broken and contrite heart, O God, thou wilt not* [C. M.
  despise."

LORD, when we bend before thy throne,
 And our confessions pour,
Teach us to feel the sins we own,
 And hate what we deplore.

2 Our broken spirits, pitying, see;
 True penitence impart;
And let a kindling glance from thee
 Beam hope upon the heart.

3 When we disclose our wants in prayer,
    May we our wills resign;
And not a thought our bosom share
    Which is not wholly thine.

4 Let faith each weak petition fill,
    And waft it to the skies,
And teach our hearts 'tis goodness still
    That grants it, or denies.

70   "*Jesus Christ, the same, yesterday, to-day, and for ever.*"   [SIX 8s.

WEARY of wandering from my God,
    And now made willing to return,
I hear and bow me to the rod;
    For thee, not without hope, I mourn:
I have an advocate above,
A friend before the throne of love.

2 O Jesus, full of pardoning grace,
    More full of grace than I of sin;
Yet once again I seek thy face:
    Open thine arms and take me in;
And freely my backslidings heal,
And love the faithless sinner still.

3 Thou know'st the way to bring me back,
    My fallen spirit to restore:
O for thy truth and mercy's sake,
    Forgive, and bid me sin no more:
The ruins of my soul repair,
And make my heart a house of prayer.

71   *" God be merciful to me, a sinner."*   [L. M

WITH broken heart and contrite sigh
A trembling sinner, Lord, I cry;
Thy pardoning grace is rich and free:
O God, be merciful to me.

2 I smite upon my troubled breast,
With deep and conscious guilt oppressed;
Christ and his cross my only plea:
O God, be merciful to me.

3 Far off I stand with tearful eyes,
Nor dare uplift them to the skies;
But thou dost all my anguish see:
O God, be merciful to me.

4 Nor alms, nor deeds that I have done,
Can for a single sin atone;
To Calvary alone I flee:
O God, be merciful to me.

5 And when, redeemed from sin and hell,
With all the ransomed throng I dwell,
My raptured song shall ever be,
God has been merciful to me.

PALM SUNDAY AND PASSION WEEK.

72 *"Out of the mouth of babes and sucklings thou hast perfected praise."*   [7s. 6s. with Chorus

ALL glory, laud, and honour,
   To thee, Redeemer, King!
To whom the lips of children
   Made sweet Hosannas ring.

2 Thou art the King of Israel,
   Thou David's royal Son,
Who in the Lord's name comest,
   The King and Blessèd One.
                 All glory, etc.

3 The company of angels
   Are praising thee on high;
And mortal men, and all things
   Created, make reply.
                 All glory, etc.

4 The people of the Hebrews
   With palms before thee went:
Our praise and prayer and anthems
   Before thee we present.
                 All glory, etc.

5 To thee before thy Passion
   They sang their hymns of praise:
To thee, now high exalted
   Our melody we raise.
                 All glory, etc.

6 Thou didst accept their praises;
   Accept the prayers we bring,
  Who in all good delightest,
   Thou good and gracious King.
                    All glory, etc.

73 *"And the multitudes that went before, and that* [L. M.
*followed, cried, saying, Hosanna to the Son of
David!"*

RIDE on! ride on in majesty!
  Hark! all the tribes Hosanna cry;
 O Saviour meek, pursue thy road
 With palms and scatter'd garments strow'd.

2 Ride on! ride on in majesty!
 In lowly pomp ride on to die:
 O Christ, thy triumphs now begin
 O'er captive death and conquer'd sin.

3 Ride on! ride on in majesty!
 The wingèd armies of the sky
 Look down with sad and wondering eyes
 To see the approaching sacrifice.

4 Ride on! ride on in majesty!
 The last and fiercest strife is nigh;
 The Father on his sapphire throne
 Expects his own anointed Son.

5 Ride on! ride on in majesty!
 In lowly pomp ride on to die;
 Bow thy meek head to mortal pain,
  Then take, O God, thy power, and reign.

74   *"The precious blood of Christ."*   [6s. 5s. Double.

GLORY be to Jesus,
  Who in bitter pains
Poured for me the life-blood
  From his sacred veins!
Grace and life eternal
  In that blood I find.
Blest be his compassion
  Infinitely kind!

2 Blest through endless ages
  Be the precious stream,
Which from endless torments
  Did the world redeem!
Abel's blood for vengeance
  Pleaded to the skies;
But the blood of Jesus
  For our pardon cries.

3 Oft as earth exulting
  Wafts its praise on high,
Angel-hosts, rejoicing,
  Make their glad reply.
Lift ye then your voices;
  Swell the mighty flood;
Louder still and louder,
  Praise the precious blood.

PALM SUNDAY AND PASSION WEEK.

75   *"He was wounded for our transgressions."*   [C. M.

MY Saviour hanging on the tree,
   In agonies and blood,
Methought once turn'd his eyes on me,
   As near his cross I stood.

2 Sure, never till my latest breath
   Can I forget that look;
It seem'd to charge me with his death,
   Though not a word he spoke.

3 My conscience felt and own'd the guilt,
   And plunged me in despair;
I saw my sins his blood had spilt,
   And help'd to nail him there.

4 Alas! I knew not what I did;
   But now my tears are vain:
Where shall my trembling soul be hid?
   For I the Lord have slain.

5 A second look he gave, which said,
   "I freely all forgive;
This blood is for thy ransom paid,
   I die that thou may'st live."

6 Thus, while his death my sin displays
   In all its blackest hue—
 Such is the mystery of grace—
   It seals my pardon too.

76 *"Who, when he had purged our sins, sat down on the right hand of the Majesty on high."* [8s. 7s. Double.

HAIL, thou once-despisèd Jesus;
   Hail, thou Galilean King;
 Thou didst suffer to release us;
   Thou didst free salvation bring!
 Hail, thou agonizing Saviour,
   Bearer of our sin and shame;
 By thy merit we find favour;
   Life is given through thy name.

2 Paschal Lamb, by God appointed,
   All our sins were on thee laid;
 By Almighty love anointed,
   Thou hast full atonement made.
 All thy people are forgiven
   Through the virtue of thy blood;
 Open'd is the gate of heaven,
   Peace is made 'twixt man and God.

3 Jesus, hail! enthroned in glory,
   There for ever to abide,
 All the heavenly hosts adore thee,
   Seated at thy Father's side;

There for sinners thou art pleading;
   There thou dost our place prepare;
Ever for us interceding,
   Till in glory we appear.

4 Worship, honour, power, and blessing
   Thou art worthy to receive;
Loudest praises, without ceasing,
   Meet it is for us to give!
Help, ye bright angelic spirits,
   Bring your sweetest, noblest lays;
Help to sing our Saviour's merits,
   Help to chant Emmanuel's praise.

77 *"Who is this that cometh from Edom, with*   [8s. 7s. 7s.
     dyed garments from Bozrah?"

WHO is this that comes from Edom,
   All his raiment stained with blood,
To the captive speaking freedom,
   Bringing and bestowing good;
Glorious in the garb he wears,
Glorious in the spoil he bears?

2 'Tis the Saviour, now victorious,
   Travelling onward in his might;
'Tis the Saviour; O how glorious
   To his people, is the sight!
Satan conquered, and the grave,
Jesus now is strong to save.

3 Why that blood his raiment staining?
   'Tis the blood of many slain;
Of his foes there's none remaining,
   None, the contest to maintain:
Fallen they are, no more to rise;
All their glory prostrate lies.

4 Mighty Victor, reign for ever;
   Wear the crown so dearly won;
Never shall thy people, never,
   Cease to sing what thou hast done;
Thou hast fought thy people's foes;
Thou hast healed thy people's woes.

78 *"The preaching of the cross is unto us who are saved the power of God."* [L. M.

WE sing the praise of him who died,
   Of him who died upon the cross:
The sinner's hope let men deride:
   For this we count the world but loss.

2 Inscribed upon the cross we see
   In shining letters, God is love:
He bears our sins upon the tree:
   He brings us mercy from above.

3 The cross—it takes our guilt away;
   It holds the fainting spirit up;
It cheers with hope the gloomy day,
   And sweetens every bitter cup.

4 It makes the coward spirit brave,
 And nerves the feeble arm for fight;
It takes its terror from the grave,
 And gilds the bed of death with light.

5 The balm of life, the cure of woe,
 The measure and the pledge of love,
The sinner's refuge here below,
 The angels' theme in heaven above.

79 *" God forbid that I should glory save in the cross* [L. M.
 of our Lord Jesus Christ."

THE Royal Banners forward go,
 The Cross shines forth in mystic glow;
Where he, in flesh, our flesh who made,
Our sentence bore, our ransom paid.

2 There whilst he hung, his sacred side
By soldier's spear was opened wide,
To cleanse us in the precious flood
Of water mingled with his blood.

3 O tree of glory, tree most fair,
Ordained those holy limbs to bear,
How bright in purple robe it stood,
The purple of a Saviour's blood!

4 Upon its arms, like balance true,
He weighed the price for sinners due,
The price which none but he could pay,
And spoiled the spoiler of his prey.

5 To Thee Eternal Three in One,
　Let homage meet by all be done:
　As by the cross thou dost restore,
　So rule and guide us evermore.

80 *"Behold the Lamb of God, which taketh away the sins of the world."* [P. M

BEHOLD the Lamb of God!
　O thou for sinners slain,
　Let it not be in vain
　　That thou hast died:
Thee for my Saviour let me take,
My only refuge let me make
　　Thy piercèd side.

2 Behold the Lamb of God!
Into the sacred flood
Of thy most precious blood
　　My soul I cast:
Wash me and make me clean within,
And keep me pure from every sin,
　　Till life be past.

3 Behold the Lamb of God!
All hail, Incarnate Word,
Thou everlasting Lord,
　　Saviour most blest;
Fill us with love that never faints,
Grant us with all thy blessèd saints,
　　Eternal rest.

4 Behold the Lamb of God!
Worthy is he alone,
That sitteth on the throne
   Of God above;
One with the Ancient of all days,
One with the Comforter in praise,
   All Light and Love.

81 *"Is it nothing to you, all ye that pass by? Behold, and* [7s
see if there be any sorrow like unto my sorrow."

SEE the destined day arise!
  See, a willing sacrifice;
Jesus, to redeem our loss,
Hangs upon the shameful cross!

2 Jesus, who but thou had borne,
  Lifted on that tree of scorn,
  Every pang and bitter throe,
  Finishing thy life of woe?

3 Who but thou had dared to drain,
  Steeped in gall, the cup of pain;
  And with tender body bear
  Thorns, and nails, and piercing spear?

4 Thence the cleansing water flowed,
  Mingled from thy side with blood;
  Sign to all attesting eyes
  Of the finished sacrifice.

5 Holy Jesus, grant us grace
In that sacrifice to place
All our trust for life renewed,
Pardoned sin, and promised good.

GOOD FRIDAY.

82   *"Truly this was the Son of God."*   [TEN 7s

BOUND upon the accursèd tree,
   Faint and bleeding, who is he?
By the eyes so pale and dim,
Streaming blood, and writhing limb,
By the flesh with scourges torn,
By the crown of twisted thorn,
By the side so deeply pierced,
By the baffled, burning thirst,
By the drooping, death-dew'd brow,
Son of Man! 'tis thou! 'tis thou!

2 Bound upon the accursèd tree,
Dread and awful, who is he?
By the sun at noonday pale,
Shivering rocks, and rending veil,
By the earth enwrapt in gloom,
By the saints who burst their tomb,
Eden promised ere he died
To the felon at his side;
Lord! our suppliant knees we bow!
Son of God! 'tis thou! 'tis thou!

3 Bound upon the accursèd tree,
  Sad and dying, who is he?
  By the last and bitter cry
  Of the dying agony,
  By the lifeless body, laid
  In the chambers of the dead,
  By the mourners come to weep
  Where the bones of Jesus sleep,
  Crucified, we know thee now:
  Son of Man! 'tis thou! 'tis thou!

4 Bound upon the accursèd tree,
  Dread and awful, who is he?
  By the prayer for them that slew,
  "Lord! they know not what they do!"
  By the spoil'd and empty grave,
  By the souls he died to save,
  By the conquest he hath won,
  By the saints before his throne,
  By the rainbow round his brow,
  Son of God! 'tis thou! 'tis thou!

33 *"God forbid that I should glory, save in the cross* [L. M.
  of our Lord Jesus Christ."

WHEN I survey the wondrous cross
  On which the Prince of Glory died,
My richest gain I count but loss,
  And pour contempt on all my pride.

2 Forbid it, Lord, that I should boast,
    Save in the cross of Christ, my God:
All the vain things that charm me most,
    I sacrifice them to thy blood.

3 See, from his head, his hands, his feet,
    Sorrow and love flow mingled down!
Did e'er such love and sorrow meet?
    Or thorns compose a Saviour's crown?

4 Were the whole realm of nature mine,
    That were a tribute far too small;
Love so amazing, so divine,
    Demands my life, my soul, my all.

84   *"Unto you therefore which believe he is precious."*   [8s. 7s.

SWEET the moments, rich in blessing,
    Which before the cross I spend;
Life, and health, and peace possessing,
    From the sinner's dying Friend.

2 Here I rest, forever viewing
    Mercy poured, in streams of blood:
Precious drops, my soul bedewing,
    Plead, and claim my peace with God.

3 Truly blessèd is the station,
    Low before his cross to lie;
Whilst I see divine compassion
    Beaming in his languid eye.

4 Lord, in ceaseless contemplation
　　Fix my thankful heart on thee,
　Till I taste thy full salvation
　　And thine unveil'd glory see.

85　*"He said, It is finished: and he bowed his head,*　[L. M.
　　　and gave up the ghost."

'TIS finished; so the Saviour cried,
　And meekly bow'd his head and died:
'Tis finish'd: yes, the work is done,
The battle fought, the victory won.

2 'Tis finished: all that heaven decreed,
　And all the ancient prophets said,
　Is now fulfill'd, as long designed,
　In me, the Saviour of mankind.

3 'Tis finished: Aaron now no more
　Must stain his robes with purple gore:
　The sacred veil is rent in twain,
　And Jewish rites no more remain.

4 'Tis finished: this my dying groan
　Shall sins of every kind atone:
　Millions shall be redeem'd from death,
　By this, my last expiring breath.

5 'Tis finished: heaven is reconciled,
　And all the powers of darkness spoiled:
　Peace, love, and happiness, again
　Return and dwell with sinful men.

6 'Tis finished: let the joyful sound
 Be heard through all the nations round:
 'Tis finished: let the echo fly
 Through heaven and hell, through earth and sky.

86 *"Remembering mine affliction and my misery, the* [SIX 7s.
 wormwood and the gall."

GO to dark Gethsemane,
  Ye that feel the tempter's power,
Your Redeemer's conflict see,
  Watch with him one bitter hour;
Turn not from his griefs away,
Learn of Jesus Christ to pray.

2 Follow to the judgment-hall;
   View the Lord of life arraign'd;
 O the wormwood and the gall!
   O the pangs his soul sustain'd!
 Shun not suffering, shame, or loss;
 Learn of him to bear the cross.

3 Calvary's mournful mountain climb;
   There, adoring at his feet,
 Mark the miracle of time,
   God's own sacrifice complete;
 "It is finish'd!" hear him cry;
 Learn of Jesus Christ to die.

GOOD FRIDAY.

87   *"Who loved me and gave himself for me."*   [7s. 6s. Double.

O SACRED Head, now wounded,
   With grief and shame bowed down,
Now scornfully surrounded
   With thorns, thine only crown.
O sacred Head, what glory,
   What bliss till now was thine!
Yet, though despised and gory,
   I joy to call thee mine.

2 What thou, my Lord, hast suffered,
   Was all for sinners' gain:
Mine, mine was the transgression,
   But thine the deadly pain.
Lo, here I fall, my Saviour:
   'Tis I deserve thy place;
Look on me with thy favour,
   Vouchsafe to me thy grace.

3 The joy can ne'er be spoken,
   Above all joys beside,
When in thy body broken
   I thus with safety hide.
Lord of my life, desiring
   Thy glory now to see,
Beside thy cross expiring,
   I'd breathe my soul to thee.

4 What language shall I borrow
   To thank thee, dearest friend,
For this thy dying sorrow,
   Thy pity without end?

O make me thine for ever;
   And should I fainting be,
Lord, let me never, never
   Outlive my love for thee.

5 Be near me when I'm dying,
   O show thy cross to me:
And to my succour flying,
   Come, Lord, and set me free.
These eyes, new faith receiving,
   From Jesus shall not move;
For he, who dies believing,
   Dies safely through thy love.

88 *"It is finished."* [8s. 7s. 4

HARK! the voice of love and mercy
   Sounds aloud from Calvary;
See, it rends the rocks asunder,
   Shakes the earth, and veils the sky!
      "It is finished!"
   Hear the dying Saviour cry.

2 "It is finished!" O what pleasure
   Do the precious words afford!
Heavenly blessings, without measure,
   Flow to us from Christ the Lord.
      "It is finished!"
   Saints the dying words record.

3 Finished all the types and shadows
   Of the ceremonial law;
Finish'd all that God had promised:

GOOD FRIDAY.

    Death and hell no more shall awe:
      "It is finished!"
    Saints from hence your comfort draw.

4 Tune your harps anew, ye seraphs;
    Strike them to Emmanuel's name;
  All on earth, and all in heaven,
    Join the triumph to proclaim.
      Alleluia!
  Glory to the bleeding Lamb!

---

89   *"They crucified him."*   [L. M

O COME and mourn with me awhile;
    O come ye to the Saviour's side;
O come, together let us mourn;
    Jesus, our Lord, is crucified.

2 Have we no tears to shed for him,
    While soldiers scoff and Jews deride?
Ah! look how patiently he hangs;
    Jesus, our Lord, is crucified.

3 Seven times he spake, seven words of love;
    And all three hours his silence cried
For mercy on the souls of men;
    Jesus, our Lord, is crucified.

4 A broken heart, a fount of tears,
    Ask, and they will not be denied;
Lord Jesus, may we love and weep,
    Since thou for us art crucified.

EASTER EVEN.

90 "*And when Joseph had taken the body, he wrapped it in a clean linen cloth, and laid it in his own new tomb, which he had hewn out in the rock. . . . . And there was Mary Magdalene and the other Mary, sitting over against the sepulchre.*" [SIX 7s.

RESTING from his work to-day
In the tomb the Saviour lay;
Still he slept, from head to feet
Shrouded in the winding-sheet,
Lying in the rock alone,
Hidden by the sealèd stone.

2 Late at even there was seen
Watching long the Magdalene;
Early, ere the break of day,
Sorrowful she took her way
To the holy garden glade,
Where her buried Lord was laid.

3 So with thee, till life shall end,
I would solemn vigil spend:
Let me hew thee, Lord, a shrine
In this rocky heart of mine,
Where in pure embalmèd cell
None but thou may ever dwell.

4 Myrrh and spices will I bring,
True affection's offering;
Close the door from sight and sound
Of the busy world around;
And in patient watch remain
Till my Lord appear again.

EASTER EVEN.

91 *"Then took they the body of Jesus, and wound it in* [7s.
linen clothes with the spices."

PAIN and toil are over now;
　　Bring the spice and bring the myrrh,
Fold the limb and bind the brow,
　　In the rich man's sepulchre.

2 Sin has bruised the Victor's heel;
　　Roll the stone and guard it well;
Bring the Roman's boasted seal,
　　Bring his boldest sentinel.

3 Yet the morning's purple ray
　　Shall present a glorious sight,
Stone by earthquake roll'd away,
　　Angel guards all robed in white.

92 *"And laid him in a sepulchre which was hewn* [8s. 7s. 7s.
out of a rock."

ALL is o'er, the pain, the sorrow,
　　Human taunts and Satan's spite;
Death shall be despoiled to-morrow
　　Of the Prey he grasps to-night.
Yet once more, his own to save,
Christ must sleep within the grave.

2 Fierce and deadly was the anguish
　　On the bitter cross he bore:
How did soul and body languish,
　　Till the toil of death was o'er!
But that toil, so fierce and dread,
Bruised and crushed the serpent's head.

3 Close and still the tomb that holds him
    While in brief repose he lies;
Deep the slumber that enfolds him,
    Veiled awhile from mortal eyes:
Slumber such as needs must be
After hard-won victory.

4 So this night, with voice of sadness
    Chant the anthem soft and low;
Loftier strains of praise and gladness
    From to-morrow's harps shall flow:
Death and hell at length are slain,
Christ hath triumphed, Christ doth reign.

93   *"I would not live alway."*   [11s. 12s.

I WOULD not live alway: I ask not to stay
  Where storm after storm rises dark o'er the way;
The few lurid mornings that dawn on us here
Are enough for life's woes, full enough for its cheer.

2 I would not live alway, thus fetter'd by sin,
Temptation without and corruption within:
E'en the rapture of pardon is mingled with fears,
And the cup of thanksgiving with penitent tears.

3 I would not live alway; no, welcome the tomb:
Since Jesus hath lain there, I dread not its gloom;
There, sweet be my rest, till he bid me arise
To hail him in triumph descending the skies.

4 Who, who would live alway, away from his God;
Away from yon heaven, that blissful abode,
Where the rivers of pleasure flow o'er the bright
    plains,
And the noontide of glory eternally reigns;

5 Where the saints of all ages in harmony meet,
Their Saviour and brethren, transported, to greet;
While the anthems of rapture unceasingly roll,
And the smile of the Lord is the feast of the soul

94 *"O Lord God of my salvation, I have cried day* [L. M.
and night before thee."

From the lxxxviii. Psalm.

GOD of my life, O Lord most high,
To thee by day and night I cry;
Vouchsafe my mournful voice to hear,
To my distress incline thine ear.

2 Like those whose strength and hopes are fled,
They number me among the dead;
Like those who, shrouded in the grave,
From thee no more remembrance have.

3 Wilt thou by miracle revive
The dead, whom thou forsook'st alive?
Shall the mute grave thy love confess,
A mouldering tomb thy faithfulness?

4 To thee, O Lord, I cry forlorn,
My prayer prevents the early morn:
Why hast thou, Lord, my soul forsook,
Nor once vouchsafed a gracious look?

5 Companions dear and friends beloved
Far from my sight thou hast removed:
God of my life, O Lord most high,
Vouchsafe to hear my mournful cry!

95 *"I have set God always before me; for he is on my right hand, therefore I shall not fall."* [C. M.

From the xvi. Psalm.

MY grateful soul shall bless the Lord,
　Whose precepts give me light;
And private counsel still afford
　In sorrow's dismal night.

2 Therefore my heart all grief defies,
　My glory does rejoice;
My flesh shall rest, in hope to rise,
　Waked by his powerful voice.

3 Thou, Lord, when I resign my breath,
　My soul from hell shalt free;
Nor let thy Holy One in death
　The least corruption see.

4 Thou shalt the paths of life display
　Which to thy presence lead;
Where pleasures dwell without allay,
　And joys that never fade.

96 *"When I awake I shall be satisfied with thy likeness."* [L. M

THIS life's a dream, an empty show;
　But the bright world to which I go
Hath joys substantial and sincere:
When shall I wake and find me there?

2 O glorious hour! O blest abode!
I shall be near and like my God,
And flesh and sense no more control
The sacred pleasures of the soul.

3 My flesh shall slumber in the ground
Till the last trumpet's joyful sound;
Then burst the chains with sweet surprise,
And in my Saviour's image rise.

87   *"I shall not die, but live."*   [S. M.

IT is not death to die;
  To leave this weary road,
And midst the brotherhood on high
  To be at home with God.

2 It is not death to close
  The eye long dimmed by tears,
And wake, in glorious repose
  To spend eternal years.

3 It is not death to bear
  The wrench that sets us free
From dungeon chain, to breathe the air
  Of boundless liberty.

4 It is not death to fling
  Aside this sinful dust,
And rise, on strong exulting wing,
  To live among the just.

5 Jesus, thou Prince of life!
  Thy chosen cannot die;
Like thee, they conquer in the strife,
  To reign with thee on high.

EASTER.

98 *"He is risen."* [7s.

CHRIST the Lord is risen to-day,
　Sons of men and angels say:
Raise your joys and triumphs high,
Sing, ye heavens; and earth, reply.

2 Love's redeeming work is done,
Fought the fight, the victory won:
Jesus' agony is o'er,
Darkness veils the earth no more.

3 Vain the stone, the watch, the seal,
Christ hath burst the gates of hell;
Death in vain forbids him rise,
Christ hath open'd Paradise.

4 Soar we now where Christ hath led,
Following our exalted Head;
Made like him, like him we rise;
Ours the cross, the grave, the skies.

99 *"He is not here; he is risen."* [7s.

JESUS CHRIST is risen to-day,
　Our triumphant holy day,
Who did once upon the cross
Suffer to redeem our loss.
　　　　　Alleluia!

2 Hymns of praise then let us sing
  Unto Christ, our heavenly King,
  Who endured the cross and grave,
  Sinners to redeem and save.
                    Alleluia!

3 But the pains which he endured
  Our salvation have procured;
  Now above the sky he's King,
  Where the angels ever sing,
                    Alleluia!

100 *" Sing ye to the Lord; for he hath triumphed gloriously."* [7s. DOUBLE

AT the Lamb's high feast we sing
  Praise to our victorious King,
Who hath washed us in the tide
Flowing from his piercèd side;
Praise we him, whose love divine
Gives his sacred blood for wine,
Gives his body for the feast,
Christ the Victim, Christ the Priest.

2 Where the Paschal blood is poured,
  Death's dark angel sheathes his sword;
  Israel's hosts triumphant go
  Through the wave that drowns the foe.
  Praise we Christ, whose blood was shed,
  Paschal Victim, Paschal Bread;
  With sincerity and love
  Eat we manna from above.

3 Mighty Victim from the sky!
Hell's fierce powers beneath thee lie;
Thou hast conquered in the fight,
Thou hast brought us life and light:
Now no more can death appal,
Now no more the grave enthral;
Thou hast opened Paradise,
And in thee thy saints shall rise.

4 Easter triumph, Easter joy,
Sin alone can this destroy;
From sin's power do thou set free
Souls new-born, O Lord, in thee.
Hymns of glory and of praise,
Risen Lord, to thee we raise;
Holy Father, praise to thee,
With the Spirit, ever be.

101 *"Now is Christ risen from the dead."* [P. M.

ANGELS, roll the rock away!
Death, yield up the mighty Prey!
See, the Saviour quits the tomb,
Glowing with immortal bloom.
 Alleluia! alleluia!
Christ the Lord is risen to-day.

2 Shout, ye seraphs; angels, raise
Your eternal song of praise;
Let the earth's remotest bound
Echo to the blissful sound.
 Alleluia! alleluia!
Christ the Lord is risen to-day.

3 Holy Father, Holy Son,
Holy Spirit, Three in One,
Glory as of old to thee,
Now and evermore, shall be.
　　Alleluia! alleluia!
Christ the Lord is risen to-day.

102　　"*The First-begotten of the dead.*"　　[8s. 8s. 6.

COME see the place where Jesus lay,
And hear angelic watchers say,
"He lives, who once was slain:
Why seek the living 'midst the dead?
Remember how the Saviour said
　That he would rise again."

2 O joyful sound! O glorious hour,
When by his own Almighty power
　He rose, and left the grave!
Now let our songs his triumph tell,
Who burst the bands of death and hell,
　And ever lives to save.

3 The First-begotten of the dead,
For us he rose, our glorious Head,
　Immortal life to bring;
What though the saints like him shall die,
They share their Leader's victory,
　And triumph with their King.

4 No more they tremble at the grave,
For Jesus will their spirits save,
　And raise their slumbering dust:
O risen Lord, in thee we live,
To thee our ransom'd souls we give,
　To thee our bodies trust.

103 *"O Sing unto the Lord a new song; for he hath done marvellous things."* [P. M.

THE strife is o'er, the battle done!
The victory of life is won;
The song of triumph has begun,
     Alleluia!

2 The powers of Death have done their worst,
But Christ their legions hath dispersed:
Let shout of holy joy outburst,
     Alleluia!

3 The three sad days are quickly sped;
He rises glorious from the dead:
All glory to our risen Head!
     Alleluia!

4 He closed the yawning gates of hell,
The bars from heaven's high portals fell;
Let hymns of praise his triumphs tell!
     Alleluia!

5 Lord! by the stripes which wounded thee,
From Death's dread sting thy servants free,
That we may live, and sing to thee,
     Alleluia!

104 *"I am he that liveth, and was dead; and behold, I am alive for ever, Amen; and have the keys of hell and of death."* [7s. 8s.

JESUS lives: no longer now
Can thy terrors, Death, appal us;
Jesus lives: by this we know
 Thou, O grave, canst not enthral us.
     Alleluia!

2 Jesus lives: henceforth is death
   But the gate of life immortal;
This shall calm our trembling breath,
   When we pass its gloomy portal.
                Alleluia!

3 Jesus lives: for us he died:
   Then, alone to Jesus living,
Pure in heart may we abide,
   Glory to our Saviour giving.
                Alleluia!

4 Jesus lives: our hearts know well
   Nought from us his love shall sever;
Life, nor death, nor powers of hell
   Tear us from his keeping ever.
                Alleluia!

5 Jesus lives: to him the throne
   Over all the world is given:
May we go where he is gone,
   Rest and reign with him in heaven.
                Alleluia!

105   *"Jesus met them, saying 'All hail.'"*   [7s. 6s. Double.

THE day of resurrection!
   Earth, tell it out abroad!
The Passover of gladness,
   The Passover of God!
From death to life eternal,
   From this world to the sky,
Our Christ hath brought us over,
   With hymns of victory.

2 Our hearts be pure from evil,
    That we may see aright
The Lord in rays eternal
    Of resurrection-light;
And, listening to his accents,
    May hear, so calm and plain,
His own "All hail!" and, hearing,
    May raise the victor-strain.

3 Now let the heavens be joyful!
    Let earth her song begin!
Let the round world keep triumph,
    And all that is therein!
Invisible and visible,
    Their notes let all things blend,
For Christ the Lord hath risen,
    Our Joy that hath no end.

106 *"Alleluia! for the Lord God Omnipotent reigneth."* [7s.

CHRIST the Lord is risen again;
    Christ hath broken every chain;
Hark, angelic voices cry,
Singing evermore on high,
              Alleluia!

2 He who gave for us his life,
    Who for us endured the strife,
Is our Paschal Lamb to-day;
We too sing for joy, and say
              Alleluia!

3 He who bore all pain and loss
  Comfortless upon the cross,
  Lives in glory now on high,
  Pleads for us and hears our cry;
                Alleluia!

4 He who slumbered in the grave
  Is exalted now to save;
  Now through Christendom it rings
  That the Lamb is King of kings.
                Alleluia!

5 Now he bids us tell abroad
  How the lost may be restored,
  How the penitent forgiven.
  How we too may enter heaven.
                Alleluia!

6 Thou, our Paschal Lamb indeed,
  Christ thy ransomed people feed:
  Take our sins and guilt away,
  Let us sing by night and day
                Alleluia!

107 *"The Lord is risen indeed."* [8s. 7s. 7s.

HE is risen! he is risen!
  Tell it with a joyful voice,
He has burst his three days' prison,
  Let the whole wide earth rejoice;
Death is vanquish'd, man is free,
Christ has won the victory.

2 Tell it to the sinners, weeping
   Over deeds in darkness done,
Weary fast and vigil keeping;
   Brightly breaks their Easter sun;
Christ has borne our sins away,
Christ has conquer'd hell to-day.

3 He is risen! he is risen!
   He has oped the eternal gate;
We are loosed from sin's dark prison,
   Risen to a holier state,
Where a brightening Easter beam
On our longing eye shall stream.

108   *"Sing unto the Lord, for he hath triumphed gloriously."*   [P. M.

LIFT your glad voices in triumph on high,
   For Jesus hath risen, and man cannot die.
Vain were the terrors that gathered around him,
   And short the dominion of death and the grave;
He burst from the fetters of darkness that bound him,
   Resplendent in glory to live and to save.
Loud was the chorus of angels on high,
"The Saviour hath risen, and man shall not die."

2 Glory to God, in full anthems of joy!
The being he gave us, death cannot destroy;
Sad were the life we must part with to-morrow,
   If tears were our birthright, and death were our end?
But Jesus hath cheered the dark valley of sorrow,
   And bade us, immortal, to heaven ascend.
Lift your glad voices in triumph on high,
Jesus hath risen, and man shall not die.

109 *"Now is Christ risen from the dead, and become the first-fruits of them that slept."* [P. M.

TO him who for our sins was slain,
To him for all his dying pain,
  Sing we Alleluia!
To him the Lamb our Sacrifice,
Who gave his blood our ransom-price,
  Sing we Alleluia!

2 To him who died that we might die
To sin, and live with him on high,
  Sing we Alleluia!
To him who rose that we might rise,
And reign with him beyond the skies,
  Sing we Alleluia!

3 To him who now for us doth plead,
And helpeth us in all our need,
  Sing we Alleluia!
To him who doth prepare on high
Our home in immortality,
  Sing we Alleluia!

4 To him be glory evermore:
Ye heavenly hosts, your Lord adore;
  Sing we Alleluia!
To Father, Son, and Holy Ghost,
Our God most great, our joy, our boast,
  Sing we Alleluia!

110 *"Thou art my Son, this day have I begotten thee."* [C. M.

From the ii. Psalm.

THUS God declares his sovereign will:
"The King that I ordain,
Whose throne is fix'd on Sion's hill,
Shall there securely reign."

2 Attend, O earth, whilst I declare
God's uncontroll'd decree:
"Thou art my Son, this day my heir
Have I begotten thee.

3 "Ask, and receive thy full demands:
Thine shall the heathen be;
The utmost limits of the lands
Shall be possess'd by thee."

111 *"Christ our Passover is sacrificed for us; therefore let us keep the feast."* [Six 7s.

ONCE the angel started back,
When he saw the blood-stain'd door,
Pausing on his vengeful track,
And the dwelling passing o'er.
Once the sea from Israel fled,
Ere it roll'd o'er Egypt's dead.

2 Now our Passover is come,
Dimly shadow'd in the past,
And the very Paschal Lamb,
Christ the Lord, is slain at last.
Then, with hearts and hands made meet,
Our unleaven'd bread we'll eat.

3 Blessed Victim sent from heaven,
   Whom all angel hosts obey,
To whose will all earth is given,
   At whose word hell shrinks away,
     Thou hast conquer'd death's dread strife,
     Thou hast brought us light and life.

112 *"The Lord is my strength, and my song; and is become my salvation."* [C. M.

From the cxviii. Psalm.

JOY fills the dwelling of the just,
   Whom God has saved from harm;
For wondrous things are brought to pass
   By his Almighty arm.

2 Then open wide the temple gates
   To which the just repair,
That I may enter in, and praise
   My great Deliverer there.

3 That which the builders once refused,
   Is now the Corner-stone:
This is the wondrous work of God,
   The work of God alone.

4 This day is God's; let all the lands
   Exalt their cheerful voice:
"Lord, we beseech thee, save us now,
   And make us still rejoice."

5 O then with me give thanks to God,
   Who still does gracious prove;
And let the tribute of our praise
   Be endless as his love.

ASCENSION.

113   *"Who is gone into heaven."*   [D. S. M.

THOU art gone up on high
  To mansions in the skies;
And round thy throne unceasingly
  The songs of praise arise:
  But we are lingering here,
  With sin and care oppressed;
Lord, send thy promised Comforter,
  And lead us to thy rest.

2 Thou art gone up on high;
  But thou didst first come down,
Through earth's most bitter misery,
  To pass unto thy crown;
  And girt with griefs and fears
  Our onward course must be;
But only let that path of tears
  Lead us at last to thee.

3 Thou art gone up on high;
  But thou shalt come again,
With all the bright ones of the sky
  Attendant in thy train.
  O by thy saving power,
  So make us live and die,
That we may stand, in that dread hour
  At thy right hand on high.

114   *"We see Jesus crowned with glory and honour."*   [C. M.

THE Head, that once was crown'd with thorns,
  Is crown'd with glory now;
A royal diadem adorns
  The mighty Victor's brow.

2 The highest place that heaven affords
   Is his, is his by right,
 The King of kings and Lord of lords,
   And heaven's eternal light.

3 The joy of all who dwell above;
   The joy of all below,
 To whom he manifests his love
   And grants his name to know.

4 To them the cross with all its shame,
   With all its grace is given;
 Their name an everlasting name,
   Their joy the joy of heaven.

5 They suffer with their Lord below,
   They reign with him above,
 Their profit and their joy to know
   The mystery of his love.

6 The cross he bore is life and health,
   Though shame and death to him:
 His people's hope, his people's wealth,
   Their everlasting theme.

115 *"By his own blood he entered in once into the holy place."* [8s. 7s. 4.

LOOK, ye saints; the sight is glorious;
   See the "Man of sorrows" now;
 From the fight returned victorious,
   Every knee to him shall bow;
     Crown him! Crown him!
 Crowns become the Victor's brow.

2 Crown the Saviour, angels crown him;
    Rich the trophies Jesus brings;
On the seat of power enthrone him,
    While the vault of heaven rings;
        Crown him! Crown him!
Crown the Saviour King of kings.

3 Sinners in derision crowned him,
    Mocking thus the Saviour's claim;
Saints and angels crowd around him,
    Own his title, praise his name:
        Crown him! Crown him!
Spread abroad the Victor's fame!

4 Hark! those bursts of acclamation!
    Hark! those loud triumphant chords!
Jesus takes the highest station;
    O what joy the sight affords!
        Crown him! Crown him!
King of kings, and Lord of lords.

116   *"And on his head were many crowns."*   [D. S. M.

CROWN him with many crowns,
    The Lamb upon his throne;
Hark! how the heavenly anthem drowns
    All music but its own!
    Awake, my soul, and sing
    Of him who died for thee;
And hail him as thy matchless King
    Through all eternity.

ASCENSION.

2 Crown him the Virgin's Son!
   The God incarnate born,
Whose arm those crimson trophies won
   Which now his brow adorn.
   Fruit of the Mystic Rose,
   True Branch of Jesse's stem,
The Root whence mercy ever flows,—
   The Babe of Bethlehem!

3 Crown him the Lord of love!
   Behold his hands and side,—
Those wounds, yet visible above,
   In beauty glorified:
   No angel in the sky
   Can fully bear that sight,
But downward bends his wondering eye
   At mysteries so bright.

4 Crown him the Lord of peace!
   Whose power a sceptre sways
In heaven and earth, that wars may cease,
   And all be prayer and praise.
   His reign shall know no end;
   And round his piercèd feet
Fair flowers of Paradise extend
   Their fragrance ever sweet.

5 Crown him the Lord of heaven!
   One with the Father known,—
And the blest Spirit, through him given
   From yonder Triune throne!
   All hail, Redeemer, hail!
   For thou hast died for me:
Thy praise and glory shall not fail
   Throughout eternity.

117 *"Thou hast led captivity captive."* L. M.

OUR Lord is risen from the dead;
 Our Jesus is gone up on high;
The powers of hell are captive led,
 Dragg'd to the portals of the sky.

2 There his triumphal chariot waits,
 And angels chant the solemn lay:
Lift up your heads, ye heavenly gates,
 Ye everlasting doors, give way.

3 Loose all your bars of massy light,
 And wide unfold the radiant scene;
He claims those mansions as his right;
 Receive the King of Glory in.

4 Who is the King of Glory, who?
 The Lord that all his foes o'ercame,
The world, sin, death, and hell o'erthrew;
 And Jesus is the Conqueror's name.

5 Lo! his triumphal chariot waits,
 And angels chant the solemn lay;
Lift up your heads, ye heavenly gates,
 Ye everlasting doors, give way.

6 Who is the King of Glory, who?
 The Lord, of boundless power possess'd,
The King of saints and angels too,
 God over all, for ever bless'd.

118 *"We have a great High Priest that is passed into the heavens."* [6s. 8s.

THE atoning work is done,
  The Victim's blood is shed,
And Jesus now is gone
  His people's cause to plead;
He stands in heaven, their great High Priest,
He bears their names upon his breast.

2 He sprinkles with his blood
  The mercy-seat above;
For justice had withstood
  The purposes of love;
But justice now withstands no more,
And mercy yields her boundless store.

3 No temple made with hands,
  His place of service is;
In heaven itself he stands,
  A heavenly priesthood his.
In him the shadows of the law
Are all fulfill'd, and now withdraw.

4 And though a while he be
  Hid from the eyes of men,
His people look to see
  Their great High Priest again;
In brightest glory he will come,
And take his waiting people home.

119   *"The King of Glory shall come in."*   [L. M.

THE rising God forsakes the tomb;
   Up to his Father's court he flies;
Cherubic legions guard him home,
   And shout him welcome to the skies.

2 Break off your tears, ye saints, and tell
   How high our great Deliverer reigns;
Sing how he spoil'd the hosts of hell,
   And led the tyrant death in chains.

3 Say, "Live for ever, glorious King,
   Born to redeem, and strong to save!"
Then ask—"O death, where is thy sting?
   And where thy victory, O grave?"

120   *"O clap your hands together, all ye people; O sing*   [L. M.
    unto God with the voice of melody."

From the xlvii. Psalm.

O ALL ye people, clap your hands,
   And with triumphant voices sing;
No force the mighty power withstands
   Of God the universal King.

2 He shall assaulting foes repel,
   And with success our battles fight;
Shall fix the place where we must dwell,
   The pride of Jacob, his delight.

3 God is gone up, our Lord and King,
   With shouts of joy, and trumpet's sound;
To him repeated praises sing,
   And let the cheerful song rebound.

4 Your utmost skill in praise be shown,
    For him who all the world commands;
Who sits upon his righteous throne,
    And spreads his sway o'er heathen lands.

121 *"Lift up your heads, O ye gates; and be ye lift* [C. M
*up, ye everlasting doors; and the King of
Glory shall come in."*

From the xxiv. Psalm.

LIFT up your heads, eternal gates,
    Unfold, to entertain
The King of Glory! see, he comes
    With his celestial train.

2 Who is the King of Glory? who?
    The Lord for strength renown'd;
In battle mighty; o'er his foes
    Eternal Victor crown'd.

3 Lift up your heads, ye gates; unfold,
    In state to entertain
The King of Glory! see, he comes
    With all his shining train.

4 Who is the King of Glory? who?
    The Lord of hosts renown'd;
Of glory he alone is King,
    Who is with glory crown'd.

122 *"O sing unto God, and sing praises unto his name."* [L. M.

From the lxviii. Psalm.

THE servants of Jehovah's will
   His favour's gentle beams enjoy;
Their upright hearts let gladness fill,
   And cheerful songs their tongues employ.

2 To him your voice in anthems raise,
   Jehovah's awful name he bears;
In him rejoice, extol his praise,
   Who rides upon high-rolling spheres.

3 His chariots numberless, his powers
   Are heavenly hosts, that wait his will;
His presence now fills Sion's towers,
   As once it honour'd Sinai's hill.

4 Ascending high, in triumph thou
   Captivity hast captive led,
And on thy people didst bestow
   Thy gifts and graces freely shed.

123 *"We see Jesus crowned with glory and honour."* [C. M.

BEHOLD the glories of the Lamb
   Amid his Father's throne;
Prepare new honours for his name,
   And songs before unknown.

2 Let elders worship at his feet,
   The Church adore around,
With vials full of odours sweet,
   And harps of sweeter sound.

3 Now to the Lamb that once was slain
    Be endless blessings paid;
  Salvation, glory, joy, remain
    For ever on thy head.

4 Thou hast redeem'd our souls with blood,
    Hast set the prisoners free,
  Hast made us kings and priests to God,
    And we shall reign with thee.

5 The worlds of nature and of grace
    Are put beneath thy power;
  Then shorten these delaying days,
    And bring the promised hour.

124 *"Father, I will that they whom thou hast given* [L. M.
          me be with me where I am."

STAND up, my soul, shake off thy fears,
  And gird the Gospel armour on;
March to the gates of endless joy,
  Where Jesus thy great Captain's gone.

2 Hell and thy sins resist thy course,
    But hell and sin are vanquish'd foes;
  Thy Saviour nail'd them to the cross,
    And sung the triumph when he rose.

3 Then let my soul march boldly on,
    Press forward to the heavenly gate;
  There peace and joy eternal reign,
    And glittering robes for conquerors wait.

4 There shall I wear a starry crown,
    And triumph in Almighty grace,
  While all the armies of the skies
    Join in my glorious Leader's praise.

WHITSUNTIDE.

125   *"The Comforter, which is the Holy Ghost."*   [C. M.

HE'S come, let every knee be bent,
    All hearts new joy resume;
Sing, ye redeem'd, with one consent,
    "The Comforter is come."

2 What greater gift, what greater love,
    Could God on man bestow?
Angels for this rejoice above,
    Let man rejoice below.

3 Hail, blessed Spirit! may each soul
    Thy sacred influence feel;
Do thou each sinful thought control,
    And fix our wavering zeal.

4 Thou to the conscience dost convey
    Those checks which we should know;
Thy motions point to us the way;
    Thou giv'st us strength to go.

126   *"I will pour out my Spirit upon all flesh."*   [L. M.

O SPIRIT of the living God,
    In all thy plenitude of grace,
Where'er the foot of man hath trod,
    Descend on our apostate race.

WHITSUNTIDE.

2 Give tongues of fire and hearts of love,
    To preach the reconciling word;
Give power and unction from above,
    Where'er the joyful sound is heard.

3 Be darkness, at thy coming, light;
    Confusion, order, in thy path;
Souls without strength inspire with might;
    Bid mercy triumph over wrath.

4 Convert the nations! far and nigh
    The triumphs of the cross record;
The name of Jesus glorify,
    Till every people call him Lord.

127   *"He shall give you another Comforter, that he*   [C. M
      may abide with you for ever."

COME, Holy Ghost, Creator, come,
    Inspire these souls of thine;
Till every heart which thou hast made
    Be fill'd with grace divine.

2 Thou art the Comforter, the gift
    Of God, and fire of love;
The everlasting spring of joy,
    And unction from above.

3 Thy gifts are manifold, thou writ'st
    God's law in each true heart;
The promise of the Father, thou
    Dost heavenly speech impart.

4 Enlighten our dark souls, till they
    Thy sacred love embrace;
Assist our minds, by nature frail,
    With thy celestial grace.

5 Drive far from us the mortal foe,
   And give us peace within;
 That, by thy guidance blest, we may
   Escape the snares of sin.

6 Teach us the Father to confess,
   And Son, from death revived,
 And thee, with both, O Holy Ghost,
   Who art from both derived.

128 *"The love of God is shed abroad in our hearts by the Holy Ghost."* [C. M.

COME, Holy Spirit, heavenly Dove,
   With all thy quickening powers;
 Kindle a flame of sacred love
   In these cold hearts of ours.

2 See how we grovel here below,
   Fond of these earthly toys:
 Our souls, how heavily they go,
   To reach eternal joys.

3 In vain we tune our lifeless songs,
   In vain we strive to rise:
 Hosannas languish on our tongues
   And our devotion dies.

4 Come, Holy Spirit, heavenly Dove,
   With all thy quickening powers;
 Come, shed abroad a Saviour's love,
   And that shall kindle ours.

WHITSUNTIDE.

129 *"The Spirit of God moved on the face of waters."*

CREATOR SPIRIT, by whose
 The world's foundations first
Come, visit every humble mind;
Come, pour thy joys on human ki
From sin and sorrow set us free,
And make thy temples worthy the

2 O source of uncreated light,
 The Father's promised Paraclete,
 Thrice holy fount, thrice holy fire
 Our hearts with heavenly love in:
 Come, and thy sacred unction bri
 To sanctify us while we sing.

3 Plenteous of grace, descend from
 Rich in thy seven-fold energy;
 Make us eternal truth receive,
 And practise all that we believe;
 Give us thyself, that we may see
 The Father and the Son by thee.

4 Immortal honour, endless fame,
 Attend the Almighty Father's nai
 The Saviour Son be glorified,
 Who for lost man's redemption di
 And equal adoration be,
 Eternal Paraclete, to thee.

130 *"They were all filled with the Holy Ghost."* [D. S. M.

LORD GOD, the Holy Ghost,
  In this accepted hour,
As on the day of Pentecost,
  Descend in all thy power;
  We meet with one accord
  In our appointed place,
And wait the promise of our Lord,
  The Spirit of all grace.

2 Like mighty rushing wind
  Upon the waves beneath,
Move with one impulse every mind,
  One soul, one feeling breathe:
  The young, the old, inspire
  With wisdom from above;
And give us hearts and tongues of fire
  To pray, and praise, and love.

3 Spirit of light, explore
  And chase our gloom away,
With lustre shining more and more
  Unto the perfect day:
  Spirit of truth, be thou
  In life and death our Guide;
O Spirit of adoption, now
  May we be sanctified.

131 *"As many as are led by the Spirit of God, they* [L. M.
  are the sons of God."

COME, gracious Spirit, heavenly Dove,
  With light and comfort from above;

Be thou our Guardian, thou our Guide,
O'er every thought and step preside.

2 The light of truth to us display,
And make us know and choose thy way;
Plant holy fear in every heart,
That we from thee may ne'er depart.

3 Lead us to Christ, the living way,
Nor let us from his precepts stray;
Lead us to holiness, the road
That we must take to dwell with God.

4 Lead us to heaven, that we may share
Fulness of joy for ever there:
Lead us to God, our final rest,
To be with him for ever blest.

132 *"If I go not away, the Comforter will not come unto* [P. M
you; but if I depart, I will send him unto you."

OUR blest Redeemer, ere he breathed
His tender last farewell,
A Guide, a Comforter, bequeathed
With us to dwell.

2 He came in semblance of a dove
With sheltering wings outspread,
The holy balm of peace and love
On earth to shed.

3 He came sweet influence to impart,
A gracious, willing guest,
While he can find one humble heart
Wherein to rest.

4 And his that gentle voice we hear,
    Soft as the breath of even,
That checks each thought, that calms each fear.
    And speaks of heaven.

5 And every virtue we possess,
    And every victory won,
And every thought of holiness
    Are his alone.

6 Spirit of purity and grace,
    Our weakness, pitying, see:
O make our hearts thy dwelling-place,
    And meet for thee.

7 O praise the Father; praise the Son;
    Blest Spirit, praise to thee;
All praise to God, the Three in One,
    The One in Three.

133 *"And the same day there were added unto them three thousand souls."*   [L. M.

SPIRIT of mercy, truth, and love,
O shed thine influence from above;
And still from age to age convey
The wonders of this sacred day.

2 In every clime, by every tongue,
Be God's surpassing glory sung:
Let all the listening earth be taught
The wonders by our Saviour wrought.

3 Unfailing Comfort, heavenly Guide
Still o'er thy holy Church preside;
Still let mankind thy blessings prove;
Spirit of mercy, truth, and love.

WHITSUNTIDE.

134 *"And the Spirit and the bride say, Come."* [S. M.

THE Spirit, in our hearts,
  Is whispering, Sinner, come:
The Bride, the Church of Christ, proclaims
  To all his children, Come.

2 Let him that heareth, say
  To all about him, Come:
Let him that thirsts for righteousness,
  To Christ, the fountain, come.

3 Yes, whosoever will,
  O let him freely come,
And freely drink the stream of life:
  'Tis Jesus bids him come.

4 Lo, Jesus, who invites,
  Declares, I quickly come.
Lord! even so; I wait thy hour:
  Jesus, my Saviour, come.

135 *"He dwelleth with you, and shall be in you."* [S. M.

COME, Holy Spirit, come;
  Let thy bright beams arise;
Dispel the sorrow from our minds,
  The darkness from our eyes.

2 Revive our drooping faith,
  Our doubts and fears remove,
And kindle in our breasts the flame
  Of never-dying love.

3 Convince us of our sin;
  Then lead to Jesus' blood,
And to our wondering view reveal
  The mercies of our God.

4 'Tis thine to cleanse the heart,
  To sanctify the soul,
To pour fresh life in every part,
  And new-create the whole.

5 Dwell therefore in our hearts,
  Our minds from bondage free;
Then shall we know, and praise, and love
  The Father, Son, and thee.

136 *"And suddenly there came a sound from heaven, as of a rushing mighty wind."* [C. M.

WHEN God of old came down from heaven,
  In power and wrath he came;
Before his feet the clouds were riven,
  Half darkness and half flame;

2 But when he came the second time,
  He came in power and love;
Softer than gale at morning prime
  Hovered his holy Dove.

3 The fires that rush'd on Sinai down
  In sudden torrents dread,
Now gently light, a glorious crown,
  On every sainted head.

4 And as on Israel's awe-struck ear
  The voice exceeding loud,
The trump, that angels quake to hear,
  Thrill'd from the deep, dark cloud;

5 So, when the Spirit of our God
   Came down his flock to find,
A voice from heaven was heard abroad,
   A rushing, mighty wind.

6 It fills the Church of God; it fills
   The sinful world around;
Only in stubborn hearts and wills
   No place for it is found.

7 Come, Lord, come, Wisdom, Love, and Power,
   Open our ears to hear;
Let us not miss th' accepted hour;
   Save, Lord, by love or fear.

137   *"He breathed on them, and saith unto them,*   [P. M
        Receive ye the Holy Ghost."

COME, Holy Ghost, our souls inspire,
And lighten with celestial fire.

Thou the anointing Spirit art,
Who dost thy sevenfold gifts impart.

Thy blessèd unction from above
Is comfort, life, and fire of love.

Enable with perpetual light
The dulness of our blinded sight.

Anoint and cheer our soilèd face
With the abundance of thy grace.

Keep far our foes, give peace at home:
Where thou art guide, no ill can come.

Teach us to know the Father, Son,
And thee of both to be but One,

That, through the ages all along,
This may be our unending song;

Praise to thy eternal merit,
Father, Son, and Holy Spirit.

TRINITY SUNDAY.

138 *"They rest not day and night, saying, Holy, holy,* [P. M.
*holy, Lord God Almighty, which was, and is,
and is to come."*

HOLY, holy, holy! Lord God Almighty!
　Early in the morning our song shall rise to thee:
Holy, holy, holy! merciful and mighty!
　God in Three Persons, blessed Trinity!

2 Holy, holy, holy! All the saints adore thee,
　Casting down their golden crowns around the glassy sea;
Cherubim and seraphim falling down before thee,
　Which wert, and art, and evermore shalt be.

3 Holy, holy, holy! though the darkness hide thee,
　Though the eye of sinful man thy glory may not see,
Only thou art holy; there is none beside thee
　Perfect in power, in love, and purity.

4 Holy, holy, holy! Lord God Almighty!
　All thy works shall praise thy name, in earth, and sky, and sea:
Holy, holy, holy! merciful and mighty!
　God in Three Persons, blessed Trinity!

139 *"Who shall not fear thee, O Lord, and glorify* [L. M.
thy name?"

O HOLY, holy, holy Lord,
   Bright in thy deeds and in thy name,
For ever be thy name adored,
   Thy glories let the world proclaim.

2 O Jesus, Lamb once crucified
   To take our load of sins away,
Thine be the hymn that rolls its tide
   Along the realms of upper day.

3 O Holy Spirit from above,
   In streams of light and glory given,
Thou source of ecstacy and love,
   Thy praises ring through earth and heaven.

4 O God Triune, to thee we owe
   Our every thought, our every song;
And ever may thy praises flow
   From saint and seraph's burning tongue.

140 *"From everlasting to everlasting thou art God."* [SIX 7s.

HOLY, holy, holy, Lord
   God of hosts, eternal King,
By the heavens and earth adored;
   Angels and archangels sing,
Chanting everlastingly
To the blessed Trinity.

2 Thousands, tens of thousands, stand,
   Spirits blest, before thy throne,
Speeding thence at thy command;
   And when thy command is done,
Singing everlastingly
 To the blessed Trinity.

3 Cherubim and seraphim
   Veil their faces with their wings;
Eyes of angels are too dim
   To behold the King of kings,
While they sing eternally
To the blessed Trinity.

4 Thee, apostles, prophets, thee,
   Thee, the noble martyr band,
Praise with solemn jubilee;
   Thee the Church in every land;
Singing everlastingly
To the blessed Trinity.

5 Alleluia! Lord, to thee,
   Father, Son, and Holy Ghost,
Three in One, and One in Three,
   Join we with the heavenly host,
Singing everlastingly
To the blessed Trinity.

141   *"This is my name for ever, and this is my*   [P. M.
     memorial unto all generations."

THE God of Abraham praise,
   Who reigns enthroned above;
Ancient of everlasting days,
   And God of love;

TRINITY SUNDAY.

   Jehovah, great I AM,
     By earth and heaven confess'd;—
I bow and bless the sacred name,
     For ever bless'd.

2 The God of Abraham praise,
   At whose supreme command
From earth I rise, and seek the joys
   At his right hand:
   I all on earth forsake,
   Its wisdom, fame, and power;
And him my only portion make,
   My shield and tower.

3 He by himself hath sworn,
   I on his oath depend,
I shall, on angel-wings upborne,
   To heaven ascend:
   I shall behold his face,
   I shall his power adore,
And sing the wonders of his grace
   For evermore.

4 There dwells the Lord, our King,
   The Lord, our righteousness,
Triumphant o'er the world and sin,
   The Prince of Peace;
   On Sion's sacred height
   His kingdom he maintains,
And, glorious with his saints in light,
   For ever reigns.

5 The God who reigns on high
   The great archangels sing;
And, "Holy, holy, holy," cry,
   "Almighty King,

      Who was, and is the same,
        And evermore shall be;
      Jehovah, Father, great I AM,
        We worship thee."

6 The whole triumphant host
    Give thanks to God on high;
Hail, Father, Son, and Holy Ghost,
      They ever cry:
  Hail, Abraham's God and mine,
    I join the heavenly lays;
All might and majesty are thine,
    And endless praise.

142   *"The grace of the Lord Jesus Christ, and the love*   [L. M.
*of God, and the communion of the Holy Ghost,
be with you all."*

FATHER of all, whose love profound
    A ransom for our souls hath found,
Before thy throne we sinners bend;
To us thy pardoning love extend.

2 Almighty Son, incarnate Word,
  Our Prophet, Priest, Redeemer, Lord,
Before thy throne we sinners bend;
To us thy saving grace extend.

3 Eternal Spirit, by whose breath
  The soul is raised from sin and death,
Before thy throne we sinners bend;
To us thy quickening power extend.

4 Jehovah,—Father, Spirit, Son,—
Mysterious Godhead, Three in One!
Before thy throne we sinners bend;
Grace, pardon, life, to us extend.

143 *"Of him and through him and to him are all things: to whom be glory for ever. Amen."* [6s. 8s.

WE give immortal praise
    To God the Father's love,
For all our comforts here,
    And all our hopes above:
He sent his own Eternal Son
To die for sins that man had done.

2 To God the Son belongs
    Immortal glory too,
Who saved us by his blood
    From everlasting woe:
And now he lives, and now he reigns,
And sees the fruit of all his pains.

3 To God the Spirit praise
    And endless worship give,
Whose new-creating power
    Makes the dead sinner live:
His work completes the great design,
And fills the soul with joy divine.

4 Almighty God, to thee
    Be endless honours done;
The sacred Persons Three,
    The Godhead only One;
Where reason fails with all her powers,
There faith prevails, and love adores.

144 *"And one cried unto another, and said, Holy,* [7s. DOUBLE.
holy, holy is the Lord of Hosts."

HOLY, holy, holy Lord
  God of hosts! When heaven and earth,
Out of darkness, at thy word,
  Issued into glorious birth,
All thy works before thee stood,
And thine eye beheld them good,
While they sang, with one accord,
Holy, holy, holy Lord!

2 Holy, holy, holy! Thee,
  One Jehovah evermore,
Father, Son, and Spirit, we,
  Dust and ashes, would adore;
Lightly by the world esteemed,
From that world by thee redeemed,
Sing we here, with glad accord,
Holy, holy, holy Lord!

3 Holy, holy, holy! All
  Heaven's triumphant choir shall sing,
When the ransomed nations fall
  At the footstool of their King:
Then shall saints and seraphim,
Hearts and voices, swell one hymn,
Round the throne with full accord,
Holy, holy, holy Lord!

TRINITY SUNDAY.

145   "*Sing unto the Lord, and praise his name.*"   [8s. 7s. 4.

HOLY Father, great Creator,
   Source of mercy, love, and peace,
Look upon the Mediator,
   Clothe us with his righteousness;
      Heavenly Father,
Through the Saviour hear and bless.

2 Holy Jesus, Lord of glory,
   Whom angelic hosts proclaim,
While we hear thy wondrous story,
   Meet and worship in thy name,
      Dear Redeemer,
In our hearts thy peace proclaim.

3 Holy Spirit, Sanctifier,
   Come with unction from above,
Raise our hearts to raptures higher,
   Fill them with the Saviour's love!
      Source of comfort,
Cheer us with the Saviour's love.

4 God the Lord, through every nation
   Let thy wondrous mercies shine!
In the song of thy salvation
   Every tongue and race combine!
      Great Jehovah,
Form our hearts and make them thine.

146 *"Let there be light."* [6s. 4s.

THOU, whose Almighty word
  Chaos and darkness heard,
    And took their flight;
Hear us, we humbly pray,
And, where the Gospel's day
Sheds not its glorious ray,
    Let there be light!

2 Thou who didst come to bring
  On thy redeeming wing
    Healing and sight,
Health to the sick in mind,
Sight to the inly-blind,
O now, to all mankind,
    Let there be light!

3 Spirit of truth and love,
  Life-giving, holy Dove,
    Speed forth thy flight!
Move on the waters' face,
Bearing the lamp of grace,
And, in earth's darkest place
    Let there be light!

4 Holy and Blessèd Three,
  Glorious Trinity,
    Wisdom, Love, Might,
Boundless as ocean's tide,
Rolling in fullest pride,
Through the world, far and wide,
    Let there be light!

THE LORD'S DAY.

147 *"A day in thy courts is better than a thousand."* [S. M.

WELCOME, sweet day of rest,
   That saw the Lord arise;
Welcome to this reviving breast,
   And these rejoicing eyes.

2 The King himself comes near
   To feast his saints to-day;
Here may we sit, and see him here,
   And love, and praise, and pray.

3 One day amidst the place
   Where Jesus is within,
Is better than ten thousand days
   Of pleasure and of sin.

4 My willing soul would stay
   In such a frame as this,
Till it is call'd to soar away,
   To everlasting bliss.

148 *"This is the day which the Lord hath made."* [6s. 8s.

AWAKE, ye saints, awake,
   And hail this sacred day;
In loftiest songs of praise
   Your joyful homage pay:
Welcome the day that God hath blest,
The type of heaven's eternal rest.

2 On this auspicious morn
 The Lord of life arose;
He burst the bars of death,
 And vanquish'd all our foes:
And now he pleads our cause above,
And reaps the fruits of all his love.

3 All hail, triumphant Lord!
 Heaven with hosannas rings,
And earth, in humbler strains,
 Thy praise responsive sings:
Worthy the Lamb that once was slain,
Through endless years to live and reign.

4 Great King, gird on thy sword,
 Ascend thy conquering car;
While justice, truth, and love
 Maintain thy glorious war:
This day let sinners own thy sway,
And rebels cast their arms away.

149   *"The first day of the week."*   [C. M.

BLEST day of God! most calm, most bright,
 The first, the best of days;
The labourer's rest, the saint's delight,
 The day of prayer and praise.

2 My Saviour's face made thee to shine;
 His rising thee did raise,
And made thee heavenly and divine
 Beyond all other days.

THE LORD'S DAY.

3 The first-fruits oft a blessing prove
    To all the sheaves behind;
And they the day of Christ who love,
    A happy week shall find.

4 This day I must with God appear;
    For, Lord, the day is thine;
Help me to spend it in thy fear,
    And thus to make it mine.

150   *"Thou, Lord, hast made me glad through thy works."*   [L. M.

SWEET is the work, my God, my King,
To praise thy name, give thanks, and sing;
To show thy love by morning light,
And talk of all thy truth at night.

2 Sweet is the day of sacred rest;
No mortal cares shall seize my breast;
O may my heart in tune be found,
Like David's harp of solemn sound!

3 My heart shall triumph in my Lord,
And bless his works, and bless his word;
His works of grace, how bright they shine!
How deep his counsels, how divine!

4 I then shall share a glorious part,
When grace hath well refined my heart,
And fresh supplies of joy are shed,
Like holy oil, to cheer my head.

5 Then shall I see, and hear, and know,
All I desired or wished below;
And every power find sweet employ
In that eternal world of joy.

151 "*This is the day which the Lord hath made.*" [SIX 8s.

GREAT God, this sacred day of thine
   Demands the soul's collected powers:
Gladly we now to thee resign
   These solemn, consecrated hours:
O may our souls adoring own
The grace that calls us to thy throne!

2 All-seeing God! thy piercing eye
   Can every secret thought explore;
May worldly cares our bosoms fly,
   And where thou art intrude no more:
O may thy grace our spirits move,
And fix our minds on things above!

3 Thy Spirit's powerful aid impart,
   And bid thy word, with life divine,
Engage the ear and warm the heart:
   Then shall the day indeed be thine;
Then shall our souls adoring own
The grace that calls us to thy throne.

152   *"The Lord is in this place."*   [6s. 8s.

IN loud exalted strains,
  The King of Glory praise;
O'er heaven and earth he reigns,
  Through everlasting days;
But Sion, with his presence blest,
Is his delight, his chosen rest.

2 O King of Glory, come;
  And with thy favour crown
This temple as thy home,
  This people as thy own;
Beneath this roof vouchsafe to show
How God can dwell with men below.

3 Now let thine ear attend
  Our supplicating cries;
Now let our praise ascend,
  Accepted, to the skies:
Now let thy Gospel's joyful sound
Spread its celestial influence round.

4 Here may the listening throng
  Imbibe thy truth and love;
Here Christians join the song
  Of seraphim above:
Till all who humbly seek thy face
Rejoice in thy abounding grace.

153 *"There remaineth a rest for the people of God."* [L. M.

ANOTHER six days' work is done,
Another Lord's day has begun;
Return, my soul, enjoy thy rest,
Improve the hours thy God hath blest.

2 This day may our devotion rise,
As grateful incense to the skies;
And heaven that sweet repose bestow,
Which none but they who feel it know.

3 This peaceful calm within the breast
Is the sure pledge of heavenly rest,
Which for the Church of God remains
The end of cares, the end of pains.

4 In holy duties, let the day,
In holy pleasures pass away:
How sweet a sabbath thus to spend,
In hope of one that ne'er shall end!

154 *"There I will meet with thee; and I will commune with thee from above the mercy seat."* [C. M.

LORD! in the morning thou shalt hear
My voice ascending high;
To thee will I direct my prayer,
To thee lift up mine eye;

2 Up to the hills, where Christ is gone
To plead for all his saints,
Presenting at his Father's throne
Our songs and our complaints.

3 Thou art a God before whose sight
   The wicked shall not stand;
Sinners shall ne'er be thy delight,
   Nor dwell at thy right hand.

4 But to thy house will I resort,
   To taste thy mercies there;
I will frequent thy holy court,
   And worship in thy fear.

5 O may thy Spirit guide my feet,
   In ways of righteousness,
Make every path of duty straight,
   And plain before my face.

---

155   *"Like as the hart desireth the water-brooks. so*   [108.
        longeth my soul after thee, O God."

From the xlii. Psalm.

AS pants the wearied hart for cooling springs,
   That sinks exhausted in the summer's chase,
So pants my soul for thee, great King of kings,
   So thirsts to reach thy sacred dwelling-place.

2 Lord, thy sure mercies, ever in my sight,
   My heart shall gladden through the tedious day
And 'midst the dark and gloomy shades of night,
   To thee, my God, I'll tune the grateful lay.

3 Why faint, my soul? why doubt Jehovah's aid?
   Thy God the God of mercy still shall prove;
Within his courts thy thanks shall yet be paid:
   Unquestion'd be his faithfulness and love.

156   *"Now is Christ risen from the dead."*   [C. M.

AGAIN the Lord of life and light
   Awakes the kindling ray,
Unseals the eyelids of the morn,
   And pours increasing day.

2 O what a night was that which wrapt
   A heathen world in gloom!
O what a sun, which broke this day
   Triumphant from the tomb!

3 The powers of darkness leagued in vain
   To bind our Lord in death;
He shook their kingdom, when he fell,
   By his expiring breath.

4 And now his conquering chariot wheels
   Ascend the lofty skies;
Broken beneath his powerful cross,
   Death's iron sceptre lies.

5 This day be grateful homage paid,
   And loud hosannas sung;
Let gladness dwell in every heart,
   And praise on every tongue.

6 Ten thousand differing voices join
   To hail this welcome morn,
Which scatters blessings from its wings
   On nations yet unborn.

157   "*My soul longeth, yea, even fainteth for the courts of the Lord.*"   [6s. 4s.

LORD of the worlds above,
   How pleasant and how fair
The dwellings of thy love,
   Thy earthly temples are!
To thine abode | With warm desires
My heart aspires | To see my God.

2 O happy souls, that pray
   Where God appoints to hear!
O happy men, that pay
   Their constant service there!
They praise thee still: | That love the way
And happy they | To Sion's hill.

3 They go from strength to strength
   Through this dark vale of tears,
Till each arrives at length,
   Till each in heaven appears:
O glorious seat; | Shall thither bring
When God our King | Our willing feet.

4 God is our sun and shield,
   Our light and our defence;
With gifts his hands are fill'd,
   We draw our blessings thence:
Thrice happy he, | Whose spirit trusts,
O God of hosts, | Alone in thee.

158 *"This is the day which the Lord hath made, we* [L. M.
will rejoice and be glad in it."

MY opening eyes with rapture see
    The dawn of thy returning day;
My thoughts, O God, ascend to thee,
    While thus my early vows I pay.

2 I yield my heart to thee alone,
    Nor would receive another guest;
Eternal King! erect thy throne,
    And reign sole monarch in my breast.

3 O bid this trifling world retire,
    And drive each carnal thought away;
Nor let me feel one vain desire,
    One sinful thought, through all the day.

4 Then, to thy courts when I repair,
    My soul shall rise on joyful wing,
The wonders of thy love declare,
    And join the strains which angels sing.

159 *"I was in the Spirit on the Lord's day."* [S. M.

THIS is the day of light:
    Let there be light to-day;
O Day-Spring, rise upon our night,
    And chase its gloom away.

2 This is the day of rest:
    Our failing strength renew;
On weary brain and troubled breast
    Shed thou thy freshening dew.

3 This is the day of peace:
   Thy peace our spirits fill;
 Bid thou the blasts of discord cease,
   The waves of strife be still.

4 This is the day of prayer:
   Let earth to heaven draw near:
 Lift up our hearts to seek thee there;
   Come down to meet us here.

5 This is the first of days:
   Send forth thy quickening breath,
 And wake dead souls to love and praise,
   O Vanquisher of death!

160   *"The Lord's day."*   [7s. 6s. Double.

O DAY of rest and gladness,
   O day of joy and light,
 O balm of care and sadness,
   Most beautiful, most bright:
 On thee, the high and lowly,
   Through ages join'd in tune
 Sing, Holy, holy, holy,
   To the great God Triune.

2 On thee, at the creation,
   The light first had its birth;
 On thee, for our salvation,
   Christ rose from depths of earth;
 On thee, our Lord victorious
   The Spirit sent from heaven,
 And thus on thee, most glorious,
   A triple light was given.

3 Thou art a port protected
   From storms that round us rise;
 A garden intersected
   With streams of Paradise;
 Thou art a cooling fountain
   In life's dry dreary sand;
 From thee, like Pisgah's mountain,
   We view our promised land.

4 To-day on weary nations
   The heavenly manna falls;
 To holy convocations
   The silver trumpet calls,
 Where Gospel light is glowing
   With pure and radiant beams,
 And living water flowing
   With soul-refreshing streams.

5 New graces ever gaining
   From this our day of rest,
 We reach the rest remaining
   To spirits of the blest;
 To Holy Ghost be praises,
   To Father, and to Son;
 The Church her voice upraises
   To thee, blest Three in One.

161 *"I will commune with thee from above the mercy seat."* [L. M.

FAR from my thoughts, vain world, begone;
  Let my religious hours alone:
From flesh and sense I would be free,
And hold communion, Lord, with thee.

THE LORD'S DAY.

2 My heart grows warm with holy fire,
And kindles with a pure desire
To see thy grace, to taste thy love,
And feel thine influence from above.

3 When I can say that God is mine,
When I can see thy glories shine,
I'll tread the world beneath my feet,
And all that men call rich and great.

4 Send comfort down from thy right hand,
To cheer me in this barren land;
And in thy temple let me know
The joys that from thy presence flow.

162 *"O send out thy light and thy truth, that they may* [L. M. *lead me, and bring me unto thy holy hill, and to thy dwelling."*

From the xliii. Psalm.

LET me with light and truth be bless'd;
   Be these my guides to lead the way,
Till on thy holy hill I rest,
   And in thy sacred temple pray.

2 Then will I there fresh altars raise
   To God, who is my only joy;
And well-tuned harps, with songs of praise,
   Shall all my grateful hours employ.

3 Why then cast down, my soul? and why
   So much oppress'd with anxious care?
On God, thy God, for aid rely,
   Who will thy ruin'd state repair.

163 *"Lord, I have loved the habitation of thy house."* [7s.

TO thy temple I repair;
　Lord, I love to worship there;
While thy glorious praise is sung,
Touch my lips, unloose my tongue.

2 While the prayers of saints ascend,
God of love, to mine attend;
Hear me, for thy Spirit pleads;
Hear, for Jesus intercedes.

3 While I hearken to thy law,
Fill my soul with humble awe,
Till thy Gospel bring to me
Life and immortality.

4 While thy ministers proclaim
Peace and pardon in thy name,
Through their voice, by faith, may I
Hear thee speaking from the sky.

5 From thy house when I return,
May my heart within me burn;
And at evening let me say,
"I have walk'd with God to-day."

164 *"He that keepeth thee will not slumber."* [7s.

NOW may he who from the dead
　Brought the Shepherd of the sheep,
Jesus Christ, our King and Head,
　All our souls in safety keep!

2 May he teach us to fulfil
 What is pleasing in his sight;
Perfect us in all his will,
 And preserve us day and night.

3 To that dear Redeemer's praise,
 Who the covenant sealed with blood,
Let our hearts and voices raise
 Loud thanksgivings to our God!

AFTER SERMON.

165 *"While he blessed them, he was parted from them."* [8s. 7s. 4.

LORD, dismiss us with thy blessing,
 Fill our hearts with joy and peace;
Let us each, thy love possessing,
 Triumph in redeeming grace;
  O refresh us,
 Travelling through this wilderness.

2 Thanks we give, and adoration,
 For the Gospel's joyful sound;
May the fruits of thy salvation
 In our hearts and lives abound:
  May thy presence
 With us evermore be found.

166 *"Thy word is a lamp unto my feet, and a light unto my path."* [L. M.

ALMIGHTY FATHER, bless the word,
 Which through thy grace we now have heard;

O may the precious seed take root,
Spring up, and bear abundant fruit.

2 We praise thee for the means of grace,
Thus in thy courts to seek thy face:
Grant, Lord, that we who worship here
May all, at last, in heaven appear.

167 *"The Lord will bless his people with peace."* [L. M.

DISMISS us with thy blessing, Lord,
Help us to feed upon thy word;
All that has been amiss forgive,
And let thy truth within us live.

Though we are guilty, thou art good;
Wash all our works in Jesus' blood;
Give every fetter'd soul release,
And bid us all depart in peace.

168 *"Go in peace."* [8s. 7s

MAY the grace of Christ our Saviour,
And the Father's boundless love,
With the Holy Spirit's favour,
Rest upon us from above!

2 Thus may we abide in union
With each other and the Lord,
And possess, in sweet communion,
Joys which earth can not afford.

169   *"The Lord shall give his people the blessing*   [10s
          of peace."

SAVIOUR, again to thy dear name we raise
   With one accord our parting hymn of praise;
We stand to bless thee ere our worship cease,
Then, lowly kneeling, wait thy word of peace.

2 Grant us thy peace upon our homeward way;
With thee began, with thee shall end the day;
Guard thou the lips from sin, the hearts from shame,
That in this house have called upon thy name.

3 Grant us thy peace, Lord, through the coming night,
Turn thou for us its darkness into light;
From harm and danger keep thy children free,
For dark and light are both alike to thee.

4 Grant us thy peace throughout our earthly life,
Our balm in sorrow, and our stay in strife;
Then, when thy voice shall bid our conflict cease,
Call us. O Lord, to thine eternal peace.

EMBER DAYS.

170   *"Unto every one of us is given grace, according*   [S. M.
          to the measure of the gift of Christ."

LORD of the harvest, hear
   Thy needy servants' cry;
Answer our faith's effectual prayer,
   And all our wants supply.

2 On thee we humbly wait,
   Our wants are in thy view;
 The harvest, Lord, is truly great,
   The labourers are few.

3 Anoint and send forth more
   Into thy Church abroad,
 Thy Spirit on their spirits pour,
   And make them strong for God.

4 O let them spread thy name,
   Their mission fully prove;
 Thy universal grace proclaim,
   Thine all-redeeming love.

171 *"Blessed are those servants whom the Lord when* [S. M.
he cometh shall find watching."

YE servants of the Lord,
   Each in your office, wait,
 Observant of his heavenly word,
   And watchful at his gate.

2 Let all your lamps be bright,
   And trim the golden flame;
 Gird up your loins as in his sight,
   For awful is his name.

3 Watch! 'tis your Lord's command,
   And while we speak he's near;
 Mark the first signal of his hand,
   And ready all appear.

4 O happy servant he
   In such a posture found;
 He shall his Lord with rapture see,
   And be with honour crown'd.

ROGATION DAYS.

MONDAY.

172   *"The eyes of all wait upon thee, O Lord; and*   [C. M.
thou givest them their meat in due season."

LORD, in thy name thy servants plead,
    And thou hast sworn to hear;
Thine is the harvest, thine the seed,
    The fresh and fading year.

2 Grant us, with precious things brought forth
    By sun and moon below,
A place in thy new heavens and earth,
    Where richer harvests grow.

TUESDAY.

173   *"Spare thy people, O Lord."*   [C. M.

LORD, spare and save our sinful race
    From death in direst form;
From pestilence that flies apace,
    From earthquake, fire, and storm.

2 Let every land bemoan its sin,
    That wars and crimes may cease;
And may thy pardoning grace bring in
    Sweet times of health and peace.

WEDNESDAY.

174 *"Mercy and truth shall go before thy face."* [C. M.

GREAT is our guilt, our fears are great,
  But naught shall prompt despair,
While open is the mercy-seat
  To penitence and prayer.

2 Kind Intercessor! to thy love
  This blest resource we owe:
Thy merits plead for us above,
  While we implore below.

OTHER HOLY DAYS.

175 *"Great and marvellous are thy works, Lord God* [7s. 6s.
  Almighty: just and true are thy ways, thou Double
  King of saints."

FROM all thy saints in warfare, for all thy saints at rest,
To thee, O blessèd Jesus, all praises be address'd.
Thou, Lord, didst win the battle, that they might conquerors be;
Their crowns of living glory are lit with rays from thee.

[*Insert here the stanza for the special Saint's Day to be celebrated.*]

OTHER HOLY DAYS.

SAINT ANDREW.

2 Praise, Lord, for thine Apostle, the first to welcome thee,
The first to lead his brother the very Christ to see.
With hearts for thee made ready, watch we throughout the year,
Forward to lead our brethren to own thine advent near.

SAINT THOMAS.

3 All praise for thine Apostle, whose short-lived doubtings prove
Thy perfect twofold nature, the fulness of thy love.
On all who wait thy coming shed forth thy peace, O Lord,
And grant us faith to know thee, true Man, true God, adored.

SAINT STEPHEN.

4 Praise for the first of Martyrs, who saw thee ready stand
To aid in midst of torments, to plead at God's right hand.
Share we with him, if summon'd by death our Lord to own,
On earth the faithful witness, in heaven the martyr crown.

SAINT JOHN THE EVANGELIST.

5 Praise for the loved Disciple, exile on Patmos' shore;
Praise for the faithful record he to thy Godhead bore;
Praise for the mystic vision, through him to us reveal'd.
May we, in patience waiting, with thine elect be seal'd.

THE INNOCENTS' DAY.

6 Praise for thine infant Martyrs, by thee with tenderest love
Call'd early from the warfare to share the rest above.
O Rachel! cease thy weeping, they rest from pains and cares.
Lord, grant us hearts as guileless, and crowns as bright as theirs.

THE CONVERSION OF ST. PAUL.

7 Praise for the light from heaven, praise for the voice of awe,
Praise for the glorious vision the persecutor saw.
Thee, Lord, for his Conversion, we glorify to-day:
So lighten all our darkness with thy true Spirit's ray.

SAINT MATTHIAS.

8 Lord, thine abiding presence directs the wondrous choice;
For one in place of Judas the faithful now rejoice.
Thy Church from false Apostles for evermore defend,
And by thy parting promise be with her to the end.

SAINT MARK.

9 For him, O Lord, we praise thee, the weak by grace made strong,
Whose labours and whose Gospel enrich our triumph-song.
May we in all our weakness find strength from thee supplied,
And all, as fruitful branches, in thee, the Vine, abide.

SAINT PHILIP AND SAINT JAMES.

10 All praise for thine Apostle, bless'd guide to Greek and Jew,
And him surnamed thy brother; keep us thy brethren true,
And grant the grace to know thee, the Way, the Truth, the Life;
To wrestle with temptations till victors in the strife.

SAINT BARNABAS.

11 The Son of Consolation, moved by thy law of love,
   Forsaking earthly treasures, sought riches from above.
   As earth now teems with increase, let gifts of grace descend,
   That thy true consolations may through the world extend.

SAINT JOHN BAPTIST.

12 We praise thee for the Baptist, forerunner of the Word,
   Our true Elias, making a highway for the Lord.
   Of prophets last and greatest, he saw thy dawning ray.
   Make us the rather blessèd, who love thy glorious day.

SAINT PETER.

13 Praise for thy great Apostle, the eager and the bold;
   Thrice falling, yet repentant, thrice charged to keep thy fold.
   Lord, make thy pastors faithful, to guard their flocks from ill,
   And grant them dauntless courage, with humble, earnest will.

SAINT JAMES.

14 For him, O Lord, we praise thee, who, slain by Herod's sword,
Drank of thy cup of suffering, fulfilling thus thy word.
Curb we all vain impatience to read thy veil'd decree,
And count it joy to suffer, if so brought nearer thee.

SAINT BARTHOLOMEW.

15 All praise for thine Apostle, the faithful, pure, and true,
Whom underneath the fig tree thine eye all-seeing knew.
Like him may we be guileless, true Israelites indeed,
That thy abiding presence our longing souls may feed.

SAINT MATTHEW.

16 Praise, Lord, for him whose Gospel thy human life declared,
Who, worldly gains forsaking, thy path of suffering shared.
From all unrighteous mammon O give us hearts set free,
That we, whate'er our calling, may rise and follow thee.

SAINT LUKE.

17 For that "Beloved Physician," all praise, whose Gospel shows
The Healer of the nations, the sharer of our woes.
Thy wine and oil, O Saviour, on bruised hearts deign to pour,
And with true balm of Gilead anoint us evermore.

SAINT SIMON AND SAINT JUDE.

18 Praise, Lord, for thine Apostles, who seal'd their faith to-day:
One love, one zeal impell'd them to tread the sacred way.
May we with zeal as earnest the faith of Christ maintain,
And, bound in love as brethren, at length thy rest attain.

GENERAL ENDING.

19 Apostles, Prophets, Martyrs, and all the sacred throng,
Who wear the spotless raiments, who raise the ceaseless song;
For these, pass'd on before us, Saviour, we thee adore,
And, walking in their footsteps, would serve thee more and more.

20 Then praise we God the Father, and praise we
    God the Son,
And God the Holy Spirit, Eternal Three in
    One;
Till all the ransom'd number fall down before
    the throne,
And honour, power, and glory ascribe to God
    alone.

176   *"The armies in heaven followed him."*   [C. M.

THE Son of God goes forth to war,
    A kingly crown to gain;
His blood-red banner streams afar:
    Who follows in his train?
Who best can drink his cup of woe,
    Triumphant over pain,
Who patient bear his cross below—
    He follows in his train.

2 The martyr first, whose eagle eye
    Could pierce beyond the grave,
Who saw his Master in the sky,
    And call'd on him to save:
Like him, with pardon on his tongue,
    In midst of mortal pain,
He pray'd for them that did the wrong:
    Who follows in his train?

3 A glorious band, the chosen few,
    On whom the Spirit came:
Twelve valiant saints, their hope they knew,
    And mock'd the cross and flame:

>   They met the tyrant's brandish'd steel,
>   The lion's gory mane;
>   They bow'd their necks the death to feel:
>   Who follows in their train?
>
> 4 A noble army, men and boys,
>   The matron and the maid,
>   Around the Saviour's throne rejoice,
>   In robes of light array'd:
>   They climb'd the steep ascent of heaven
>   Through peril, toil, and pain:
>   O God! to us may grace be given
>   To follow in their train!

177 *"These are they which came out of great tribulation, and have washed their robes, and made them white in the blood of the Lamb."* [D.C.M.

> HOW bright these glorious spirits shine!
>   Whence all their white array?
>   How came they to the blissful seats
>   Of everlasting day?
>   Lo, these are they from sufferings great,
>   Who came to realms of light:
>   And in the blood of Christ have washed
>   Those robes which shine so bright.
>
> 2 Now with triumphal palms they stand
>   Before the throne on high,
>   And serve the God they love amidst
>   The glories of the sky.

His presence fills each heart with joy,
    Tunes every mouth to sing;
By day, by night, the sacred courts
    With glad hosannas ring.

3 The Lamb which reigns upon the throne
    Shall o'er them still preside;
Feed them with nourishment divine,
    And all their footsteps guide.
'Mong pastures green he'll lead his flock,
    Where living streams appear;
And God the Lord from every eye
    Shall wipe off every tear.

HOLY INNOCENTS.

178   *"These are they which follow the Lamb*   [L. M.
      whithersoever he goeth."

O LORD, the Holy Innocents
    Laid down for thee their infant life,
And martyrs brave and patient saints
    Have stood for thee in fire and strife.

2 We wear the cross they wore of old,
    Our lips have learn'd like vows to make;
We need not die; we cannot fight;
    What may we do for Jesus' sake?

3 O day by day each Christian child
    Has much to do, without, within;
A death to die for Jesus' sake,
    A weary war to wage with sin.

4 When deep within our swelling hearts,
    The thoughts of pride and anger rise,
  When bitter words are on our tongues,
    And tears of passion in our eyes;

5 Then we may stay the angry blow,
    Then we may check the hasty word,
  Give gentle answers back again,
    And fight a battle for our Lord.

6 With smiles of peace and looks of love,
    Light in our dwellings we may make,
  Bid kind good-humour brighten there,
    And do all still for Jesus' sake.

7 There's not a child so weak and small
    But has his little cross to take,
  His little work of love and praise,
    That he may do for Jesus' sake.

179 *"They are without fault before the throne* [S. M.
  of God."

GLORY to thee, O Lord,
  Who from this world of sin,
By cruel Herod's ruthless sword
  Those precious ones didst win.

2 Glory to thee for all
    The ransomed infant band,
  Who since that hour have heard thy call,
    And reach'd the quiet land.

3 O that our hearts within,
    Like theirs, were pure and bright;
  O that, as free from deeds of sin,
    We shrank not from thy sight.

4 Lord, help us every hour
    Thy cleansing grace to claim;
  In life to glorify thy power,
    In death to praise thy name.

THE PRESENTATION OF CHRIST IN THE TEMPLE.

180 *"The glory of this latter house shall be greater* [S. M
         than of the former."

BEHOLD a humble train
    The courts of God draw near;
  A Virgin Mother and her babe
    Before the Lord appear.

2 O wondrous, blessèd sight!
    To faithful eyes made known,
  That lowly babe—the mighty God,
    The Prince of Peace, they own.

3 And now this temple shines
    With glory far more bright
  Than e'er the former temple saw,
    E'en at its greatest height.

4 The cloud indeed was there,
    The symbol of the Lord;
  But here the Lord himself appears,
    The true, incarnate Word.

5 Blest Saviour, come once more
   With power and grace divine;
Our hearts thy living temples make,
   Wholly and ever thine.

ANNUNCIATION OF THE BLESSED VIRGIN MARY.

181 *"Behold, a virgin shall be with child, and shall bring forth a Son, and they shall call his name Emmanuel, which being interpreted is, God with us."* [S. M

PRAISE we the Lord this day,
   This day so long foretold,
Whose promise shone with cheering ray
   On waiting saints of old.

2 The prophet gave the sign
   For faithful men to read;
A virgin born of David's line,
   Shall bear the promised Seed.

3 Ask not how this should be,
   But worship and adore,
Like her whom heaven's majesty
   Came down to shadow o'er.

4 Meekly she bowed her head
   To hear the gracious word,
Mary, the pure and lowly maid,
   The favoured of the Lord.

5 Blessèd shall be her name
   In all the Church on earth,
Through whom that wondrous mercy came,
   The incarnate Saviour's birth.

SAINT MICHAEL AND ALL ANGELS.

182 "*O praise the Lord, all ye his hosts: ye servants of his that do his pleasure.*" [7s.

PRAISE to God who reigns above,
  Binding earth and heaven in love;
All the armies of the sky
Worship his dread sovereignty.

2 Seraphim his praises sing,
  Cherubim on fourfold wing,
  Thrones, Dominions, Princes, Powers,
  Ranks of Might that never cowers.

3 Angel hosts his word fulfil,
  Ruling nature by his will:
  Round his throne archangels pour
  Songs of praise for evermore.

4 Yet on man they joy to wait,
  All that bright celestial state,
  For true Man their Lord they see,
  Christ, the incarnate Deity.

5 On the throne our Lord who died
  Sits in manhood glorified,
  Where his people faint below
  Angels count it joy to go.

II. THE COMMUNION OF SAINTS.

183   *"Seeing we also are compassed about with so great a cloud of witnesses."*   [C. M.

LO! what a cloud of witnesses
    Encompass us around!
Men once like us with suffering tried,
    But now with glory crown'd.

2 Let us, with zeal like theirs inspired,
    Strive in the Christian race;
And, freed from every weight of sin,
    Their holy footsteps trace.

3 Behold a witness nobler still,
    Who trod affliction's path—
Jesus, the Author, Finisher,
    Rewarder of our faith:

4 He, for the joy before him set,
    And moved by pitying love,
Endured the cross, despised the shame,
    And now he reigns above.

5 Thither, forgetting things behind,
    Press we, to God's right hand;
There, with the Saviour and his saints,
    Triumphantly to stand.

THE COMMUNION OF SAINTS.

184   *"He hath prepared for them a city."*   [C. M.

NOT to the terrors of the Lord,
   The tempest, fire, and smoke:
Not to the thunder of that word
   Which God on Sinai spoke;

2 But we are come to Sion's hill,
   The city of our God;
Where milder words declare his will,
   And spread his love abroad.

3 Behold th' innumerable host
   Of angels clothed in light:
Behold the spirits of the just,
   Whose faith is changed to sight.

4 Behold the bless'd assembly there
   Whose names are writ in heaven;
Hear God, the Judge of all, declare
   Their sins, through Christ, forgiven.

5 Angels, and living saints and dead,
   But one communion make:
All join in Christ, their living Head,
   And of his love partake.

185   *"Behold, how good and joyful a thing it is,*   [C. M.
      brethren, to dwell together in unity."

      From the cxxxiii. Psalm.

HOW vast must their advantage be,
   How great their pleasure prove,
Who live like brethren, and consent
   In offices of love!

2 True love is like the precious oil,
    Which, poured on Aaron's head,
  Ran down his beard, and o'er his robes
    Its costly fragrance shed.

3 'Tis like refreshing dew, which does
    On Hermon's top distil;
  Or like the early drops that fall
    On Sion's favour'd hill.

4 For Sion is the chosen seat
    Where the Almighty King
  The promised blessing has ordain'd,
    And life's eternal spring.

186 *"Their sound went into all the earth, and their words unto the ends of the world."* [P. M

FOR the Apostles' glorious company,
  Who, bearing forth the cross o'er land and sea,
Shook all the mighty world, we sing to thee,
                                Alleluia.

2 For the Evangelists, by whose blest word,
  Like fourfold streams, the garden of the Lord
  Is fair and fruitful, be thy name adored.
                                Alleluia.

3 For Martyrs, who, with rapture-kindled eye,
  Saw the bright crown descending from the sky,
  And died to grasp it, thee we glorify.
                                Alleluia.

187   *"We are compassed about with so great a*   P. M.
          cloud of witnesses."

FOR all the saints, who from their labours rest,
 Who thee by faith before the world confess'd,
Thy name, O Jesus, be forever bless'd.
                              Alleluia.

2 Thou wast their rock, their fortress, and their might;
 Thou, Lord, their Captain in the well-fought fight;
 Thou, in the darkness drear, the Light of light.
                              Alleluia.

3 O may thy soldiers, faithful, true, and bold,
 Fight as the saints who nobly fought of old,
 And win, with them, the victor's crown of gold.
                              Alleluia.

4 O blest Communion, fellowship divine!
 We feebly struggle, they in glory shine;
 Yet all are one in thee, for all are thine.
                              Alleluia.

5 And when the strife is fierce, the warfare long,
 Steals on the ear the distant triumph-song,
 And hearts are brave again, and arms are strong.
                              Alleluia.

6 The golden evening brightens in the west;
 Soon, soon to faithful warriors comes the rest;
 Sweet is the calm of Paradise the bless'd.
                              Alleluia.

7 But lo! there breaks a yet more glorious day;
   The saints triumphant rise in bright array;
   The King of Glory passes on his way.
                        Alleluia.

8 From earth's wide bounds, from ocean's farthest coast,
   Through gates of pearl streams in the countless host,
   Singing to Father, Son, and Holy Ghost,
                        Alleluia.

188   *"Of whom the whole family in heaven and earth is named."*   [C. M.

COME, let us join our friends above
   That have obtained the prize,
And on the eagle wings of love
   To joys celestial rise.

2 Let all the saints terrestrial sing,
   With those to glory gone;
For all the servants of our King,
   In earth and heaven are one.

3 One family, we dwell in him,
   One Church, above, beneath;
Though now divided by the stream,
   The narrow stream of death.

4 One army of the living God,
   To his command we bow;
Part of his host have cross'd the **flood,**
   And part are crossing now.

5 Ten thousand to their endless home,
   This solemn moment fly;
And we are to the margin come,
   And we expect to die.

6 Then, Lord of hosts, be thou our guide,
   And we, at thy command,
Through waves that part on either side,
   Shall reach thy blessèd land.

189 *And after this I beheld, and lo, a great multitude, which no man could number, of all nations and kindred and people and tongues, stood before the throne, and before the Lamb, clothed with white robes, and palms in their hands."* [8s. 7s. Double.

HARK! the sound of holy voices,
   Chanting o'er the crystal sea,
Alleluia, alleluia,
   Alleluia, Lord, to thee:
Multitude, which none can number,
   Like the stars in glory stands,
Clothed in white apparel, holding
   Palms of victory in their hands.

2 Patriarch, and holy Prophet,
   Who prepared the way of Christ,
King, Apostle, Saint, Confessor,
   Martyr and Evangelist,
Saintly maiden, godly matron,
   Widows who have watched to prayer,
Joined in holy concert, singing
   To the Lord of all, are there.

3 They have come from tribulation,
    And have wash'd their robes in blood,
Wash'd them in the blood of Jesus;
    Tried they were, and firm they stood;
Mock'd, imprison'd, stoned, tormented,
    Sawn asunder, slain with sword,
They have conquer'd death and Satan
    By the might of Christ the Lord.

4 Marching with thy cross their banner,
    They have triumph'd, following
Thee, the Captain of salvation,
    Thee, their Saviour and their King,
Gladly, Lord, with thee they suffer'd;
    Gladly, Lord, with thee they died;
And by death to life immortal
    They were born and glorified.

5 Now they reign in heavenly glory,
    Now they walk in golden light,
Now they drink, as from a river,
    Holy bliss and infinite:
Love and peace they taste for ever,
    And all truth and knowledge see
In the beatific vision
    Of the blessèd Trinity.

III. THE CHURCH.

190   "*Glorious things are spoken of thee, O city of God.*"   [8s. 7s Double

GLORIOUS things of thee are spoken,
  Zion, city of our God:
He, whose word cannot be broken,
  Form'd thee for his own abode;
On the Rock of Ages founded,
  What can shake thy sure repose?
With salvation's walls surrounded,
  Thou may'st smile at all thy foes.

2 See, the streams of living waters,
  Springing from eternal love,
Well supply thy sons and daughters,
  And all fear of want remove;
Who can faint, while such a river
  Ever flows their thirst t' assuage?
Grace, which like the Lord, the giver,
  Never fails from age to age.

3 Round each habitation hovering,
  See the cloud and fire appear,
For a glory and a covering,
  Showing that the Lord is near.
Blest inhabitants of Zion,
  Wash'd in the Redeemer's blood!
Jesus, whom their souls rely on,
  Makes them kings and priests to God.

191 *"O pray for the peace of Jerusalem: they shall prosper that love thee."* [S. M.

I LOVE thy kingdom, Lord,
  The house of thine abode,
The Church our blest Redeemer saved
  With his own precious blood.

2 I love thy Church, O God;
  Her walls before thee stand,
Dear as the apple of thine eye,
  And graven on thy hand.

3 For her my tears shall fall;
  For her my prayers ascend;
To her my cares and toils be given,
  Till toils and cares shall end.

4 Beyond my highest joy
  I prize her heavenly ways,
Her sweet communion, solemn vows,
  Her hymns of love and praise.

5 Jesus, thou Friend divine,
  Our Saviour and our King,
Thy hand from every snare and foe
  Shall great deliverance bring.

6 Sure as thy truth shall last,
  To Sion shall be given
The brightest glories earth can yield,
  And brighter bliss of heaven.

192 *"Awake, awake; put on thy strength, O Sion."* [L. M.

TRIUMPHANT Sion! lift thy head
From dust, and darkness, and the dead:
Though humbled long, awake at length,
And gird thee with thy Saviour's strength.

2 Put all thy beauteous garments on,
And let thy excellence be known:
Deck'd in the robes of righteousness,
The world thy glories shall confess.

3 No more shall foes unclean invade,
And fill thy hallow'd walls with dread;
No more shall hell's insulting host
Their victory and thy sorrows boast.

4 God from on high has heard thy prayer,
His hand thy ruins shall repair:
Nor will thy watchful Monarch cease
To guard thee in eternal peace.

193 *"Very excellent things are spoken of thee, thou* [Six 8s.
city of God."

From the lxxxvii. Psalm.

GOD'S temple crowns the holy mount,
The Lord there condescends to dwell:
His Sion's gates, in his account,
Our Israel's fairest tents excel:
Yea, glorious things of thee we sing,
O city of th' Almighty King!

2 Of honour'd Sion we aver,
   Illustrious throngs from her proceed;
The Almighty shall establish her,
   And shall enrol her holy seed:
Yea, for his people he shall count
The children of his favour'd mount.

3 He'll Sion find with numbers fill'd
   Who celebrate his matchless praise;
Who, here in alleluias skill'd,
   In heaven their harps and hymns shall raise:
O Sion, seat of Israel's King,
Be mine to drink thy living spring!

194 *" God is our hope and strength, a very present help in trouble."* [Six 8s.

From the xlvi. Psalm.

GOD is our refuge in distress,
  A present help when dangers press,
   In him, undaunted, we'll confide;
Though earth were from her centre tost,
And mountains in the ocean lost,
   Torn piecemeal by the roaring tide.

2 A gentler stream with gladness still
  The city of our Lord shall fill,
   The royal seat of God most high:
God dwells in Sion, whose fair towers
Shall mock th' assaults of earthly powers,
   While his Almighty aid is nigh.

3 Submit to God's Almighty sway,
   For him the heathen shall obey,
     And earth her sovereign Lord confess:
   The God of hosts conducts our arms,
   Our tower of refuge in alarms,
     As to our fathers in distress.

195 *"We which have believed do enter into rest."* [S. M.

LIKE Noah's weary dove,
   That soar'd the earth around,
 But not a resting-place above
   The cheerless waters found;

2 O cease, my wandering soul,
   On restless wing to roam;
 All the wide world, to either pole,
   Has not for thee a home.

3 Behold the Ark of God,
   Behold the open door;
 Hasten to gain that dear abode,
   And rove, my soul, no more.

4 There, safe thou shalt abide,
   There, sweet shall be thy rest,
 And every longing satisfied,
   With full salvation blest.

5 And, when the waves of ire
   Again the earth shall fill,
 The Ark shall ride the sea of fire,
   Then rest on Sion's hill.

196 *"The hill of Sion is a fair place, and the joy of the whole earth."* [C. M.

From the xlviii. Psalm.

THE Lord, the only God, is great,
   And greatly to be praised
In Sion, on whose happy mount
   His sacred throne is raised.

2 In Sion we have seen perform'd
   A work that was foretold,
In pledge that God, for times to come,
   His city will uphold.

3 Let Sion's mount with joy resound;
   Her daughters all be taught
In songs his judgments to extol,
   Who this deliverance wrought.

4 Compass her walls in solemn pomp,
   Your eyes quite round her cast;
Count all her towers, and see if there
   You find one stone displaced.

5 Her forts and palaces survey,
   Observe their order well,
That to the ages yet to come
   His wonders you may tell.

6 This God is ours, and will be ours,
   Whilst we in him confide;
Who, as he has preserved us now,
   Till death will be our guide.

197   *"That they all may be one."*   [6s. 8s.

ONE sole baptismal sign,
  One Lord, below, above,
One faith, one hope divine,
  One only watchword—Love:
From different temples though it rise,
One song ascendeth to the skies.

2 Our sacrifice is one,
  One Priest before the throne,
The slain, the risen Son,
  Redeemer, Lord alone!
And sighs from contrite hearts that spring
Our chief, our choicest offering.

3 Head of thy Church beneath,
  The catholic, the true,
On all her members breathe,
  Her broken frame renew!
Then shall thy perfect will be done,
When Christians love and live as one.

198   *"Christ is the Head of the Church."*   [P. M.

HEAD of the hosts in glory!
  We joyfully adore thee,
    Thy Church below,
Blending with those on high—
Where through the azure sky
Thy saints in ecstasy
    For ever glow!

2 Angels! archangels! glorious
   Guards of the Church victorious!
      Worship the Lamb!
   Crown him with crowns of light,
   One of the Three by right—
   Love, majesty, and might—
      The great I AM!

3 Martyrs! whose mystic legions
   March o'er yon heavenly regions
      In triumph round:
   Wave high your banners, wave!
   Your God, our Saviour, clave
   For death itself a grave,
      In hell profound!

4 Saints! in fair circles, casting
   Rich trophies everlasting
      At Jesus' feet,
   Amidst our rude alarms,
   We stretch forth suppliant arms,
   That we, too, safe from harms,
      In heaven may meet!

5 Saviour! in glory beaming,
   With radiance brightly streaming,
      Enthroned in power,
   Grant, by thy awful name,
   That we through flood and flame
   The Gospel may proclaim,
      Till life's last hour.

199   *"Our feet shall stand in thy gates, O Jerusalem."*   [8s. 6s.

From the cxxii. Psalm.

WITH joy shall I behold the day
That calls my willing soul away,
    To dwell among the blest:
For, lo! my great Redeemer's power
Unfolds the everlasting door,
    And points me to his rest.

2 Ev'n now, to my expecting eyes
The heaven-built towers of Salem rise;
    Their glory I survey;
I view her mansions that contain
The angel host, a beauteous train,
    And shine with cloudless day.

3 Thither, from earth's remotest end,
Lo! the redeem'd of God ascend,
    Borne on immortal wing;
There, crown'd with everlasting joy,
In ceaseless hymns their tongues employ,
    Before th' Almighty King.

4 Mother of cities! o'er thy head
Bright peace, with healing wings outspread,
    For evermore shall dwell:
Let me, blest seat! my name behold
Among thy citizens enroll'd,
    And bid the world farewell.

200   "*O how amiable are thy dwellings, thou Lord of hosts.*"   [7s. DOUBLE.

PLEASANT are thy courts above,
In the land of light and love;
Pleasant are thy courts below,
In this land of sin and woe.
O my spirit longs and faints
For the converse of thy saints,
For the brightness of thy face,
King of glory, God of grace!

2 Happy birds that sing and fly
Round thy altars, O Most High!
Happier souls, that find a rest,
In a heavenly Father's breast!
Like the wandering dove, that found
No repose on earth around,
They can to their ark repair,
And enjoy it ever there.

3 Happy souls! their praises flow,
Ever in this vale of woe;
Waters in the desert rise,
Manna feeds them from the skies;
On they go from strength to strength,
Till they reach thy throne at length;
At thy feet adoring fall,
Who hast led them safe through all.

4 Lord, be mine this prize to win;
Guide me through a world of sin,
Keep me by thy saving grace,
Give me at thy side a place;

Sun and shield alike thou art;
Guide and guard my erring heart;
Grace and glory flow from thee;
Shower, O shower them, Lord, on me.

201   *"Under the shadow of thy wings shall be my refuge."*   Six 8s.

FORTH from the dark and stormy sky,
  Lord, to thine altar's shade we fly;
Forth from the world, its hope and fear,
Saviour, we seek thy shelter here:
Weary and weak, thy grace we pray;
Turn not, O Lord, thy guests away.

2 Long have we roamed in want and pain,
Long have we sought thy rest in vain;
Wildered in doubt, in darkness lost,
Long have our souls been tempest-tost;
Low at thy feet our sins we lay;
Turn not O Lord! thy guests away.

202   *"Jesus Christ himself being the chief corner stone."*   [7s. 6s. Double

THE Church's one foundation
  Is Jesus Christ her Lord;
She is his new creation
  By water and the word:
From heaven he came and sought her
  To be his holy bride;
With his own blood he bought her,
  And for her life he died.

2 Elect from every nation,
　　Yet one o'er all the earth,
　Her charter of salvation
　　One Lord, one faith, one birth;
　One holy name she blesses,
　　Partakes one holy food,
　And to one hope she presses,
　　With every grace endued.

3 Though with a scornful wonder,
　　Men see her sore opprest,
　By schisms rent asunder,
　　By heresies distrest;
　Yet saints their watch are keeping,
　　Their cry goes up, "How long?"
　And soon the night of weeping
　　Shall be the morn of song.

4 'Mid toil and tribulation,
　　And tumult of her war,
　She waits the consummation
　　Of peace for evermore;
　Till with the vision glorious
　　Her longing eyes are blest,
　And the great Church victorious
　　Shall be the Church at rest.

5 Yet she on earth hath union
　　With God the Three in One,
　And mystic sweet communion
　　With those whose rest is won:
　O happy ones and holy!
　　Lord, give us grace that we
　Like them, the meek and lowly,
　　On high may dwell with thee.

IV. THE SACRAMENTS.

THE LORD'S SUPPER.

203 *"Worthy is the Lamb that was slain to receive power, and riches, and wisdom, and strength, and honour, and glory, and blessing."* [C. M.

THOU, God, all glory, honour, power
    Art worthy to receive;
Since all things by thy power were made,
    And by thy bounty live.

2 And worthy is the Lamb all power,
    Honour, and wealth to gain,
Glory and strength; who for our sins
    A sacrifice was slain.

3 All worthy thou, who hast redeem'd
    And ransom'd us to God,
From every nation, every coast,
    By thy most precious blood.

4 Blessing and honour, glory, power,
    By all in earth and heaven,
To him that sits upon the throne,
    And to the Lamb, be given.

204 *"Jesus Christ, who gave himself for our sins."* [L. M.

TO Jesus, our exalted Lord,
    That name in heaven and earth adored,
Fain would our hearts and voices raise
A cheerful song of sacred praise.

2 But all the notes which mortals know
 Are weak, and languishing, and low;
 Far, far above our humble songs,
 The theme demands immortal tongues.

3 Yet whilst around his board we meet,
 And worship at his sacred feet,
 O let our warm affections move
 In glad returns of grateful love.

4 Yes, Lord, we love, and we adore,
 But long to know and love thee more;
 And, whilst we take the bread and wine,
 Desire to feed on joys divine.

205 *"Come, for all things are now ready."* [L. M.

MY God, and is thy table spread,
   And does thy cup with love o'erflow?
Thither be all thy children led,
   And let them thy sweet mercies know.

2 Hail! sacred feast, which Jesus makes,
   Rich banquet of his flesh and blood:
Thrice happy he who here partakes
   That sacred stream, that heavenly food.

3 Why are its bounties all in vain
   Before unwilling hearts display'd?
Was not for you the victim slain?
   Are you forbid the children's bread?

4 Oh, let thy table honour'd be,
   And furnish'd well with joyful guests:
And may each soul salvation see,
   That here its holy pledges tastes!

5 Drawn by thy quickening grace, O Lord,
   In countless numbers let them come;
And gather from their Father's board
   The bread that lives beyond the tomb.

6 Nor let thy spreading Gospel rest,
   Till through the world thy truth has run,
Till with this bread all men be blest,
   Who see the light or feel the sun.

206   *"We will go into his tabernacles; we will*   [C. M.
       worship at his footstool."

AND are we now brought near to God,
   Who once at distance stood?
And, to effect this glorious change,
   Did Jesus shed his blood?

2 O for a song of ardent praise,
   To bear our souls above!
What should allay our lively hope,
   Or damp our flaming love?

3 Then let us join the heavenly choirs,
   To praise our heavenly King:
O may that love which spread this board,
   Inspire us while we sing·

4 "Glory to God in highest strains,
   And to the earth be peace·
Good-will from heaven to men is come,
   And let it never cease."

207 *"Jesus said unto them, I am the Bread of Life."* [P. M

BREAD of the world, in mercy broken,
   Wine of the soul, in mercy shed,
By whom the words of life were spoken,
   And in whose death our sins are dead;

2 Look on the heart by sorrow broken,
   Look on the tears by sinners shed;
And be thy feast to us the token
   That by thy grace our souls are fed.

208 *"To him be glory and dominion."* [C. M.

COME let us join our cheerful songs
   With angels round the throne.
Ten thousand thousand are their tongues,
   But all their joys are one.

2 "Worthy the Lamb that died," they cry,
   "To be exalted thus:"
"Worthy the Lamb," our lips reply,
   For he was slain for us.

3 Jesus is worthy to receive
   Honour and power divine;
And blessings more than we can give,
   Be, Lord, for ever thine.

4 Let all that dwell above the sky,
   And air, and earth, and seas,
Conspire to lift thy glories high,
   And speak thine endless praise!

5 The whole creation join in one,
  To bless the sacred name
Of him that sits upon the throne,
  And to adore the Lamb.

209 *"Whoso eateth my flesh and drinketh my blood* [Six 7s.
hath eternal life."

BREAD of heaven, on thee we feed,
  For thy flesh is meat indeed:
Ever may our souls be fed
With this true and living bread;
Day by day with strength supplied,
Through the life of him who died.

2 Vine of heaven, thy blood supplies
This blest cup of sacrifice,
Lord, thy wounds our healing give,
To thy cross we look and live:
Jesus, may we ever be
Grafted, rooted, built in thee.

210 *"I am that bread of life."* [C M

SHEPHERD of souls, refresh and bless
  Thy chosen pilgrim flock,
With manna in the wilderness,
  With water from the rock.

2 Hungry and thirsty, faint and weak,
  As thou when here below,
Our souls the joys celestial seek
  Which from thy sorrows flow.

3 We would not live by bread alone,
    But by that word of grace,
  In strength of which we travel on
    To our abiding-place.

4 Be known to us in breaking bread,
    But do not then depart;
  Saviour, abide with us, and spread
    Thy table in our heart.

5 Lord, sup with us in love divine;
    Thy body and thy blood,
  That living bread, that heavenly wine,
    Be our immortal food.

211   *"This do in remembrance of me."*   [C. M.

ACCORDING to thy gracious word,
    In meek humility,
  This will I do, my dying Lord,
    I will remember thee.

2 Thy body, broken for my sake,
    My bread from heaven shall be;
  Thy sacramental cup I take,
    And thus remember thee.

3 Can I Gethsemane forget?
    Or there thy conflict see,
  Thine agony and bloody sweat,
    And not remember thee?

4 When to the cross I turn mine eyes,
    And rest on Calvary,
  O Lamb of God, my sacrifice,
    I must remember thee.

5 Remember thee, and all thy pains,
　　And all thy love to me;
　Yes, while a breath, a pulse remains,
　　Will I remember thee.

6 And when these failing lips grow dumb,
　　And mind and memory flee,
　When thou shalt in thy kingdom come,
　　Jesus, remember me.

BAPTISM.

BAPTISM OF INFANTS.

212　　*'Suffer little children to come unto me, and forbid them not."*　　[S. M

THE gentle Saviour calls
　　Our children to his breast;
He folds them in his gracious arms,
　　Himself declares them blest.

2 "Let them approach," he cries,
　　"Nor scorn their humble claim;
The heirs of heaven are such as these,
　　For such as these I came."

3 Gladly we bring them, Lord,
　　Devoting them to thee,
Imploring that, as we are thine,
　　Thine may our offspring be.

213 *"He took them up in his arms, put his hands* [8s. 7s.
upon them, and blessed them."

SAVIOUR, who thy flock art feeding,
  With the shepherd's kindest care,
All the feeble gently leading,
  While the lambs thy bosom share;

2 Now, *these* little *ones* receiving,
  Fold *them* in thy gracious arm;
There, we know, thy word believing,
  Only there secure from harm.

3 Never from thy pasture roving,
  Let *them* be the lion's prey;
Let thy tenderness, so loving,
  Keep *them* all life's dangerous way

4 Then, within thy fold eternal,
  Let *them* find a resting-place;
Feed in pastures ever vernal,
  Drink the rivers of thy grace.

214 *"That he may please him who hath chosen him* [C. M.
to be a soldier."

IN token that thou shalt not fear
  Christ crucified to own,
We print the cross upon thee here,
  And stamp thee his alone.

2 In token that thou shalt not blush
  To glory in his name,
We blazon here upon thy front,
  His glory and his shame

3 In token that thou too shalt tread
    The path he travell'd by,
Endure the cross, despise the shame,
    And sit thee down on high;

4 Thus outwardly and visibly
    We seal thee for his own:
And may the brow that wears his cross
    Hereafter share his crown.

BAPTISM OF A YOUNG PERSON.

215 "*Remember thy Creator in the days of thy youth.*" [C. M

O, IN the morn of life, when youth
    With vital ardour glows,
And shines in all the fairest charms
    That beauty can disclose;

2 Deep in thy soul, before its powers
    Are yet by vice enslaved,
Be thy Creator's glorious Name
    And character engraved:

3 Ere yet the shades of sorrow cloud
    The sunshine of thy days;
And cares and toils, in endless round,
    Encompass all thy ways;

4 Ere yet thy heart the woes of age,
    With vain regret, deplore,
And sadly muse on former joys,
    That now return no more.

5 True wisdom, early sought and gain'd,
    In age will give thee rest:
O then, improve the morn of life,
    To make its evening blest.

THE SACRAMENTS.

BAPTISM OF ADULTS.

216   *"Be strong in the Lord, and in the power of his might."*   [S. M

SOLDIERS of Christ, arise,
  And put your armour on;
Strong in the strength which God supplies
  Through his eternal Son.

2 Strong in the Lord of hosts,
  And in his mighty power;
Who in the strength of Jesus trusts,
  Is more than conqueror.

3 Stand then in his great might,
  With all his strength endued;
And take, to arm you for the fight,
  The panoply of God;

4 That having all things done,
  And all your conflicts past,
Ye may behold your victory won,
  And stand complete at last.

217   *"Kept by the power of God through faith unto salvation."*   [C. M

MY God, thy covenant of love
  Abides for ever sure;
And in its matchless grace I feel
  My happiness secure.

2 Since thou, the everlasting God,
    My Father art become,
Jesus, my Guardian and my Friend,
    And heaven my final home,—

3 I welcome all thy sovereign will,
    For all that will is love;
And when I know not what thou dost,
    I wait the light above.

4 Thy covenant in darkest gloom
    Shall heavenly rays impart,
Which, when my eyelids close in death,
    Shall warm my chilling heart.

218   *"I am not ashamed, for I know whom I have*   [L. M
        believed."

JESUS, and shall it ever be,
    A mortal man ashamed of thee?
Ashamed of thee, whom angels praise,
Whose glories shine through endless days?

2 Ashamed of Jesus! sooner far
    Let night disown each radiant star;
'Tis midnight with my soul, till he,
Bright Morning Star, bid darkness flee.

3 Ashamed of Jesus! O as soon
    Let morning blush to own the sun;
He sheds the beams of light divine
O'er this benighted soul of mine.

4 Ashamed of Jesus! that dear Friend
On whom my hopes of heaven depend?
No; when I blush, be this my shame,
That I no more revere his name.

5 Ashamed of Jesus! empty pride;
I'll boast a Saviour crucified;
And O may this my portion be,
My Saviour not ashamed of me.

V. OFFICES OF THE CHURCH.

CATECHISM.

219 *"Jesus saith, Have ye never read, Out of the mouth of babes and sucklings thou hast perfected praise."* [7s. 6s. Double, with Chorus

WHEN, his salvation bringing,
  To Zion Jesus came,
The children all stood singing
  Hosanna to his name;
Nor did their zeal offend him,
  But as he rode along,
He let them still attend him,
  And smiled to hear their song.
    Hosanna to Jesus they sang.

2 And since the Lord retaineth
   His love to children still,
Though now as King he reigneth
   On Zion's heavenly hill;
We'll flock around his banner,
   Who sits upon the throne,
And cry aloud, Hosanna
   To David's royal Son:
     Hosanna to Jesus we'll sing.

3 For should we fail proclaiming
   Our great Redeemer's praise,
The stones, our silence shaming,
   Might well hosannas raise.
But shall we only render
   The tribute of our words?
No; while our hearts are tender,
   They too shall be the Lord's.
     Hosanna to Jesus, our King.

220   *"Sing unto the Lord, and praise his name."*   [7a.

GLORY to the Father give,
   God in whom we move and live;
Children's prayers he deigns to hear,
Children's songs delight his ear.

2 Glory to the Son we bring,
   Christ our Prophet, Priest, and King;
Children, raise your sweetest strain
To the Lamb, for he was slain.

3 Glory to the Holy Ghost,
   He reclaims the sinner lost;
   Children's minds may he inspire,
   Touch their tongues with holy fire.

4 Glory in the highest be
   To the blessèd Trinity,
   For the Gospel from above,
   For the word that "God is love."

221 *"Blessed are they that keep his testimonies, and* [C. M.
   seek him with their whole heart."

From the cxix. Psalm.

How bless'd are they who always keep
   The pure and perfect way;
Who never from the sacred paths
   Of God's commandments stray!

2 How bless'd, who to his righteous laws
   Have still obedient been;
And have with fervent, humble zeal
   His favour sought to win!

3 Such men their utmost caution use
   To shun each wicked deed;
But in the path which he directs
   With constant care proceed.

4 Thou strictly hast enjoin'd us, Lord,
   To learn thy sacred will;
And all our diligence employ
   Thy statutes to fulfil.

5 O then that thy most holy will
　　Might o'er my ways preside;
　And I the course of all my life
　　By thy direction guide!

222　*"Her ways are ways of pleasantness and all　　*[C. M
　　　　her paths are peace."

O HAPPY is the man who hears
　　Religion's warning voice,
And who celestial wisdom makes
　　His early, only choice.

2 For she has treasures greater far
　　Than east or west unfold;
　More precious are her bright rewards
　　Than gems, or stores of gold.

3 Her right hand offers to the just
　　Immortal, happy days;
　Her left, imperishable wealth
　　And heavenly crowns displays.

4 And, as her holy labours rise,
　　So her rewards increase;
　Her ways are ways of pleasantness,
　　And all her paths are peace.

223　*"That signs and wonders may be done by the*　[8s. 7s.
　　　　name of the holy child Jesus."

WHAT a strange and wondrous story
　　From the book of God is read;—
How the Lord of life and glory
　　Had not where to lay his head;—

2 How he left his throne in heaven,
    Here to suffer, bleed, and die,
That my soul might be forgiven,
    And ascend to God on high!

3 Father! let thy Holy Spirit
    Still reveal a Saviour's love,
And prepare me to inherit
    Glory where he reigns above.

4 There, with saints and angels dwelling,
    May I that great love proclaim,
And with them be ever telling
    All the wonders of his name.

224 *"The child grew, and waxed strong in spirit,* [C. M
*filled with wisdom; and the grace of God
was upon him."*

BY cool Siloam's shady rill
    How fair the lily grows!
How sweet the breath, beneath the hill,
    Of Sharon's dewy rose!

2 Lo! such the child, whose early feet
    The paths of peace have trod,
Whose secret heart, with influence sweet,
    Is upward drawn to God.

3 By cool Siloam's shady rill
    The lily must decay;
The rose that blooms beneath the hill
    Must shortly fade away.

4 And soon, too soon, the wintry hour
    Of man's maturer age
Will shake the soul with sorrow's power,
    And stormy passion's rage.

5 O thou, whose infant feet were found
    Within thy Father's shrine,
Whose years, with changeless virtue crown'd,
    Were all alike divine:

6 Dependent on thy bounteous breath,
    We seek thy grace alone,
In childhood, manhood, age and death,
    To keep us still thine own.

225   *"Little children keep yourselves from idols."*   [6s. 5s.

JESUS, meek and gentle
    Son of God most high,
Pitying, loving Saviour,
    Hear thy children's cry.

2 Pardon our offences,
    Loose our captive chains,
Break down every idol
    Which our soul detains.

3 Give us holy freedom,
    Fill our hearts with love;
Draw us, holy Jesus,
    To the realms above.

4 Lead us on our journey,
　　Be thyself the way,
　Through terrestrial darkness
　　To celestial day.

5 Jesus, meek and gentle
　　Son of God most high,
　Pitying, loving Saviour,
　　Hear thy children's cry.

226　　*"Of such is the kingdom of God."*　　[P.M.

I THINK when I read that sweet story of old,
　　When Jesus was here among men,
How he call'd little children as lambs to his fold,
　　I should like to have been with them then.

2 I wish that his hands had been placed on my head,
　　That his arm had been thrown around me,
　And that I might have seen his kind look when he said,
　　Let the little ones come unto me.

3 Yet still to his footstool in prayer I may go,
　　And ask for a share in his love;
　And if I thus earnestly seek him below,
　　I shall see him and hear him above,

4 In that beautiful place he has gone to prepare
　　For all who are washed and forgiven;
　And many dear children shall be with him there,
　　For of such is the kingdom of heaven.

5 But thousands and thousands who wander and fall,
  Never heard of that heavenly home;
I wish they could know there is room for them all,
  And that Jesus has bid them to come.

227 *"Other fell into good ground, and brought* [8s. 7s. 4
      forth fruit."

IN the vineyard of our Father
  Daily work we find to do;
Scatter'd gleanings we may gather,
  Though we are but young and few;
    Little clusters
  Help to fill the garners too.

2 Toiling early in the morning,
    Catching moments through the day
  Nothing small or lowly scorning
    While we work, and watch, and pray;
      Gathering gladly
    Free-will offerings by the way.

3 Not for selfish praise or glory,
    Not for objects nothing worth,
  But to send the blessèd story
    Of the Gospel o'er the earth,
      Telling mortals
    Of our Lord and Saviour's birth.

4 Up and ever at our calling,
    Till in death our lips are dumb,
  Or till—sin's dominion falling—

Christ shall in his kingdom come,
And his children
Reach their everlasting home.

5 Steadfast, then, in our endeavour,
Heavenly Father, may we be;
And for ever, and for ever,
We will give the praise to thee;
Alleluia!
Singing, all eternity.

228 *"Write them upon the table of thine heart."* [L. M.

O WRITE upon my memory, Lord,
The text and doctrine of thy word;
That I may break thy laws no more,
But love thee better than before.

2 With thoughts of Christ and things divine,
Fill up this sinful heart of mine;
That hoping pardon through his blood,
I may lie down and wake with God.

229 *"He shall feed his flock like a shepherd; he* [8s. 7s. 4.
shall gather the lambs with his arm, and
carry them in his bosom."

SAVIOUR, like a shepherd lead us,
Much we need thy tender care;
In thy pleasant pastures feed us;
For our use thy folds prepare:
Blessèd Jesus!
Thou hast bought us, thine we are.

2 Thou hast promised to receive us,
   Poor and sinful though we be;
Thou hast mercy to relieve us;
   Grace to cleanse, and power to free:
      Blessèd Jesus!
   Let us early turn to thee.

3 Early let us seek thy favour,
   Early let us learn thy will;
Do thou, Lord, our only Saviour,
   With thy love our bosoms fill:
      Blessèd Jesus!
   Thou hast loved us,—love us still.

230   *"He shall grow up before him as a*   [D. C. M.
               tender plant."

WHEN Jesus left his Father's throne,
   He chose an humble birth;
Like us, unhonour'd and unknown,
   He came to dwell on earth.
Like him may we be found below,
   In wisdom's path of peace;
Like him in grace and knowledge grow,
   As years and strength increase.

2 Sweet were his words and kind his look,
   When mothers round him press'd;
Their infants in his arms he took,
   And on his bosom bless'd.
Safe from the world's alluring harms,
   Beneath his watchful eye,
Thus in the circle of his arms
   May we for ever lie.

3 When Jesus into Salem rode,
   The children sang around;
For joy they pluck'd the palms, and strow'd
   Their garments on the ground.
Hosanna our glad voices raise,
   Hosanna to our King!
Should we forget our Saviour's praise,
   The stones themselves would sing.

231 *"While we were yet sinners, Christ died for us."* (C. M.

THERE is a green hill far away,
   Without a city wall,
Where the dear Lord was crucified
   Who died to save us all.

2 We may not know, we cannot tell,
   What pains he had to bear,
But we believe it was for us
   He hung and suffered there.

3 He died that we might be forgiven,
   He died to make us good,
That we might go at last to heaven,
   Saved by his precious blood.

4 There was no other good enough
   To pay the price of sin,
He only could unlock the gate
   Of heaven, and let us in.

5 O, dearly, dearly has he loved,
   And we must love him too,
And trust in his redeeming blood,
   And try his works to do.

232 "*Be strong and of a good courage... And the Lord, he it is that doth go before thee.*" [6s. 5s. with Chorus.

ONWARD, Christian soldiers,
   Marching as to war,
With the cross of Jesus,
   Going on before.
Christ the royal Master
   Leads against the foe;
Forward into battle,
   See, his banners go.
      Onward, Christian soldiers,
         Marching as to war,
      With the cross of Jesus
         Going on before.

2 At the sign of triumph
   Satan's host doth flee;
On, then, Christian soldiers,
   On to victory.
Hell's foundations quiver
   At the shout of praise;
Brothers, lift your voices,
   Loud your anthems raise.
      Onward, &c.

3 Like a mighty army
   Moves the Church of God;
Brothers, we are treading
   Where the saints have trod;
We are not divided,
   All one body we,
One in hope and doctrine,
   One in charity.
      Onward, &c.

4 Crowns and thrones may perish,
    Kingdoms rise and wane,
  But the Church of Jesus
    Constant will remain;
  Gates of hell can never
    'Gainst that Church prevail;
  We have Christ's own promise,
    And that cannot fail.
        Onward, &c.

5 Onward, then, ye people,
    Join our happy throng,
  Blend with ours your voices
    In the triumph-song;
  Glory, laud, and honour,
    Unto Christ the King;
  This through countless ages
    Men and angels sing.
        Onward, Christian soldiers,
          Marching as to war,
        With the cross of Jesus
          Going on before.

233   *"The child Jesus."*   [8s. 7s. 7s.

ONCE in royal David's city
  Stood a lowly cattle shed,
Where a mother laid her baby,
  In a manger for his bed;
Mary was that mother mild,
Jesus Christ her little child.

2 He came down to earth from heaven
    Who is God and Lord of all,
 And his shelter was a stable,
    And his cradle was a stall;
 With the poor, and mean, and lowly,
 Lived on earth our Saviour holy.

3 And, through all his wondrous childhood,
    He would honour and obey,
 Love, and watch the lowly maiden
    In whose gentle arms he lay;
 Christian children all must be
 Mild, obedient, good as he.

4 For he is our childhood's pattern,
    Day by day like us he grew;
 He was little, weak, and helpless,
    Tears and smiles like us he knew;
 And he feeleth for our sadness,
 And he shareth in our gladness.

5 And our eyes at last shall see him,
    Through his own redeeming love,
 For that child so dear and gentle
    Is our Lord in heaven above;
 And he leads his children on
 To the place where he is gone.

6 Not in that poor lowly stable,
    With the oxen standing by,
 We shall see him; but in heaven,
    Set at God's right hand on high;
 When like stars his children crowned
 All in white shall wait around.

CONFIRMATION.

234 *"With my whole heart have I sought thee."* [C. M.

MY God, accept my heart this day,
  And make it always thine,
That I from thee no more may stray,
  No more from thee decline.

2 Before the cross of him who died,
  Behold, I prostrate fall;
Let every sin be crucified,
  And Christ be all in all.

3 Anoint me with thy heavenly grace,
  And seal me for thine own;
That I may see thy glorious face,
  And worship near thy throne.

4 Let every thought, and work, and word,
  To thee be ever given;
Then life shall be thy service, Lord,
  And death the gate of heaven!

235 *"My heart is fixed, O God, my heart is fixed."* [L. M

O HAPPY day, that stays my choice
  On thee, my Saviour and my God:
Well may this glowing heart rejoice,
  And tell thy goodness all abroad.

2 O happy bond, that seals my vows,
  To him who merits all my love;
Let cheerful anthems fill his house,
  While to his sacred throne I move.

3 'Tis done, the great transaction's done;
    Deign, gracious Lord, to make me thine;
  Help me, through grace, to follow on,
    Glad to confess thy voice divine.

4 Here rest, my oft-divided heart,
    Fix'd on thy God, thy Saviour, rest;
  Who with the world would grieve to part
    When call'd on angels' food to feast?

5 High heaven, that heard the solemn vow,
    That vow renew'd shall daily hear,
  Till in life's latest hour I bow,
    And bless in death a bond so dear.

236 *"What things were gain to me, those I counted loss for Christ."* [8s. 7s. Double.

JESUS, I my cross have taken,
    All to leave and follow thee;
Destitute, despised, forsaken,
    Thou from hence my all shalt be:
Perish every fond ambition,
    All I've sought, or hoped, or known;
Yet how rich is my condition!
    God and heaven are still my own.

2 Man may trouble and distress me,
    'Twill but drive me to thy breast;
  Life with trials hard may press me,
    Heaven will bring me sweeter rest.
  O 'tis not in grief to harm me,
    While thy love is left to me;
  O 'twere not in joy to charm me,
    Were that joy unmix'd with thee.

3 Take, my soul, thy full salvation;
    Rise o'er sin, and fear, and care;
Joy to find in every station
    Something still to do or bear:
Think what Spirit dwells within thee;
    What a Father's smile is thine;
What a Saviour died to win thee;
    Child of heaven, shouldst thou repine?

4 Haste then on from grace to glory,
    Arm'd by faith, and wing'd by prayer;
Heaven's eternal day's before thee,
    God's own hand shall guide thee there.
Soon shall close thy earthly mission,
    Swift shall pass thy pilgrim days;
Hope soon change to glad fruition,
    Faith to sight, and prayer to praise.

237   *"My grace is sufficient for thee."*   [6s. 4s.

MY faith looks up to thee,
    Thou Lamb of Calvary,
  Saviour divine!
Now hear me while I pray:
Take all my guilt away;
O let me from this day
  Be wholly thine.

2 May thy rich grace impart
    Strength to my fainting heart,
      My zeal inspire;

  As thou hast died for me,
  O may my love to thee
  Pure, warm, and changeless be,
   A living fire.

3 While life's dark maze I tread,
 And griefs around me spread,
  Be thou my guide;
 Bid darkness turn to day;
 Wipe sorrow's tears away,
 Nor let me ever stray
  From thee aside.

4 When ends life's transient dream,
 When death's cold, sullen stream
  Shall o'er me roll,
 Blest Saviour, then in love,
 Fear and distrust remove;
 O bear me safe above,
  A ransom'd soul.

238 *"And they shall be mine, saith the Lord of hosts, in* [7s.
  that day when I make up my jewels."

THINE for ever:—God of love,
 Hear us from thy throne above;
Thine for ever may we be,
Here and in eternity.

2 Thine for ever:—Lord of life,
Shield us through our earthly strife:
Thou the life, the truth, the way,
Guide us to the realms of day.

3 Thine for ever:—O how bless'd
They who find in thee their rest!
Saviour, guardian, heavenly friend,
O defend us to the end.

4 Thine for ever:—Saviour, keep
These thy frail and trembling sheep;
Safe alone beneath thy care,
Let us all thy goodness share.

5 Thine for ever:—thou our guide,
All our wants by thee supplied,
All our sins by thee forgiven,
Lead us, Lord, from earth to heaven.

239 *"Thou hast avouched the Lord this day to be thy God."* [C. M.

WITNESS, ye men and angels; now
  Before the Lord we speak;
To him we make our solemn vow,
  A vow we dare not break:

2 That long as life itself shall last,
  Ourselves to Christ we yield;
Nor from his cause will we depart,
  Or ever quit the field.

3 We trust not in our native strength,
  But on his grace rely,
That, with returning wants, the Lord
  Will all our need supply.

4 Lord, guide our doubtful feet aright,
  And keep us in thy ways;
And, while we turn our vows to prayers,
  Turn thou our prayers to praise.

CONFIRMATION.

240 *"He dwelleth with you, and shall be in you."* [L. M.

DRAW, Holy Ghost, thy seven-fold veil
  Between us and the fires of youth;
Breathe, Holy Ghost, thy fresh'ning gale
  Our fevered brow in age to soothe.

2 For ever on our souls be traced
  This blessing from the Saviour's hand,
A sheltering rock in memory's waste,
  O'ershadowing all the weary land.

241 *"He that cometh unto me, I will in no wise cast out."* [Six 8s.

LORD, shall thy children come to thee?
  A boon of love divine we seek:
Brought to thine arms in infancy,
  Ere heart could feel, or tongue could speak,
Thy children pray for grace, that they
May come themselves to thee to-day.

2 Lord, shall we come? and come again,
  Oft as we see thy table spread,
And, tokens of thy dying pain,
  The wine pour'd out, the broken bread?
Bless, bless, O Lord, thy children's prayer,
That they may come and find thee there.

3 Lord, shall we come? not thus alone
  At holy time, or solemn rite;
But every hour till life be flown,
  Through weal or woe, in gloom or light,
Come to thy throne of grace, that we
In faith, hope, love, confirm'd may be.

4 Lord, shall we come? come yet again?
    Thy children ask one blessing more:
To come, not now alone;—but then,
    When life, and death, and time are o'er;
Then, then to come, O Lord, and be
Confirm'd in heaven, confirm'd by thee.

242   *"Put on the whole armour of God."*   [D. L. M

ARM these thy soldiers, mighty Lord,
    With shield of faith and Spirit's sword;
Forth to the battle may they go,
And boldly fight against the foe,
With banner of the cross unfurl'd,
And by it overcome the world;
And so at last receive from thee
The palm and crown of victory.

2 Come, ever-blessed Spirit, come,
And make thy servants' hearts thy home;
May each a living temple be,
Hallow'd for ever, Lord, to thee;
Enrich that temple's holy shrine
With sevenfold gifts of grace divine;
With wisdom, light, and knowledge bless,
Strength, counsel, fear, and godliness.

243   *"Show me thy ways, O Lord, and teach me*   [S. M
    thy paths."

From the xxv. Psalm.

HIS mercy and his truth
    The righteous Lord displays,
In bringing wandering sinners home,
    And teaching them his ways.

2 He those in justice guides
   Who his direction seek;
And in his sacred paths shall lead
   The humble and the meek.

3 Through all the ways of God
   Both truth and mercy shine,
To such as, with religious hearts,
   To his blest will incline.

4 For God to all his saints
   His secret will imparts,
And does his gracious covenant write
   In their obedient hearts.

244   *"And I will accept thee, saith the Lord."*   [S. M.

From the xx. Psalm.

MAY God accept our vow,
   Our sacrifice receive,
Our heart's devout request allow,
   Our holy wishes give!

2 O Lord, thy saving grace
   We joyfully declare;
Our banner in thy name we raise—
   "The Lord fulfil our prayer!"

3 Now know we that the Lord
   His chosen will defend;
From heaven will strength divine afford,
   And will their prayer attend.

245   "*O Lord God of hosts, blessed is the man that*   [C. M.
putteth his trust in thee."

From the lxxxiv. Psalm.

O GOD of hosts, the mighty Lord,
    How lovely is the place
Where thou, enthroned in glory, show'st
    The brightness of thy face!

2 My longing soul faints with desire
    To view thy blest abode;
My panting heart and flesh cry out
    For thee, the living God.

3 Thrice happy they whose choice has thee
    Their sure protection made,
Who long to tread the sacred ways
    That to thy dwelling lead.

4 Thus they proceed from strength to strength,
    And still approach more near;
Till all on Sion's holy mount
    Before their God appear.

5 For God, who is our sun and shield,
    Will grace and glory give;
And no good thing will he withhold
    From them that justly live.

6 Thou God, whom heavenly hosts obey,
    How highly bless'd is he,
Whose hope and trust, securely placed,
    Are still reposed on thee!

HOLY MATRIMONY.

246   *"What shall separate us from the love of Christ?"*   [C. M.

AS by the light of opening day
   The stars are all conceal'd,
So earthly pleasures fade away
   When Jesus is reveal'd.

2 Creatures no more divide my choice,
   I bid them all depart;
His name, and love, and gracious voice
   Shall fix my roving heart.

3 Now, Lord, I would be thine alone,
   And wholly live to thee;
Yet worthless still myself I own,
   Thy worth is all my plea.

HOLY MATRIMONY.

247   *" God blessed them."*   [SIX 7s.

DEIGN this union to approve,
   And confirm it, God of love.

Bless thy servants; on their head
Now the oil of gladness shed;
In this nuptial bond, to thee
Let them consecrated be.

2 In prosperity, be near,
To preserve them in thy fear;
In affliction, let thy smile
All the woes of life beguile;
And when every change is past,
Take them to thyself at last.

248   *"A threefold cord is not quickly broken."*   [7s. 6s.

THE voice that breathed o'er Eden,
　That earliest wedding-day,
The primal marriage blessing,
　It hath not pass'd away.

2 Still in the pure espousal
　Of Christian man and maid,
The holy Three are with us,
　The threefold grace is said.

3 Be present, awful Father,
　To give away this bride,
As Eve thou gav'st to Adam
　Out of his own pierced side:

4 Be present, Son of Mary,
　To join their loving hands,
As thou didst bind two natures
　In thine eternal bands!

5 Be present, holiest Spirit,
    To bless them as they kneel,
As thou, for Christ the Bridegroom,
    The heavenly spouse dost seal!

6 O spread thy pure wing o'er them,
    Let no ill power find place,
When onward to thine altar
    Their hallowed path they trace,

7 To cast their crowns before thee
    In perfect sacrifice,
Till to the home of gladness
    With Christ's own bride they rise.

VISITATION OF THE SICK.

249   *"I look for the Lord; my soul doth wait for*   [L. M.
         him; in his word is my trust."

BE still, my heart, these anxious cares
    To thee are burdens, thorns, and snares;
They cast dishonour on thy Lord,
And contradict his gracious word.

2 Brought safely by his hand thus far,
Why wilt thou now give place to fear?
How canst thou want if he provide,
Or lose thy way with such a guide?

3 When first before his mercy-seat,
  Thou didst to him thy all commit;
  He gave thee warrant from that hour,
  To trust his wisdom, love, and power.

4 Did ever trouble yet befall,
  And he refuse to hear thy call?
  And has he not his promise passed,
  That thou shalt overcome at last?

5 Though rough and thorny be the road,
  It leads thee home apace to God;
  Then count thy present trials small,
  For heaven will make amends for all.

250 *"Who is this that cometh up from the wilderness, leaning upon her Beloved."* [SIX 8s.

WHEN gathering clouds around I view,
  And days are dark, and friends are few,
On him I lean, who not in vain
Experienced every human pain;
He sees my wants, allays my fears,
And counts and treasures up my tears.

2 If aught should tempt my soul to stray
  From heavenly wisdom's narrow way,
  To fly the good I would pursue,
  Or do the ill I would not do;
  Still he who felt temptation's power,
  Shall guard me in that dangerous hour.

3 If vexing thoughts within me rise,
And, sore dismay'd, my spirit dies;
Still he who once vouchsafed to bear
Such bitter conflict with despair,
Shall sweetly soothe, shall gently dry,
The throbbing heart, the streaming eye.

4 When sorrowing o'er some stone I bend,
Which covers what was once a friend,
And from his voice, his hand, his smile,
Divides me for a little while,
Thou Saviour, mark'st the tears I shed,
For thou didst weep o'er Lazarus dead.

5 And O, when I have safely past
Through every conflict but the last,
Still, still, unchanging, watch beside
My bed of death, for thou hast died:
Then point to realms of cloudless day,
And wipe the latest tear away.

251 *"Let this mind be in you, which was also in Christ Jesus."* [C. M.

LORD, as to thy dear cross we flee,
 And plead to be forgiven,
So let thy life our pattern be,
 And form our souls for heaven.

2 Help us, through good report and ill,
 Our daily cross to bear;
Like thee, to do our Father's will,
 Our brethren's griefs to share.

3 Let grace our selfishness expel,
  Our earthliness refine;
And kindness in our bosoms dwell,
  As free and true as thine.

4 If joy shall at thy bidding fly,
  And grief's dark day come on,
We in our turn would meekly cry,
  "Father, thy will be done."

5 Kept peaceful in the midst of strife,
  Forgiving and forgiven,
O may we lead the pilgrim's life,
  And follow thee to heaven.

252 *"Surely he hath borne our griefs and carried our sorrows."* [7s

WHEN our heads are bowed with woe,
  When our bitter tears o'erflow,
When we mourn the lost, the dear,
Jesus, Son of Mary, hear.

2 Thou our throbbing flesh hast worn,
Thou our mortal griefs hast borne,
Thou hast shed the human tear;
Jesus, Son of Mary, hear.

3 When the solemn death-bell tolls
For our own departing souls,
When our final doom is near,
Jesus, Son of Mary, hear.

4 Thou hast bowed the dying head,
　Thou the blood of life hast shed,
　Thou hast filled a mortal bier;
　　Jesus, Son of Mary, hear.

5 When the heart is sad within
　With the thought of all its sin,
　When the spirit shrinks with fear,
　　Jesus, Son of Mary, hear.

6 Thou the shame, the grief, hast known,
　Though the sins were not thine own;
　Thou hast deigned their load to bear,
　　Jesus, Son of Mary, hear.

253　　*"Thou art my hiding-place."*　　[D. C. M.

THOU art my hiding-place, O Lord!
　　In thee I put my trust,
Encouraged by thy holy word,
　　A feeble child of dust.
I have no argument beside,
　　I urge no other plea;
And 'tis enough the Saviour died,
　　The Saviour died for me.

2 When storms of fierce temptation beat,
　　And furious foes assail,
　My refuge is the mercy-seat,
　　My hope within the veil.
　From strife of tongues and bitter words
　　My spirit flies to thee:
　Joy to my heart the thought affords,
　　My Saviour died for me.

3 Mid trials heavy to be borne,
   When mortal strength is vain,
A heart with grief and anguish torn,
   A body rack'd with pain,—
Ah! what could give the sufferer rest,
   Bid every murmur flee,
But this, the witness in my breast
   That Jesus died for me?

4 And when thine awful voice commands
   This body to decay,
And life, in its last lingering sands,
   Is ebbing fast away,—
Then, though it be in accents weak,
   And faint and tremblingly,
O give me strength in death to speak,
   My Saviour died for me.

254 *"Make thy way straight before my face."* [6s. DOUBLE.

THY way, not mine, O Lord
   However dark it be:
Lead me by thine own hand,
   Choose out the path for me.
Smooth let it be or rough,
   It will be still the best;
Winding or straight, it leads
   Right onward to thy rest.

2 I dare not choose my lot;
   I would not, if I might;
Choose thou for me, my God;
   So shall I walk aright.

Take thou my cup, and it
  With joy or sorrow fill,
As best to thee may seem;
  Choose thou my good and ill.

3 Choose thou for me my friends,
   My sickness or my health;
  Choose thou my cares for me,
   My poverty or wealth.
  Not mine, not mine the choice,
   In things or great or small;
  Be thou my guide, my strength,
   My wisdom, and my all.

255 *"Having a desire to depart, and to be with* [C. M.
Christ, which is far better."

WHEN musing sorrow weeps the past,
  And mourns the present pain,
How sweet to think of peace at last,
  And feel that death is gain!

2 'Tis not that murmuring thoughts arise,
   And dread a Father's will;
  'Tis not that meek submission flies,
   And would not suffer still;

3 It is that heaven-taught faith surveys
   The path that leads to light,
  And longs her eagle plumes to raise,
   And lose herself in sight.

4 It is that hope with ardour glows
    To see him face to face,
Whose dying love no language knows
    Sufficient art to trace.

5 It is that tortur'd conscience feels
    The pangs of struggling sin;
Sees, though afar, the hand that heals,
    And ends her war within.

6 O let me wing my hallow'd flight
    From earth-born woe and care,
And soar above these clouds of night
    My Saviour's bliss to share!

256   *"Thy will be done."*   [P. M.

MY God, my Father, while I stray,
    Far from my home, on life's rough way,
O teach me from my heart to say,
    "Thy will be done."

2 Though dark my path, and sad my lot,
Let me be still and murmur not,
And breathe the prayer divinely taught,
    "Thy will be done."

3 What though in lonely grief I sigh
For friends beloved no longer nigh,
Submissive still would I reply,
    "Thy will be done."

4 If thou shouldst call me to resign
  What most I prize—it ne'er was mine;
  I only yield thee what is thine—
    "Thy will be done."

5 Renew my will from day to day,
  Blend it with thine, and take away
  All that now makes it hard to say,
    "Thy will be done."

6 Let but my fainting heart be blest
  With thy sweet Spirit for its guest,
  My God, to thee I leave the rest;
    "Thy will be done."

257 *"My meditation of him shall be sweet."* [P. M.

WHATE'ER my God ordains is right;
  His will is ever just;
Howe'er he orders now my cause,
  I will be still and trust.
    He is my God;
    Though dark my road,
He holds me that I shall not fall,
Wherefore to him I leave it all.

2 Whate'er my God ordains is right;
    He never will deceive;
  He leads me by the proper path,
    And so to him I cleave,
      And take content
      What he hath sent;
  His hand can turn my griefs away,
  And patiently I wait his day.

3 Whate'er my God ordains is right;
    Though I the cup must drink
  That bitter seems to my faint heart,
    I will not fear nor shrink;
      Tears pass away
      With dawn of day;
  Sweet comfort yet shall fill my heart,
  And pain and sorrow all depart.

4 Whate'er my God ordains is right;
    My Light, my Life is he,
  Who cannot will me aught but good;
    I trust him utterly;
      For well I know,
      In joy or woe,
  We soon shall see, as sunlight clear,
  How faithful was our Guardian here.

5 Whate'er my God ordains is right;
    Here will I take my stand,
  Though sorrow, need, or death make earth
    For me a desert land.
      My Father's care
      Is round me there,
  He holds me that I shall not fall;
  And so to him I leave it all.

BURIAL OF THE DEAD.

258   *"Lord, let me know my end, and the number of*   [C. M.
my days."

From the xxxix. Psalm.

LORD, let me know my term of days,
    How soon my life will end:
The numerous train of ills disclose,
    Which this frail state attend.

2 My life, thou know'st, is but a span,
    A cipher sums my years;
And every man, in best estate,
    But vanity appears.

3 Man, like a shadow, vainly walks,
    With fruitless cares oppress'd;
He heaps up wealth, but cannot tell
    By whom 'twill be possess'd.

4 Why then should I on worthless toys
    With anxious cares attend?
On thee alone my steadfast hope
    Shall ever, Lord, depend.

5 Lord, hear my cry, accept my tears,
    And listen to my prayer,
Who sojourn like a stranger here,
    As all my fathers were.

6 O spare me yet a little time;
    My wasted strength restore,
Before I vanish quite from hence,
    And shall be seen no more.

259   *"Ye sorrow not even as others which have*   [C. M.
no hope."

HEAR what the voice from heaven declares
  To those in Christ who die:
Released from all their earthly cares,
  They'll reign with him on high.

2 Then why lament departed friends,
  Or shake at death's alarms?
Death's but the servant Jesus sends
  To call us to his arms.

3 If sin be pardon'd, we're secure,
  Death hath no sting beside;
The law gave sin its strength and power,
  But Christ, our ransom, died.

4 The grave of all his saints he bless'd,
  When in the grave he lay:
And, rising thence, their hopes he raised
  To everlasting day.

5 Then, joyfully, while life we have,
  To Christ, our life, we'll sing,
"Where is thy victory, O grave?
  And where, O death, thy sting?"

260   *"They which sleep in Jesus, will God bring*   [L. M.
with him."

ASLEEP in Jesus! blessèd sleep!
  From which none ever wakes to weep;
A calm and undisturb'd repose,
Unbroken by the last of foes.

BURIAL OF THE DEAD.

2 Asleep in Jesus! O how sweet
To be for such a slumber meet;
With holy confidence to sing
That death hath lost its painful sting!

3 Asleep in Jesus! peaceful rest!
Whose waking is supremely blest;
No fear, no woe shall dim that hour
That manifests the Saviour's power.

4 Asleep in Jesus! O for me
May such a blissful refuge be!
Securely shall my ashes lie,
Waiting the summons from on high.

5 Asleep in Jesus! far from thee
Thy kindred and their graves may be;
But there is still a blessèd sleep,
From which none ever wakes to weep.

261   *"He shall enter into peace."*   [C. M.

NOT for the dead in Christ we weep;
   Their sorrows now are o'er;
The sea is calm, the tempest past,
   On that eternal shore.

2 Their peace is seal'd, their rest is sure,
   Within that better home;
A while we weep and linger here,
   Then follow to the tomb.

3 And though no vision'd dream of bliss
    Nor trance of rapture show
Where, on the bosom of their God,
    They rest from human woe;

4 Jesus! our shadowy path illume,
    And teach the chasten'd mind
To welcome all that's left of good,
    To all that's lost resign'd.

BURIAL OF A CHILD.

262   *"Of such is the kingdom of heaven."*   [L. M.

AS the sweet flower that scents the morn,
    But withers in the rising day;
Thus lovely was this infant's dawn,
    Thus swiftly fled its life away.

2 It died ere its expanding soul
    Had ever burnt with wrong desires,
Had ever spurn'd at heaven's control,
    Or ever quench'd its sacred fires.

3 It died to sin, it died to cares,
    But for a moment felt the rod:
O mourner, such, the Lord declares,
    Such are the children of our God.

FOR THOSE AT SEA.

263 *"There is hope in thine end, saith the Lord,* [7s. 8s. 7s.
*that thy children shall come again to
their own border."*

TENDER Shepherd, thou hast still'd
   Now thy little lamb's brief weeping;
Ah, how peaceful, pale, and mild
   In its narrow bed 'tis sleeping,
     And no sigh of anguish sore
     Heaves that little bosom more.

2 In this world of care and pain,
   Lord, thou wouldst no longer leave it;
To the sunny heavenly plain
   Thou dost now with joy receive it;
     Clothed in robes of spotless white,
     Now it dwells with thee in light.

3 Ah, Lord Jesus, grant that we
   Where it lives may soon be living,
And the lovely pastures see
   That its heavenly food are giving;
     Then the gain of death we prove,
     Though thou take what most we love.

FOR THOSE AT SEA.

264 *"The bright and morning star."* [8s. 7s. 4.

STAR of peace, to wanderers weary,
   Bright the beams, that smile on me;
Cheer the pilot's vision dreary,
     Far, far at sea.

2 Star of hope, gleam on the billow,
    Bless the soul that sighs for thee,
  Bless the sailor's lonely pillow,
    Far, far at sea.

3 Star of faith, when winds are mocking
    All his toil, he flies to thee;
  Save him, on the billows rocking,
    Far, far at sea.

4 Star divine, O safely guide him,
    Bring the wanderer home to thee;
  Sore temptations long have tried him,
    Far, far at sea.

265 *"Be of good cheer, it is I; be not afraid."* [6s. 4s. Double.

FIERCE was the wild billow;
    Dark was the night,
  Oars laboured heavily,
    Foam glimmered white;
  Mariners trembled,
    Peril was nigh!
  Then said the God of God,
    "Peace! It is I."

2 Ridge of the mountain-wave,
    Lower thy crest;
  Wail of the tempest-wind,
    Be thou at rest;

Peril can none be,
  Sorrow must fly—
Where saith the Light of light,
  "Peace! It is I."

3 Jesus, Deliverer,
  Come thou to me:
Soothe thou my voyaging
  Over life's sea:
Thou, when the storm of death
  Roars, sweeping by,
Whisper, O Truth of truth—
  "Peace! It is I!"

266   *"Save, Lord, or we perish."*   [12s

WHEN through the torn sail the wild tempest is streaming,
When o'er the dark wave the red lightning is gleaming,
Nor hope lends a ray the poor seaman to cherish,
We fly to our Maker: "Save, Lord, or we perish."

2 O Jesus, once rock'd on the breast of the billow,
Aroused by the shriek of despair from thy pillow,
Now seated in glory, the mariner cherish,
Who cries in his anguish, "Save, Lord, or we perish."

3 And O, when the whirlwind of passion is raging,
When sin in our hearts its wild warfare is waging,
Then send down thy Spirit thy redeemèd to cherish,
Rebuke the destroyer: "Save, Lord, or we perish."

267   *"These men see the works of the Lord, and his wonders in the deep."*   [Six 8s.

ETERNAL Father! strong to save,
Whose arm hath bound the restless wave,
Who bid'st the mighty ocean deep
Its own appointed limits keep;
   O hear us when we cry to thee
   For those in peril on the sea.

2 O Christ! whose voice the waters heard,
And hushed their raging at thy word,
Who walkedst on the foaming deep,
And calm amidst its rage didst sleep;
   O hear us when we cry to thee
   For those in peril on the sea.

3 Most Holy Spirit! who didst brood
Upon the chaos dark and rude,
And bid its angry tumult cease,
And give, for wild confusion, peace;
   O hear us when we cry to thee
   For those in peril on the sea.

4 O Trinity of love and power!
 Our brethren shield in danger's hour;
 From rock and tempest, fire and foe,
 Protect them wheresoe'er they go;
  Thus evermore shall rise to thee
  Glad hymns of praise from land and sea.

268 *"Jesus went unto them, walking on the sea."* [S. M

O THOU who didst prepare
  The ocean's sounding deep,
 And bid the gathering waters there
  In mighty concourse sweep:

2 Toss'd in our reeling bark
  On this tumultuous sea,
 Thy wondrous ways, O Lord, we mark,
  And lift our hearts to thee.

3 Jesus is nigh, who trod
  Of old that foaming spray,
 Whose billows own'd the incarnate God,
  And died in calm away.

4 Though swells the threatening tide,
  Mounting to heaven above,
 We know in whom our souls confide,
  And fearless trust his love.

269 *"I will keep thee in all places whither thou goest."* [C M.

[Which may be used at Sea or on Land.]

LORD, for the just thou dost provide,
　Thou art their sure defence;
Eternal Wisdom is their guide,
　Their help, Omnipotence.

2 Though they through foreign lands should roam
　And breathe the tainted air
In burning climates, far from home,
　Yet thou, their God, art there.

3 Thy goodness sweetens every soil,
　Makes every country please;
Thou on the snowy hills dost smile,
　And smooth'st the rugged seas.

4 When waves on waves, to heaven uprear'd,
　Defied the pilot's art;
When terror in each face appear'd,
　And sorrow in each heart;

5 To thee I raised my humble prayer,
　To snatch me from the grave:
I found thine ear not slow to hear,
　Nor short thine arm to save.

6 Thou gav'st the word, the winds did cease.
　The storms obey'd thy will,
The raging sea was hush'd in peace,
　And every wave was still.

7 For this, my life, in every state,
    A life of praise shall be;
And death, when death shall be my fate,
    Shall join my soul to thee.

ORDINATION OR INSTITUTION OF MINISTERS.

270   *"Let thy priests be clothed with righteousness."*   [L. M.

LORD, pour thy Spirit from on high,
    And thine ordainèd servants bless;
Graces and gifts to each supply,
    And clothe thy priests with righteousness.

2 Within thy temple when they stand,
    To teach the truth as taught by thee,
Saviour, like stars in thy right hand
    Let all thy Church's pastors be.

3 Wisdom, and zeal, and love impart,
    Firmness and meekness from above,
To bear thy people in their heart,
    And love the souls whom thou dost love;

4 To love, and pray, and never faint,
    By day and night their guard to keep,
To warn the sinner, form the saint,
    To feed thy lambs, and tend thy sheep.

5 So, when their work is finish'd here,
    They may in hope their charge resign;
So, when their Master shall appear,
    They may with crowns of glory shine.

271 *"Unto every one of us is given grace; according to the measure of the gift of Christ."* [L. M.

FATHER of mercies, bow thine ear,
Attentive to our earnest prayer:
We plead for those who plead for thee;
Successful pleaders may they be.

2 How great their work, how vast their charge!
Do thou their anxious souls enlarge:
Their best acquirements are our gain;
We share the blessings they obtain.

3 Clothe, then, with energy divine
Their words, and let those words be thine;
To them thy sacred truth reveal,
Suppress their fear, inflame their zeal.

4 Teach them to sow the precious seed,
Teach them thy chosen flock to feed;
Teach them immortal souls to gain—
Souls that will well reward their pain.

5 Let thronging multitudes around
Hear from their lips the joyful sound;
In humble strains thy grace implore,
And feel thy new-creating power.

6 Let sinners break their massy chains,
Distressèd souls forget their pains;
Let light through distant realms be spread,
And Sion rear her drooping head.

272   *"And a river went out of Eden to water the garden; and from thence it was parted, and became into four heads."*   [8s. 7s. Six Lines.

COME pure hearts, in sweetest measures
Sing of those who spread the treasures
  In the holy Gospels shrined;
Blessèd tidings of salvation,
Peace on earth their proclamation,
  Love from God to lost mankind.

2 See the Rivers four that gladden
With their streams the better Eden
  Planted by our Lord most dear;
Christ the fountain, these the waters;
Drink, O Sion's sons and daughters,
  Drink and find salvation here.

3 O that we, thy truth confessing,
And thy holy word possessing,
  Jesus, may thy love adore;
Unto thee our voices raising,
Thee with all thy ransomed praising,
  Ever and for evermore.

273   *"To proclaim the unsearchable riches of Christ."*   [L. M.

GO forth, ye heralds, in my name,
  Sweetly the Gospel trumpet sound;
The glorious jubilee proclaim,
  Where'er the human race is found.

2 The joyful news to all impart,
    And teach them where salvation lies;
With care bind up the broken heart,
    And wipe the tears from weeping eyes

3 Be wise as serpents, where you go,
    But harmless as the peaceful dove;
And let your heaven-taught conduct show
    That ye're commission'd from above.

4 Freely from me ye have received,
    Freely, in love, to others give;
Thus shall your doctrines be believed,
    And, by your labours, sinners live.

CONSECRATION OF BISHOPS.

274   *"And he breathed on them, and said, Receive*   [C. M
       ye the Holy Ghost."

COME, Holy Ghost, eternal God,
    Proceeding from above,
Both from the Father and the Son,
    The God of peace and love.

2 Visit our minds, into our hearts
    Thy heavenly grace inspire;
That truth and godliness we may
    Pursue with full desire.

3 Thou in thy gifts art manifold,
    By them Christ's Church doth stand:
In faithful hearts thou writ'st thy law,
    The finger of God's hand.

4 According to thy promise, Lord,
   Thou givest speech with grace;
 That, through thy help, God's praises may
   Resound in every place.

5 O Holy Ghost, into our minds.
   Send down thy heavenly light;
 Kindle our hearts with fervent zeal,
   To serve God day and night.

6 Of strife and of dissension
   Dissolve, O Lord, the bands,
 And knit the knots of peace and love
   Throughout all Christian lands.

7 Grant us the grace that we may know
   The Father of all might,
 That we of his beloved Son
   May gain the blissful sight;

8 And that we may with perfect faith
   Ever acknowledge thee,
 The Spirit of Father and of Son,
   One God in Persons Three.

LAYING OF A CORNER STONE.

275 "*May thine eyes be opened toward this house* [L. M.
             night and day."

THIS stone to thee in faith we lay;
   We build the temple, Lord, to thee;
 Thine eye be open night and day
   To guard this house and sanctuary.

2 Here, when thy people seek thy face,
   And dying sinners pray to live,
Hear thou in heaven, thy dwelling-place,
   And when thou hearest, O forgive.

3 Here, when thy messengers proclaim
   The blessèd Gospel of thy Son,
Still by the power of his great name
   Be mighty signs and wonders done.

4 Hosanna! to their heavenly King,
   When children's voices raise that song,
Hosanna! let their angels sing
   And heaven with earth the strain prolong.

5 But will, indeed, Jehovah deign
   Here to abide, no transient guest?
Here will the world's Redeemer reign?
   And here the Holy Spirit rest?

6 That glory never hence depart;
   Yet choose not, Lord, this house alone:
Thy kingdom come to every heart,
   In every bosom fix thy throne.

276 *"The glory of Lebanon shall come unto thee, the* [L. M.
*fir tree, the pine tree, and the box together, to
beautify the place of my sanctuary."*

O LORD of hosts, whose glory fills
   The bounds of the eternal hills,
And yet vouchsafes, in Christian lands,
To dwell in temples made with hands;

2 Grant that all we who here to-day
　Rejoicing this foundation lay,
　May be in very deed thine own,
　Built on the precious Corner-stone.

3 Endue the creatures with thy grace
　That shall adorn thy dwelling-place;
　The beauty of the oak and pine,
　The gold and silver, make them thine.

4 To thee they all pertain; to thee
　The treasures of the earth and sea;
　And when we bring them to thy throne
　We but present thee with thine own.

5 The heads that guide endue with skill;
　The hands that work preserve from ill;
　That we, who these foundations lay,
　May raise the topstone in its day.

CONSECRATION OF CHURCHES AND CHAPELS.

277 *"O go your way into his gates with thanksgiving,* [L. M *and into his courts with praise."*

From the c. Psalm.

WITH one consent let all the earth
　　To God their cheerful voices raise;
Glad homage pay with awful mirth,
　　And sing before him songs of praise.

2 Convinced that he is God alone,
　　From whom both we and all proceed;
We, whom he chooses for his own,
　　The flock that he vouchsafes to feed.

3 O enter then his temple gate,
　　Thence to his courts devoutly press;
　And still your grateful hymns repeat,
　　And still his name with praises bless.

4 For he's the Lord, supremely good,
　　His mercy is for ever sure:
　His truth, which always firmly stood,
　　To endless ages shall endure.

278 "*I will wash my hands in innocency, O Lord;*　[C. M.
　　and so will I go to thine altar."

　　　From the xxvi. Psalm.

I'LL wash my hands in innocence,
　And round thine altar go;
Pour the glad hymn of triumph thence,
　And thence thy wonders show.

2 My thanks I'll publish there, and tell
　　How thy renown excels;
　That seat affords me most delight,
　　In which thine honour dwells.

279 "*The Lord said unto him, I have hallowed this*　[6s. 4s.
　　house to put my name there for ever, and
　　mine eyes and mine heart shall be there per-
　　petually."

CHRIST is our corner-stone,
　On him alone we build;
With his true saints alone
　The courts of heaven are filled:

On his great love
 Our hopes we place
 Of present grace
And joys above.

2 O then with hymns of praise
 These hallowed courts shall ring,
Our voices we will raise
 The Three in One to sing;
 And thus proclaim
  In joyful song
  Both loud and long
 That glorious name.

3 Here, gracious God, do thou
 For evermore draw nigh;
Accept each faithful vow,
 And mark each suppliant sigh:
 In copious shower
  On all who pray
  Each holy day
 Thy blessings pour.

4 Here may we gain from heaven
 The grace which we implore;
And may that grace, once given,
 Be with us evermore,
 Until that day
  When all the blest
  To endless rest
 Are called away.

R

280   *"Arise, O Lord, into thy resting-place."*   [C. M.

From the cxxxii. Psalm.

O WITH due reverence let us all
    To God's abode repair;
And prostrate at his footstool fall,
    To breathe our humble prayer.

2 Arise, O Lord, and now possess
    Thy constant place of rest;
Be that not only with thy ark,
    But with thy presence bless'd.

3 Clothe thou thy priests with righteousness,
    Make thou thy saints rejoice;
And, for thy servant David's sake,
    Hear thy anointed's voice.

281   *"O pray for the peace of Jerusalem; they shall*   [C. M.
                prosper that love thee."

From the cxxii. Psalm.

O 'TWAS a joyful sound to hear
    Our tribes devoutly say,
Up, Israel! to the temple haste,
    And keep your festal-day.

2 At Salem's courts we must appear,
    With our assembled powers,
In strong and beauteous order ranged,
    Like her united towers.

3 O ever pray for Salem's peace;
　For they shall prosp'rous be,
Thou holy city of our God,
　Who bear true love to thee.

4 May peace within thy sacred walls
　A constant guest be found;
With plenty and prosperity
　Thy palaces be crown'd.

5 For my dear brethren's sake, and friends
　No less than brethren dear,
I'll pray, May peace in Salem's towers
　A constant guest appear.

6 But most of all I'll seek thy good,
　And ever wish thee well,
For Sion and the temple's sake,
　Where God vouchsafes to dwell.

282 *"Behold, I lay in Sion a chief corner-stone,* [8s. 7s.
　　elect, precious." Six Lines

CHRIST is made the sure foundation,
　Christ the head and corner-stone,
Chosen of the Lord, and precious,
　Binding all the Church in one,
Holy Sion's help forever,
　And her confidence alone.

2 All that dedicated city,
    Dearly loved of God on high,
  In exultant jubilation
    Pours perpetual melody;
  God the One in Three adoring
    In glad hymns eternally.

3 To this temple, where we call thee,
    Come, O Lord of hosts, to-day:
  With thy wonted loving-kindness,
    Hear thy servants as they pray;
  And thy fullest benediction
    Shed within its walls alway.

4 Here vouchsafe to all thy servants
    What they ask of thee to gain,
  What they gain from thee for ever
    With the blessèd to retain,
  And hereafter in thy glory
    Evermore with thee to reign.

5 Praise and honour to the Father,
    Praise and honour to the Son,
  Praise and honour to the Spirit,
    Ever Three, and ever One,
  One in might, and One in glory,
    While eternal ages run.

VI. MISSIONS AND CHARITIES.

283   *"Come over and help us."*   [7s. 6s Double.

FROM Greenland's icy mountains,
   From India's coral strand,
Where Afric's sunny fountains
   Roll down their golden sand;
From many an ancient river,
   From many a palmy plain,
They call us to deliver
   Their land from error's chain.

2 What though the spicy breezes
   Blow soft o'er Ceylon's isle;
Though every prospect pleases,
   And only man is vile:
In vain with lavish kindness
   The gifts of God are strewn;
The heathen in his blindness
   Bows down to wood and stone.

3 Shall we, whose souls are lighted
   With wisdom from on high;
Shall we to men benighted
   The lamp of life deny?
Salvation, O salvation,
   The joyful sound proclaim,
Till each remotest nation
   Has learnt Messiah's name.

4 Waft, waft, ye winds. his story,
   And you, ye waters, roll,
  Till, like a sea of glory,
   It spreads from pole to pole:
  Till o'er our ransom'd nature
    The Lamb for sinners slain,
  Redeemer, King, Creator,
    In bliss returns to reign.

284 *"He shall have dominion from sea to sea."* [L. M.

JESUS shall reign where'er the sun
  Does his successive journeys run;
His kingdom stretch from shore to shore,
Till moons shall wax and wane no more.

2 To him shall endless prayer be made,
  And praises throng to crown his head;
  His name like sweet perfume shall rise
  With every morning sacrifice.

3 People and realms of every tongue
  Dwell on his love with sweetest song;
  And infant voices shall proclaim
  Their early blessings on his name.

4 Blessings abound where'er he reigns;
  The prisoner leaps to burst his chains,
  The weary find eternal rest,
  And all the sons of want are blest.

5 Let every creature rise and bring
  Peculiar honours to our King;
  Angels descend with songs again,
  And earth repeat the loud Amen.

285   *"That thy way may be known upon earth."*   [S. M.

From the lxvii. Psalm.

TO bless thy chosen race,
   In mercy, Lord, incline;
And cause the brightness of thy face
   On all thy saints to shine:

2 That so thy wondrous way
   May through the world be known;
While distant lands their tribute pay,
   And thy salvation own.

3 O let them shout and sing,
   With joy and pious mirth;
For thou, the righteous Judge and King,
   Shalt govern all the earth.

4 Let differing nations join
   To celebrate thy fame;
Let all the world, O Lord, combine
   To praise thy glorious name.

5 Then God upon our land
   Shall constant blessings shower;
And all the world in awe shall stand
   Of his resistless power.

286   *"They shall see the glory of the Lord."*   [C. M.

ON Sion and on Lebanon,
   On Carmel's blooming height,
On Sharon's fertile plains, once shone
   The glory, pure and bright.

2 From thence its mild and cheering ray
    Stream'd forth from land to land;
  And empires now behold its day;
    And still its beams expand.

3 Its brightest splendours, darting west,
    Our happy shores illume;
  Our farther regions, once unblest,
    Now like a garden bloom.

4 But ah! our deserts deep and wild
    See not this heavenly light;
  No sacred beams, no radiance mild,
    Dispel their dreary night.

5 Thou, who didst lighten Sion's hill,
    On Carmel who didst shine,
  Our deserts let thy glory fill,
    Thy excellence divine.

6 Like Lebanon, in towering pride,
    May all our forests smile;
  And may our borders blossom wide
    Like Sharon's fruitful soil.

287 *"Awake, awake; put on strength, O arm* [L. M.
          of the Lord."

ARM of the Lord, awake, awake,
  Put on thy strength, the nations shake;
And let the world adoring see
Triumphs of mercy wrought by thee.

2 Say to the heathen from thy throne,
I am Jehovah, God alone:
Thy voice their idols shall confound,
And cast their altars to the ground.

3 Let Sion's time of favour come;
O bring the tribes of Israel home;
And let our wondering eyes behold
Gentiles and Jews in Jesus' fold.

4 Almighty God, thy grace proclaim
In every clime, of every name;
Let adverse powers before thee fall,
And crown the Saviour Lord of all.

288 *' O send out thy light and truth.* [8s. 7s. 4.

O'ER the gloomy hills of darkness,
　Look, my soul, be still and gaze;
All the promises do travail
　With a glorious day of grace.
　　Blessèd jubilee,
　Let thy glorious morning dawn.

2 Kingdoms wide that sit in darkness,
　Grant them, Lord, thy glorious light,
And from eastern coast to western
　May the morning chase the night:
　　And redemption,
　Freely purchased, win the day.

3 Fly abroad, eternal Gospel,
    Win and conquer, never cease:
  May thy lasting wide dominions
    Multiply, and still increase:
      May thy sceptre
      Sway the enlighten'd world around.

289   "*O praise ye the Lord, all ye nations.*"   [L. M.
From the cxvii. Psalm.

FROM all that dwell below the skies
  Let the Creator's praise arise;
Jehovah's glorious name be sung
Through every land, by every tongue.

2 Eternal are thy mercies, Lord,
  And truth eternal is thy word:
  Thy praise shall sound from shore to shore,
  Till suns shall rise and set no more.

290   "*To preach the acceptable year of the Lord.*"   [L. M.

YE Christian heralds, go, proclaim
  Salvation in Emmanuel's name:
To distant climes the tidings bear,
And plant the rose of Sharon there.

2 God shield you with a wall of fire,
  With holy zeal your hearts inspire,
  Bid raging winds their fury cease,
  And calm the savage breast to peace.

3 And when our labours all are o'er,
   Then may we meet to part no more,—
   Meet, with the ransomed throng to fall,
   And crown the Saviour Lord of all.

291 *"And there shall be one fold and one shepherd."* [7s. 6s. Double.

HASTEN the time appointed,
   By prophets long foretold,
When all shall dwell together,
   One shepherd and one fold.
Let every idol perish,
   To moles and bats be thrown,
And every prayer be offer'd
   To God in Christ alone.

2 Let Jew and Gentile, meeting
   From many a distant shore,
Around one altar kneeling,
   One common Lord adore.
Let all that now divides us
   Remove and pass away,
Like shadows of the morning
   Before the blaze of day.

3 Let all that now unites us
   More sweet and lasting prove,
A closer bond of union,
   In a blest land of love.
Let war be learn'd no longer,
   Let strife and tumult cease,
All earth his blessèd kingdom,
   The Lord and Prince of Peace.

4 O long-expected dawning,
 Come with thy cheering ray!
When shall the morning brighten,
 The shadows flee away?
O sweet anticipation!
 It cheers the watchers on,
To pray, and hope, and labour,
 Till the dark night be gone.

292   *"And I will set my glory among the heathen."*   [8s. 7s. 4.

SOULS in heathen darkness lying,
 Where no light has broken through,
Souls that Jesus bought by dying,
 Whom his soul in travail knew—
  Thousand voices
 Call us, o'er the waters blue.

2 Christians, hearken! None has taught them
 Of his love so deep and dear;
Of the precious price that bought them;
 Of the nail, the thorn, the spear;
  Ye who know him,
 Guide them from their darkness drear.

3 Haste, O haste, and spread the tidings
 Wide to earth's remotest strand;
Let no brother's bitter chidings
 Rise against us when we stand
  In the judgment,
 From some far, forgotten land.

4 Lo! the hills for harvest whiten,
　All along each distant shore;
　Seaward far the islands brighten;
　　Light of nations! lead us o'er:
　　　When we seek them,
　　Let thy Spirit go before.

FOR MISSIONS TO THE NEW SETTLEMENTS IN THE
UNITED STATES.

293 "*So shall they fear the name of the Lord from the west, and his glory from the rising of the sun.*" [8s. 6s.

WHEN, Lord, to this our western land,
　Led by thy providential hand,
　　Our wandering fathers came,
　Their ancient homes, their friends in youth,
　Sent forth the heralds of thy truth,
　　To keep them in thy name.

2 Then, through our solitary coast,
　The desert features soon were lost;
　　Thy temples there arose;
　Our shores, as culture made them fair,
　Were hallowed by thy rites, by prayer,
　　And blossomed as the rose.

3 And O may we repay this debt
　To regions solitary yet
　　Within our spreading land:
　There, brethren, from our common home,
　Still westward, like our fathers, roam;
　　Still guided by thy hand.

4 Saviour, we own this debt of love:
   O shed thy spirit from above,
      To move each Christian breast;
   Till heralds shall thy truth proclaim,
   And temples rise to fix thy name,
      Through all our desert west.

FOR THE JEWS.

294   *"God is able to graff them in again."*   [L. M.

DISOWN'D of heaven, by man oppress'd,
   Outcasts from Sion's hallow'd ground,
Wherefore should Israel's sons, once bless'd,
   Still roam the scorning world around?

2 Lord, visit thy forsaken race,
   Back to thy fold the wanderers bring;
Teach them to seek thy slighted grace,
   And hail in Christ their promised King.

3 The veil of darkness rend in twain,
   Which hides their Shiloh's glorious light;
The sever'd olive-branch again
   Firm to its parent-stock unite.

4 Hail, glorious day, expected long!
   When Jew and Greek one prayer shall pour,
With eager feet one temple throng,
   With grateful praise one God adore.

295 *"Speak ye comfortably to Jerusalem."* [L. M.

HIGH on the bending willows hung,
  Israel, still sleeps the tuneful string?
Still mute remains the sullen tongue,
  And Sion's song denies to sing?

2 Awake! thy loudest raptures raise;
  Let harp and voice unite their strains;
Thy promised King his sceptre sways;
  Behold, thy own Messiah reigns.

3 By foreign streams no longer roam,
  And, weeping, think on Jordan's flood;
In every clime behold a home,
  In every temple see thy God.

4 No taunting foes the song require;
  No strangers mock thy captive chain;
Thy friends provoke the silent lyre,
  And brethren ask the holy strain.

5 Then why, on bending willows hung,
  Israel, still sleeps the tuneful string?
Why mute remains the sullen tongue,
  And Sion's song delays to sing?

296 *"Inasmuch as ye have done it unto one of the least of these my brethren, ye have done it unto me."* [C. M.

FOUNTAIN of good, to own thy love
  Our thankful hearts incline;
What can we render, Lord, to thee,
  When all the worlds are thine?

2 But thou hast needy brethren here,
   Partakers of thy grace,
 Whose humble names thou wilt confess
   Before thy Father's face.

3 In their sad accents of distress
   Thy pleading voice is heard;
 In them thou may'st be clothed, and fed:
   And visited, and cheer'd.

4 Thy face with reverence and with love
   We in thy poor would see;
 For, while we minister to them,
   We do it, Lord, to thee.

297 *"Lay up for yourselves treasures in heaven."* [C. M.

 RICH are the joys which cannot die,
   With God laid up in store;
 Treasures beyond the changing sky,
   Brighter than golden ore.

2 The seeds which piety and love
   Have scatter'd here below,
 In the fair fertile fields above
   To ample harvests grow.

3 All that my willing hands can give
   At Jesus' feet I lay;
 Grace shall the humble gift receive,
   Abounding grace repay.

298 *"In the morning sow thy seed, and in the evening* [S. M.
withhold not thine hand."

SOW in the morn thy seed;
  At eve hold not thy hand;
To doubt and fear give thou no heed,
  Broad-cast it o'er the land.

2 Thou know'st not which may thrive,
  The late or early sown;
Grace keeps the chosen germ alive,
  When and wherever strown.

3 And duly shall appear,
  In verdure, beauty, strength,
The tender blade, the stalk, the ear,
  And the full corn at length.

4 Thou canst not toil in vain;
  Cold, heat, and moist, and dry,
Shall foster and mature the grain
  For garners in the sky.

299 *"As every man hath received the gift, even so* [S. M.
minister the same one to another."

WE give thee but thine own,
  Whate'er the gift may be:
All that we have is thine alone,
  A trust, O Lord, from thee.

2 May we thy bounties thus
  As stewards true receive,
And gladly, as thou blessest us,
  To thee our first-fruits give.

3 O! hearts are bruised and dead,
    And homes are bare and cold,
And lambs for whom the Shepherd bled,
    Are straying from the fold.

4 To comfort and to bless,
    To find a balm for woe,
To tend the lone and fatherless
    Is angel's work below.

5 The captive to release,
    To God the lost to bring,
To teach the way of life and peace,
    It is a Christ-like thing.

6 And we believe thy word,
    Though dim our faith may be;
Whate'er for thine we do, O Lord,
    We do it unto thee.

300   *"Bear ye one another's burdens, and so fulfil*   [D. C. M.
             the law of Christ."

LORD, lead the way the Saviour went,
    By lane and cell obscure,
And let love's treasures still be spent,
    Like his, upon the poor:
Like him through scenes of deep distress,
    Who bore the world's sad weight,
We, in their crowded loneliness,
    Would seek the desolate.

2 For thou hast placed us side by side
   In this wide world of ill,
  And, that thy followers may be tried,
   The poor are with us still.
  Mean are all offerings we can make,
   But thou hast taught us, Lord,
  If given for the Saviour's sake,
   They lose not their reward.

VII. SPECIAL SEASONS.

THANKSGIVING AND HARVEST-HOME.

301 *"O come, let us sing unto the Lord; let us* [L. M
heartily rejoice in the strength of our sal-
vation."

From the xcv. Psalm.

O COME, loud anthems let us sing,
  Loud thanks to our almighty King,
 And high our grateful voices raise,
 As our Salvation's rock we praise

2 Into his presence let us haste
  To thank him for his favours past;
  To him address, in joyful songs,
  The praise that to his name belongs.

3 For God the Lord, enthroned in state,
  Is with unrivall'd glory great;
  The depths of earth are in his hand,
  Her secret wealth at his command.

4. O let us to his courts repair,
And bow with adoration there;
Low on our knees with reverence fall,
And on the Lord our Maker call.

302 *"Thou crownest the year with thy goodness."* [SIX 7s

PRAISE to God, immortal praise,
For the love that crowns our days;
Bounteous source of every joy,
Let thy praise our tongues employ:
All to thee, our God, we owe,
Source whence all our blessings flow.

2 All the blessings of the fields,
All the stores the garden yields,
Flocks that whiten all the plain,
Yellow sheaves of ripen'd grain:
Lord, for these our souls shall raise
Grateful vows and solemn praise.

3 Clouds that drop their fattening dews,
Suns that genial warmth diffuse,
All the plenty summer pours,
Autumn's rich, o'erflowing stores:
Lord, for these our souls shall raise
Grateful vows and solemn praise.

4 Peace, prosperity, and health,
Private bliss and public wealth,
Knowledge, with its gladdening streams,
Pure religion's holier beams:
Lord, for these our souls shall raise
Grateful vows and solemn praise.

303   "*O clap your hands together, all ye people: O*   [P. M.
sing unto God with the voice of melody."

NOW thank we all our God,
  With heart and hands and voices,
Who wondrous things hath done,
In whom his world rejoices;
  Who from our mother's arms
    Hath bless'd us on our way
  With countless gifts of love,
    And still is ours to-day.

2 O may this bounteous God
Through all our life be near us,
  With ever joyful hearts
And blessèd peace to cheer us;
  And keep us in his grace,
    And guide us when perplex'd,
  And free us from all ills
    In this world and the next.

3 All praise and thanks to God
The Father now be given,
  The Son, and him who reigns
With them in highest heaven,
  The One eternal God,
    Whom earth and heaven adore,
  For thus it was, is now,
    And shall be evermore.

FOR PUBLIC MERCIES AND DELIVERANCES.

304 *"Let the people praise thee, O God."* [L. M.

SALVATION doth to God belong,
His power and grace shall be our song;
From him alone all mercies flow,
His arm alone subdues the foe.

2 Then praise this God, who bows his ear
Propitious to his people's prayer;
And though deliverance he may stay,
Yet answers still in his own day.

3 O may this goodness lead our land,
Still saved by thine Almighty hand,
The tribute of its love to bring
To thee, our Saviour and our King.

305 *"Who giveth food to all flesh; for his mercy endureth for ever."* [7s.

PRAISE, O praise our God and King!
Hymns of adoration sing;
For his mercies still endure,
Ever faithful, ever sure.

2 Praise him that he made the sun
Day by day his course to run;
For his mercies still endure,
Ever faithful, ever sure:

3 And the silver moon by night,
　Shining with her gentle light;
　　For his mercies still endure,
　　Ever faithful, ever sure.

4 Praise him that he gave the rain
　To mature the swelling grain;
　　For his mercies still endure,
　　Ever faithful, ever sure:

5 And hath bid the fruitful field
　Crops of precious increase yield;
　　For his mercies still endure,
　　Ever faithful, ever sure.

6 Praise him for our harvest-store,
　He hath fill'd the garner-floor;
　　For his mercies still endure,
　　Ever faithful, ever sure:

7 And for richer food than this,
　Pledge of everlasting bliss;
　　For his mercies still endure,
　　Ever faithful, ever sure.

8 Glory to our bounteous King!
　Glory let creation sing!
　　Glory to the Father, Son,
　　And blest Spirit, Three in One.

306 *"They joy before thee, according to the joy* [7s. DOUBLE.
　　　of harvest."

COME, ye thankful people, come,
　Raise the song of Harvest-home:

All is safely gather'd in,
Ere the winter storms begin;
God, our Maker, doth provide
For our wants to be supplied;
Come to God's own temple, come,
Raise the song of Harvest-home.

2 All the world is God's own field,
Fruit unto his praise to yield;
Wheat and tares together sown,
Unto joy or sorrow grown:
First the blade, and then the ear,
Then the full corn shall appear:
Lord of harvest, grant that we
Wholesome grain and pure may be.

3 For the Lord our God shall come,
And shall take his harvest home:
From his field shall in that day
All offences purge away;
Give his angels charge at last
In the fire the tares to cast,
But the fruitful ears to store
In his garner evermore.

4 Even so, Lord, quickly come
To thy final Harvest-home:
Gather thou thy people in,
Free from sorrow, free from sin;
There for ever purified,
In thy presence to abide:
Come with all thine angels, come,
Raise the glorious Harvest-home.

NATIONAL FESTIVALS.

307 *"Praise ye the name of the Lord; praise him,* [6s. 4s.
O ye servants of the Lord."

BEFORE the Lord we bow,
   The God who reigns above,
And rules the world below,
   Boundless in power and love;
     Our thanks we bring
       In joy and praise,
      Our hearts we raise
    To heaven's high King.

2 The nation thou hast blest
   May well thy love declare,
From foes and fears at rest,
   Protected by thy care.
     For this fair land,
       For this bright day,
      Our thanks we pay—
    Gifts of thy hand.

3 May every mountain height,
   Each vale and forest green,
Shine in thy word's pure light,
   And its rich fruits be seen!
     May every tongue
       Be tuned to praise,
      And join to raise
    A grateful song.

4 Earth! hear thy Maker's voice,
   The great Redeemer own,
Believe, obey, rejoice,
   And worship him alone;

   Cast down thy pride,
    Thy sin deplore,
    And bow before
   The Crucified.

5 And when in power he comes,
  O may our native land,
 From all its rending tombs,
  Send forth a glorious band;
   A countless throng
    Ever to sing
    To heaven's high King
   Salvation's song.

308   *"This God is our God for ever and ever."*   [P. M

LORD GOD, we worship thee!
 In loud and happy chorus
We praise thy love and power,
 Whose goodness reigneth o'er us.
  To heaven our song shall soar,
   For ever shall it be
  Resounding o'er and o'er,
   Lord God, we worship thee!

2 Lord God, we worship thee!
For thou our land defendest;
 Thou pourest down thy grace,
  And strife and war thou endest.
  Since golden peace, O Lord,
   Thou grantest us to see,
  Our land, with one accord,
   Lord God, gives thanks to thee!

3 Lord God, we worship thee!
Thou didst indeed chastise us,
 Yet still thy anger spares,
  And still thy mercy tries us:

NATIONAL FASTS. 283

Once more our Father's hand
Doth bid our sorrows flee,
And peace rejoice our land:
Lord God, we worship thee!

309 *"Blessed is the nation whose God is the Lord."* [6s. 4s.

GOD bless our native land!
Firm may she ever stand,
Through storm and night;
When the wild tempests rave,
Ruler of winds and wave,
Do thou our country save
By thy great might.

2 For her our prayer shall rise
To God, above the skies;
On him we wait;
Thou who art ever nigh
Guarding with watchful eye,
To thee aloud we cry,
God save the state!

NATIONAL FASTS.

310 *"O Lord, hear; O Lord, forgive; O Lord,* [8s. 7s.
hearken and do."

DREAD Jehovah, God of nations,
From thy temple in the skies,
Hear thy people's supplications,
Now for their deliverance rise.

2 Lo, with deep contrition turning,
Humbly at thy feet we bend;
Hear us, fasting, praying, mourning;
Hear us, spare us, and defend.

3 Though our sins, our hearts confounding,
　　Long and loud for vengeance call,
　Thou hast mercy more abounding,
　　Jesus' blood can cleanse from all.

4 Let that love veil our transgression,
　　Let that blood our guilt efface:
　Save thy people from oppression,
　　Save from spoil thy holy place.

311 *"O Lord, correct me, but with judgment."* [C. M.

ALMIGHTY LORD, before thy throne
　　Thy mourning people bend;
'Tis on thy pardoning grace alone
　　Our failing hopes depend.

2 Dark judgments, from thy heavy hand,
　　Thy dreadful power display;
　Yet mercy spares our guilty land,
　　And still we live to pray.

3 How changed, alas! are truths divine
　　For error, guilt, and shame!
　What impious numbers, bold in sin,
　　Disgrace the Christian name!

4 O turn us, turn us, mighty Lord!
　　Convert us by thy grace;
　Then shall our hearts obey thy word,
　　And see again thy face.

5 Then, should oppressing foes invade,
　　We will not yield to fear,
　Secure of all-sufficient aid,
　　When thou, O God, art near.

312. *"The Lord shall give his people the blessing of peace."* [L. M.

O GOD of love, O King of peace,
　Make wars throughout the world to cease;
The wrath of sinful man restrain;
Give peace, O God, give peace again.

2 Remember, Lord, thy works of old,
　The wonders that our fathers told;
Remember not our sin's dark stain;
Give peace, O God, give peace again.

3 Whom shall we trust but thee, O Lord?
　Where rest but on thy faithful word?
None ever called on thee in vain;
Give peace, O God, give peace again.

4 Where saints and angels dwell above,
　All hearts are knit in holy love;
O bind us in that heavenly chain,
Give peace, O God, give peace again.

313 *"God be merciful unto us and bless us, and show us the light of his countenance."* [L. M.

NOW may the God of grace and power
　Attend his people's humble cry;
Defend them in the needful hour,
　And send deliverance from on high.

2 In his salvation is our hope;
　And in the name of Israel's God,
Our troops shall lift their banners up,
　Our navies spread their flags abroad.

3 Some trust in horses train'd for war,
    And some of chariots make their boasts;
Our surest expectations are
    From thee, the Lord of heavenly hosts.

4 Then save us, Lord, from slavish fear,
    And let our trust be firm and strong,
Till thy salvation shall appear,
    And hymns of peace conclude our song.

FAMILY WORSHIP.

314   *"Ask, and it shall be given you."*   [SIX 8s

WHEN, streaming from the eastern skies,
    The morning light salutes mine eyes,
O Sun of Righteousness divine,
On me with beams of mercy shine;
Chase the dark clouds of guilt away,
And turn my darkness into day.

2 When to heaven's great and glorious King
My morning sacrifice I bring,
And, mourning o'er my guilt and shame,
Ask mercy in my Saviour's name,
Then, Jesus, sprinkle with thy blood,
And be my advocate with God.

3 As every day thy mercy spares
Will bring its trials and its cares,
O Saviour, till my life shall end,
Be thou my counsellor and friend:
Teach me thy precepts, all divine.
And be thy great example mine.

FAMILY WORSHIP.

4 When pain transfixes every part,
   Or languor settles at the heart;
   When on my bed, diseased, opprest,
   I turn, and sigh, and long for rest;
   O great Physician, see my grief,
   And grant thy servant sweet relief.

5 Should poverty's consuming blow
   Lay all my worldly comforts low;
   And neither help nor hope appear,
   My steps to guide, my heart to cheer:
   Lord, pity and supply my need,
   For thou on earth wast poor indeed.

6 Should Providence profusely pour
   Its various blessings on my store;
   O keep me from the ills that wait
   On such a seeming prosperous state:
   From hurtful passions set me free,
   And humbly may I walk with thee.

7 When each day's scenes and labours close,
   And wearied nature seeks repose,
   With pardoning mercy richly blest,
   Guard me, my Saviour, while I rest;
   And as each morning sun shall rise,
   O lead me onward to the skies.

8 And at my life's last setting sun,
   My conflicts o'er, my labours done,
   Jesus, thine heavenly radiance shed,
   To cheer and bless my dying bed;
   And from death's gloom my spirit raise,
   To see thy face and sing thy praise.

SPECIAL SEASONS.

315   *"For ye are members one of another."*   [S. M.

BLEST be the tie that binds
  Our hearts in Jesus' love:
The fellowship of Christian minds
  Is like to that above.

2 Before our Father's throne
  We pour united prayers;
Our fears, our hopes, our aims are one;
  Our comforts and our cares.

3 We share our mutual woes,
  Our mutual burdens bear;
And often for each other flows
  The sympathizing tear.

4 When we at death must part,
  Not like the world's, our pain;
But one in Christ, and one in heart,
  We part to meet again.

5 From sorrow, toil, and pain,
  And sin, we shall be free;
And perfect love and friendship reign
  Throughout eternity.

316   *"I will lift up mine eyes unto the hills, from*   [C. M.
                whence cometh my help."

From the cxxi. Psalm.

TO Sion's hill I lift my eyes,
  From thence expecting aid,
From Sion's hill, and Sion's God,
  Who heaven and earth has made.

2 He will not let thy foot be moved,
   Thy guardian will not sleep;
Behold, the God who slumbers not
   Will favour'd Israel keep.

3 Shelter'd beneath th' Almighty's wings,
   Thou shalt securely rest,
Where neither sun nor moon shall thee
   By day or night molest.

4 At home, abroad, in peace, in war,
   Thy God shall thee defend;
Conduct thee through life's pilgrimage,
   Safe to thy journey's end.

317 *"There remaineth therefore a rest for the people of God."* [6s. DOUBLE.

THERE is a blessèd home
   Beyond this land of woe,
Where trials never come,
   Nor tears of sorrow flow;
Where faith is lost in sight,
   And patient hope is crown'd.
And everlasting light
   Its glory throws around.

2 There is a land of peace,
   Good angels know it well;
Glad songs that never cease
   Within its portals swell;

Around its glorious throne
 Ten thousand saints adore
Christ, with the Father One,
 And Spirit, evermore.

3 O joy all joys beyond,
 To see the Lamb who died,
And count each sacred wound
 In hands and feet and side;
To give to him the praise
 Of every triumph won,
And sing through endless days
 The great things he hath done.

4 Look up, ye saints of God,
 Nor fear to tread below
The path your Saviour trod
 Of daily toil and woe;
Wait but a little while
 In uncomplaining love,
His own most gracious smile
 Shall welcome you above.

318 *"Walk before me, and be thou perfect."* [L. M.

FORTH in thy name, O Lord, I go,
 My daily labour to pursue;
Thee, only thee, resolved to know,
 In all I think, or speak, or do.

2 The task thy wisdom hath assigned
 O let me cheerfully fulfil;
In all my works thy presence find,
 And prove thy good and perfect will.

3 Thee may I set at my right hand,
   Whose eyes my inmost substance see;
  And labour on at thy command,
   And offer all my works to thee.

4 Give me to bear thy easy yoke,
   And every moment watch and pray;
  And still to things eternal look,
   And hasten to thy glorious day.

5 Fain would I still for thee employ
   Whate'er thy bounteous grace hath given,
  Would run my course with even joy,
   And closely walk with thee to heaven.

319 *"Whoso dwelleth under the defence of the Most* [Six 8s. *High, shall abide under the shadow of the Almighty."*

From the xci. Psalm.

HE that has God his guardian made
   Shall under the Almighty's shade
  Secure and undisturb'd abide:
  Thus to my soul of him I'll say,
  He is my fortress and my stay,
   My God, in whom I will confide.

2 His tender love and watchful care
  Shall free thee from the fowler's snare,
   And from the noisome pestilence;
  He over thee his wings shall spread,
  And cover thy unguarded head;
   His truth shall be thy strong defence.

3 Because, with well-placed confidence,
   Thou mak'st the Lord thy sure defence,
     Thy refuge, even God most high;
   Therefore no ill on thee shall come,
   Nor to thy heaven-protected home
     Shall overwhelming plagues draw nigh.

320   *"O God, thou art my God; early will I*   [Six 8s.
       seek thee."

From the lxiii. Psalm.

O GOD, my gracious God, to thee
   My morning prayers shall offer'd be,
     For thee my thirsty soul doth pant;
   My fainting flesh implores thy grace,
   As in a dry and barren place,
     Where I refreshing waters want.

2 O to my longing eyes once more
   That view of glorious power restore,
     Which thy majestic house displays:
   Because to me thy wondrous love
   Than life itself does dearer prove,
     My lips shall always speak thy praise.

3 My life, while I that life enjoy,
   In blessing God I will employ,
     With lifted hands adore his name:
   As with its choicest food supplied,
   My soul shall be full satisfied,
     While I with joy his praise proclaim.

4 When down I lie, sweet sleep to find,
　Thou, Lord, art present to my mind,
　　And when I wake in dead of night,
　Because thou still dost succour bring,
　Beneath the shadow of thy wing
　　I rest with safety and delight.

321　*"Thou knowest my down-sitting and mine uprising."*　[L. M.

UP to the hills I lift mine eyes,
　The eternal hills beyond the skies;
Thence all her help my soul derives,
There my almighty refuge lives.

2 He lives—the everlasting God,
That built the world, that spread the flood;
The heavens with all their hosts he made,
And the dark regions of the dead.

3 He guides our feet, he guards our way;
His morning smiles bless all the day:
He spreads the evening veil, and keeps
The silent hours while Israel sleeps.

4 Israel, a name divinely blest,
May rise secure, securely rest;
Thy holy Guardian's wakeful eyes
Admit no slumber nor surprise.

SPECIAL SEASONS.

322   *"Except the Lord build the house, their labour*   [C. M.
        is but lost that build it."

From the cxxvii. Psalm.

WE build with fruitless cost, unless
    The Lord the pile sustain;
Unless the Lord the city keep,
    The watchman wakes in vain.

2 In vain we rise before the day,
    And late to rest repair,
Allow no respite to our toil,
    And eat the bread of care.

3 Supplies of life, with ease to them,
    He on his saints bestows;
He crowns their labours with success,
    Their nights with safe repose.

323   *' Our eyes wait upon the Lord our God."*   [P. M.

WHEN I can trust my all with God,
    In trial's fearful hour,
Bow, all resign'd, beneath his rod,
    And bless his chastening power,
A joy springs up amid distress,
A fountain in the wilderness.

2 O blessèd be the hand that gave,
    Still blessèd when it takes;
Blessèd be he who smites to save,
    Who heals the heart he breaks:
Perfect and true are all his ways,
Whom heaven adores and death obeys.

324   *"This God is our God for ever and ever."*   [L. M.

MY God, how endless is thy love!
   Thy gifts are every evening new,
And morning mercies from above
   Gently distil, like early dew.

2 Thou spread'st the curtain of the night,
   Great Guardian of my sleeping hours;
Thy sovereign word restores the light,
   And quickens all my drowsy powers.

3 I yield my powers to thy command,
   To thee I consecrate my days;
Perpetual blessings from thy hand
   Demand perpetual songs of praise.

325   *"I have set God always before me."*   [L. M.

SAVIOUR, when night involves the skies,
   My soul, adoring, turns to thee;
Thee, self-abased in mortal guise,
   And wrapt in shades of death for me.

2 On thee my waking raptures dwell,
   When crimson gleams the east adorn,
Thee, victor of the grave and hell,
   Thee, source of life's eternal morn.

3 When noon her throne in light arrays,
   To thee my soul triumphant springs;
Thee, throned in glory's endless blaze,
   Thee, Lord of lords and King of kings.

4 O'er earth, when shades of evening steal,
    To death and thee my thoughts I give;
To death, whose power I soon must feel,
    To thee, with whom I trust to live.

326   *" O Lord, thou art our God."*   [C. M.

GOD of our fathers, by whose hand
    Thy people still are blest,
Be with us through our pilgrimage;
    Conduct us to our rest.

2 Through each perplexing path of life
    Our wandering footsteps guide;
Give us each day our daily bread,
    And raiment fit provide.

3 O spread thy sheltering wings around,
    Till all our wanderings cease,
And at our Father's loved abode
    Our souls arrive in peace.

4 Such blessings from thy gracious hand
    Our humble prayers implore;
And thou, the Lord, shalt be our God,
    And portion evermore.

327   *" Boast not thyself of to-morrow."*   [S. M.

TO-MORROW, Lord, is thine,
    Lodged in thy sovereign hand;
And if its sun arise and shine,
    It shines by thy command.

2 The present moment flies,
    And bears our life away;
O make thy servants truly wise,
    That they may live to-day.

3 Since on this wingèd hour
    Eternity is hung,
Waken, by thine almighty power
    The aged and the young.

4 One thing demands our care;
    O be it still pursued,
Lest, slighted once, the season fair
    Should never be renew'd.

5 To Jesus may we fly,
    Swift as the morning light,
Lest life's young golden beam should die
    In sudden, endless night.

MORNING.

328   *"The Lord preserveth me."*   [L. M.

ARISE, my soul, with rapture rise,
    And, fill'd with love and fear, adore
The awful Sovereign of the skies,
    Whose mercy lends me one day more.

2 And may this day, indulgent Power,
    Not idly pass, nor fruitless be;
But may each swiftly-flying hour
    Still nearer bring my soul to thee.

3 But can it be? That power divine
   Is throned in light's unbounded blaze;
And countless worlds and angels join
   To swell the glorious song of praise.

4 And will he deign to lend an ear,
   When I, poor sinful mortal, pray?
Yes, boundless goodness! he will hear,
   Nor cast the meanest wretch away.

5 Then let me serve thee all my days,
   And may my zeal with years increase:
For pleasant, Lord, are all thy ways,
   And all thy paths are paths of peace.

329 *"His compassions fail not: they are new every morning."* [L. M.

NEW every morning is the love
   Our wakening and uprising prove;
Through sleep and darkness safely brought,
Restored to life, and power, and thought.

2 New mercies, each returning day,
   Hover around us while we pray;
New perils past, new sins forgiven,
New thoughts of God, new hopes of heaven.

3 If on our daily course our mind
   Be set to hallow all we find,
New treasures still of countless price,
God will provide for sacrifice.

4 The trivial round, the common task,
   Will furnish all we ought to ask:
   Room to deny ourselves: a road
   To bring us daily nearer God.

5 Only, O Lord, in thy dear love
   Fit us for perfect rest above;
   And help us this, and every day,
   To live more nearly as we pray.

330 *"In thy Light shall we see light."* [P. M.

COME, my soul, thou must be waking,
   Now is breaking
     O'er the earth another day:
Come, to him who made this splendour
See thou render
     All thy feeble strength can pay.

2 Gladly hail the sun returning:
   Ready burning
     Be the incense of thy powers:
   For the night is safely ended;
   God hath tended
     With his care thy helpless hours.

3 Pray that he may prosper ever
   Each endeavour,
     When thine aim is good and true;
   But that he may ever thwart thee,
   And convert thee,
     When thou evil wouldst pursue.

4 Think that he thy ways beholdeth,
  He unfoldeth
    Every fault that lurks within;
  He the hidden shame glossed over
  Can discover,
    And discern each deed of sin.

5 Mayest thou on life's last morrow,
  Free from sorrow,
    Pass away in slumber sweet;
  And, released from death's dark sadness,
  Rise in gladness,
    That far brighter Sun to greet.

6 Only God's free gifts abuse not,
  Light refuse not,
    But his Spirit's voice obey;
  Thou with him shalt dwell, beholding
  Light enfolding
    All things in unclouded day.

7 Glory, honour, exaltation,
  Adoration,
    Be to the eternal One:
  To the Father, Son, and Spirit
  Laud and merit,
    While unending ages run.

331 *"Unto you that fear my name shall the Sun* [Six 7s.
of Righteousness arise."

CHRIST, whose glory fills the skies,
  Christ, the true, the only light,

Sun of righteousness, arise!
   Triumph o'er the shades of night;
Day-spring from on high, be near;
Day-star, in my heart appear.

2 Dark and cheerless is the morn
   Unaccompanied by thee;
Joyless is the day's return,
   Till thy mercy's beams I see;
Till they inward light impart,
Glad my eyes, and warm my heart.

3 Visit then this soul of mine;
   Pierce the gloom of sin and grief;
Fill me, radiancy divine;
   Scatter all my unbelief;
More and more thyself display,
Shining to the perfect day.

832 *"I myself will awake right early."* [L. M.

AWAKE, my soul, and with the sun
   Thy daily course of duty run;
Shake off dull sloth, and early rise
To pay thy morning sacrifice.

2 Redeem thy mis-spent time that's past;
Live this day, as if 'twere thy last;
To improve thy talents take due care;
'Gainst the great day thyself prepare.

3 Let all thy converse be sincere,
Thy conscience as the noon-day clear;
Think how the all-seeing God, thy ways
And all thy secret thoughts surveys.

4 Wake, and lift up thyself, my heart,
   And with the angels bear thy part,
   Who all night long unwearied sing
   "Glory to thee, eternal King."

5 I wake, I wake, ye heavenly choir,
   May your devotion me inspire,
   That I, like you, my age may spend,
   Like you may on my God attend.

6 Glory to thee, who safe hast kept,
   And hast refresh'd me while I slept;
   Grant, Lord, when I from death shall wake,
   I may of endless light partake.

7 Lord, I my vows to thee renew;
   Scatter my sins as morning dew;
   Guard my first spring of thought and will,
   And with thyself my spirit fill.

8 Direct, control, suggest this day
   All I design, or do, or say;
   That all my powers, with all their might,
   In thy sole glory may unite.

9 Praise God, from whom all blessings flow;
   Praise him, all creatures here below;
   Praise him above, angelic host;
   Praise Father, Son, and Holy Ghost.

EVENING.

333   *"Under his wings shalt thou trust."*   [L. M.

GLORY to thee, my God, this night,
For all the blessings of the light:
Keep me, O keep me, King of kings,
Under thine own almight wings.

2 Forgive me, Lord, for thy dear Son,
The ills that I this day have done;
That with the world, myself, and thee,
I, ere I sleep, at peace may be.

3 Teach me to live, that I may dread
The grave as little as my bed;
Teach me to die, that so I may
Triumphing rise at the last day.

4 O may my soul on thee repose,
And with sweet sleep mine eyelids close:
Sleep, that may me more vigorous make
To serve my God, when I awake.

5 When in the night I sleepless lie,
My soul with heavenly thoughts supply:
Let no ill dreams disturb my rest,
No powers of darkness me molest.

6 O when shall I, in endless day,
Forever chase dark sleep away,
And hymns divine with angels sing,
Glory to thee, eternal King.

334   *"I will lay me down in peace."*   [S. M.

THE day is past and gone;
   The evening shades appear:
O may we all remember well
   The night of death draws near.

2 We lay our garments by,
   Upon our beds to rest;
So death shall soon disrobe us all
   Of what is here possest.

3 Lord, keep us safe this night,
   Secure from all our fears;
May angels guard us while we sleep,
   Till morning light appears.

335   *"Abide with us; for the day is far spent."*   [10s.

ABIDE with me: fast falls the eventide;
   The darkness deepens; Lord, with me abide:
When other helpers fail, and comforts flee,
Help of the helpless, O abide with me.

2 Swift to its close ebbs out life's little day;
Earth's joys grow dim, its glories pass away,
Change and decay in all around I see;
O thou who changest not, abide with me.

3 I need thy presence every passing hour;
What but thy grace can foil the tempter's power?
Who, like thyself, my guide and stay can be?
Through cloud and sunshine, Lord, abide with me.

4 I fear no foe, with thee at hand to bless:
Ills have no weight, and tears no bitterness.
Where is death's sting? where, grave, thy victory?
I triumph still, if thou abide with me.

5 Hold thou thy cross before my closing eyes;
Shine through the gloom, and point me to the skies;
Heaven's morning breaks, and earth's vain shadows flee;
In life, in death, O Lord, abide with me.

336 *"Thy sun shall no more go down."* [L. M.

SUN of my soul, thou Saviour dear,
It is not night if thou be near;
O may no earth-born cloud arise
To hide thee from thy servant's eyes.

2 When the soft dews of kindly sleep
My weary eyelids gently steep,
Be my last thought, how sweet to rest
For ever on my Saviour's breast.

3 Abide with me from morn till eve,
For without thee I cannot live;
Abide with me when night is nigh,
For without thee I dare not die.

4 If some poor wandering child of thine
Have spurn'd to-day the voice divine,
Now, Lord, the gracious work begin;
Let him no more lie down in sin.

5 Watch by the sick; enrich the poor
　With blessings from thy boundless store;
　Be every mourner's sleep to-night,
　Like infant slumbers, pure and light.

6 Come near and bless us when we wake,
　Ere through the world our way we take,
　Till in the ocean of thy love
　We lose ourselves in heaven above.

337 *"With my soul have I desired thee in the night."* [C. M.

THE shadows of the evening hours
　Fall from the darkening sky,
Upon the fragrance of the flowers
　The dews of evening lie;

2 Before thy throne, O Lord of heaven
　We kneel at close of day;
Look on thy children from on high,
　And hear us while we pray.

3 The sorrows of thy servants, Lord,
　O do not thou despise,
But let the incense of our prayers
　Before thy mercy rise;

4 The brightness of the coming night
　Upon the darkness rolls;
With hopes of future glory chase
　The shadows on our souls.

5 Slowly the rays of daylight fade;
    So fade within our heart
The hopes in earthly love and joy,
    That one by one depart;

6 Slowly the bright stars, one by one,
    Within the heavens shine:—
Give us, O Lord, fresh hopes in heaven,
    And trust in things divine.

7 Let peace, O Lord! thy peace, O God!
    Upon our souls descend,
From midnight fears, and perils, thou
    Our trembling hearts defend:

8 Give us a respite from our toil,
    Calm and subdue our woes;
Through the long day we suffer, Lord,
    O give us now repose!

338   *"The Lord is my light."*   [Six 8s.

SWEET Saviour, bless us ere we go:
    Thy word into our minds instil;
And make our lukewarm hearts to glow
    With lowly love and fervent will.
Through life's long day and death's dark night,
O gentle Jesus, be our light.

2 The day is gone, its hours have run,
    And thou hast taken count of all,
The scanty triumphs grace hath won,
    The broken vow, the frequent fall.
Through life's long day and death's dark night,
O gentle Jesus, be our light.

3 Grant us, dear Lord, from evil ways
    True absolution and release;
And bless us, more than in past days,
    With purity and inward peace.
Through life's long day and death's dark night,
O gentle Jesus, be our light.

4 Labour is sweet, for thou hast toil'd;
    And care is light, for thou hast cared;
Ah! never let our works be soil'd
    With strife, or by deceit ensnared.
Through life's long day and death's dark night,
O gentle Jesus, be our light.

5 For all we love, the poor, the sad,
    The sinful, unto thee we call;
O let thy mercy make us glad;
    Thou art our Jesus, and our all.
Through life's long day and death's dark night,
O gentle Jesus, be our light.

6 Sweet Saviour, bless us; night is come;
    Through night and darkness near us be;
Good angels watch about our home,
    And we are one day nearer thee.
Through life's long day and death's dark night,
O gentle Jesus, be our light.

339   *"Darkness and light to thee are both alike."*   [8s

INSPIRER and Hearer of prayer,
    Thou Shepherd and Guardian of thine,
My all to thy covenant care,
    I, sleeping or waking, resign.

2 If thou art my shield and my sun,
   The night is no darkness to me;
And, fast as my minutes roll on,
   They bring me but nearer to thee.

3 A sovereign protector I have,
   Unseen, yet forever at hand;
Unchangeably faithful to save,
   Almighty to rule and command.

4 His smiles and his comforts abound,
   His grace, as the dew, shall descend;
And walls of salvation surround
   The soul he delights to defend.

5 All praise to the Father, the Son,
   And Spirit, thrice holy and bless'd,
Th' eternal, supreme Three in One,
   Was, is, and shall still be address'd.

340 *"Let the lifting up of my hands be an evening sacrifice."* [7s.

SOFTLY now the light of day
   Fades upon my sight away;
Free from care, from labour free,
   Lord, I would commune with thee:

2 Thou, whose all-pervading eye
   Naught escapes, without, within,
Pardon each infirmity,
   Open fault, and secret sin.

3 Soon, for me, the light of day
   Shall for ever pass away;
   Then, from sin and sorrow free,
   Take me, Lord, to dwell with thee:

4 Thou who, sinless, yet hast known
     All of man's infirmity;
   Then, from thine eternal throne,
     Jesus, look with pitying eye.

341   *"Thou, Lord, only makest me dwell in safety."*   [P. M.

THE day is past and over:
   All thanks, O Lord, to thee!
I pray thee that offenceless
   The hours of dark may be.
O Jesus, keep me in thy sight,
And save me through the coming night!

2 The joys of day are over:
   I lift my heart to thee;
   And call on thee that sinless
     The hours of gloom may be.
   O Jesus, make their darkness light,
   And save me through the coming night!

3 The toils of day are over;
   I raise the hymn to thee,
   And ask that free from peril
     The hours of fear may be:
   O Jesus, keep me in thy sight,
   And guard me through the coming night.

4 Lighten mine eyes, O Saviour,
   Or sleep in death shall I,
And he, my wakeful tempter,
   Triumphantly shall cry
"Against him I have now prevailed:
Rejoice! the child of God has failed."

5 Be thou my soul's Preserver,
   O God! for thou dost know
How many are the perils
   Through which I have to go.
O loving Jesus, hear my call,
And guard and save me from them all!

342   "*I will lay me down in peace and take my rest.*"   [8s. /s. 7s.

THROUGH the day thy love has spared us;
   Now we lay us down to rest,
Through the silent watches guard us,
   Let no foe our peace molest;
     Jesus, thou our guardian be;
     Sweet it is to trust in thee.

2 Pilgrims here on earth, and strangers,
   Dwelling in the midst of foes;
Us and ours preserve from dangers;
   In thine arms may we repose;
     And, when life's short day is past,
     Rest with thee in heaven at last.

SPECIAL SEASONS.

343   *"The Lord is thy keeper."*   [L. M

GREAT God, to thee my evening song,
  With humble gratitude I raise:
O let thy mercy tune my tongue,
  And fill my heart with lively praise.

2 My days unclouded as they pass,
  And every onward rolling hour,
Are monuments of wondrous grace,
  And witness to thy love and power.

3 And yet this thoughtless, wretched heart,
  Too oft regardless of thy love,
Ungrateful, can from thee depart,
  And from the path of duty rove.

4 Seal my forgiveness in the blood
  Of Christ my Lord; his name alone
I plead for pardon, gracious God,
  And kind acceptance at thy throne.

5 With hope in him mine eyelids close;
  With sleep refresh my feeble frame;
Safe in thy care may I repose,
  And wake with praises to thy name.

344   *"He shall give his angels charge over thee."*   [8s. 4s

GOD, that madest earth and heaven,
  Darkness and light;
Who the day for toil hast given,
  For rest the night:

May thine angel-guards defend us,
Slumber sweet thy mercy send us,
Holy dreams and hopes attend us,
    This livelong night.

2 Guard us waking, guard us sleeping,
    And, when we die,
May we in thy mighty keeping,
    All peaceful lie:
When the last dread trump shall wake us,
Do not thou, our Lord, forsake us,
But to reign in glory take us
    With thee on high.

345   *"Whether we wake or sleep, we should live together with him."*   [P. M.

THE sun is sinking fast,
    The daylight dies;
Let love awake, and pay
    Her evening sacrifice.

2 As Christ upon the cross
    His head inclined,
And to his Father's hands
    His parting soul resign'd;

3 So now herself my soul
    Would wholly give
Into his sacred charge,
    In whom all spirits live;

4 So now beneath his eye
    Would calmly rest,
Without a wish or thought
    Abiding in the breast;

5 Save that his will be done,
    Whate'er betide;
Dead to herself, and dead
    In him to all beside.

6 Thus would I live: yet now
    Not I, but he,
In all his power and love,
    Henceforth alive in me.

7 One Sacred Trinity,
    One Lord Divine,
May I be ever his,
    And he for ever mine.

346   *"At eventide it shall be light."*   [S. M.

THE day of praise is done;
    The evening shadows fall;
Yet pass not from us with the sun,
    True light that lightenest all.

2 Around thy throne on high
    Where night can never be,
The white-robed harpers of the sky
    Bring ceaseless songs to thee

3 Too faint our anthems here;
    Too soon of praise we tire;
But oh! the strains how full and clear
    Of that eternal choir.

4 Yet, Lord, to thy dear will
    If thou attune the heart,
We in thine angels' music still
    May bear our lower part.

5 'Tis thine each soul to calm,
    Each wayward thought reclaim,
And make our daily life a psalm
    Of glory to thy name.

6 Shine thou within us, then,
    A day that knows no end,
Till songs of angels and of men
    In perfect praise shall blend.

347   *"I tell of thy truth in the night season."*   [C. M.

NOW from the altar of our hearts,
    Let flames of love arise;
Assist us, Lord, to offer up
    Our evening sacrifice.

2 Minutes and mercies multiplied
    Have made up all this day;
Minutes came quick, but mercies were
    More swift, more free than they.

3 New time, new favours, and new joys
    Do a new song require;
Till we shall praise thee as we would,
    Accept our hearts' desire.

348   *"Now is our salvation nearer than when we believed."*   [C. M

TIME hastens on; ye longing saints,
   Now raise your voices high;
And magnify that sovereign love
   Which shows salvation nigh.

2 As time departs salvation comes;
   Each moment brings it near:
Then welcome each declining day,
   Welcome each closing year.

3 Not many years their course shall run,
   Not many mornings rise,
Ere all its glories stand reveal'd
   To our transported eyes.

349   *"The darkness and light to thee are both alike."*   [Six 10s.

THE day is gently sinking to a close,
   Fainter and yet more faint the sunlight glows:
O Brightness of thy Father's glory, thou
Eternal Light of light, be with us now:
Where thou art present darkness cannot be:
Midnight is glorious noon, O Lord, with thee.

2 Our changeful lives are ebbing to an end,
Onward to darkness and to death we tend:
O Conqueror of the grave, be thou our guide,
Be thou our light in death's dark eventide;
Then in our mortal hour will be no gloom,
No sting in death, no terror in the tomb.

3 Thou, who in darkness walking didst appear
Upon the waves, and thy disciples cheer,
Come, Lord, in lonesome days, when storms assail,
And earthly hopes and human succours fail:
When all is dark may we behold thee nigh,
And hear thy voice—"Fear not, for it is I."

4 The weary world is mouldering to decay,
Its glories wane, its pageants fade away;
In that last sunset when the stars shall fall,
May we arise awaken'd by thy call,
With thee, O Lord, for ever to abide
In that blest day which has no eventide.

SATURDAY EVENING.

350 *"He that followeth me shall not walk in darkness, but shall have the light of life."* [Six 7s

SAFELY through another week,
  God has brought us on our way;
Let us now a blessing seek
  On the approaching holy day;
Day of all the week the best,
Emblem of eternal rest!

2 Mercies multiplied each hour
  Through the week our praise demand;
Guarded by almighty power,
  Fed and guided by his hand:
Though ungrateful we have been,
And repaying love with sin.

3 While we pray for pardoning grace,
    Through the dear Redeemer's name,
Show thy reconcilèd face,
    Drive away our sin and shame;
From our worldly cares set free,
May we rest this night with thee.

4 When the morn shall bid us rise,
    May we feel thy presence near;
May thy glory meet our eyes,
    When we in thy house appear:
There afford us, Lord, a taste
Of our everlasting feast.

5 May thy Gospel's joyful sound
    Conquer sinners, comfort saints;
Make the fruits of grace abound,
    Bring relief for all complaints;
Such the days of rest we love,
Till we join the Church above.

SUNDAY EVENING.

351   *"Thou, Lord, hast made me glad through thy*   [L. M.
        works."

LORD, when this holy morning broke
    O'er island, continent, and deep,
Thy far-spread family awoke,
    All round the world, the feast to keep.

2 From east to west the sun surveyed,
　　From north to south, adoring throngs;
　And still where evening stretched her shade,
　　And stars came forth, were heard their songs.

3 And not a prayer, a tear, a sigh,
　　Hath failed this day some suit to gain;
　To hearts in trouble thou wast nigh,
　　Nor one hath sought thy face in vain.

4 The poor in spirit thou hast fed,
　　Thy chastened ones have kissed the rod,
　The mourner thou hast comforted,
　　The pure in heart have seen their God.

352 *"He shall gather the lambs with his arm, and carry them in his bosom."* [8s. 7s.

JESUS, tender Shepherd, hear me;
　　Bless thy little lamb to-night;
　Through the darkness be thou near me;
　　Keep me safe till morning light.

2 All this day thy hand has led me,
　　And I thank thee for thy care;
　Thou hast warmed me, clothed and fed me,
　　Listen to my evening prayer!

3 Let my sins be all forgiven;
　　Bless the friends I love so well;
　Take us all at last to heaven,
　　Happy there with thee to dwell.

THE SEVEN HOURS.

BEFORE DAWN.

353 *"I myself will awake right early."* [L. M.

THE wingèd herald of the day
  Proclaims the morn's approaching ray:
So Christ the Lord renews his call,
To endless life awakening all.

2 "Take up thy bed," to each he cries,
Who sick, or wrapp'd in slumber, lies:
"Be chaste, and, living soberly,
Watch ye, for I the Lord am nigh."

3 With earnest cry, with tearful care,
Call we the Lord to hear our prayer;
While supplication, pure and deep,
Forbids each chastened heart to sleep.

4 O Father, that we ask be done,
Through Jesus Christ, thine only Son;
Who, with the Holy Ghost and thee,
Shall live and reign eternally.

FIRST HOUR.

354 *"Early in the morning will I direct my prayer* [L. M.
  unto thee, and will look up."

DAWN purples all the east with light;
  Day o'er the earth is gliding bright;
Morn's sparkling rays their course begin;
Farewell to darkness and to sin!

2 Each evil dream of night, depart,
Each thought of guilt, forsake the heart!
Let every ill that darkness brought
Beneath its shade, now come to naught!

3 So that last morning, dread and great,
Which we with trembling hope await,
With blessèd light for us shall glow,
Who chant the song we learnt below.

4 O Father, that we ask be done,
Through Jesus Christ, thine only Son;
Who, with the Holy Ghost and thee,
Shall live and reign eternally.

THIRD HOUR.

355 *"It is but the third hour of the day."* [L. M.

COME, Holy Ghost, with God the Son,
And God the Father, ever One;
Shed forth thy grace within our breast,
And dwell with us, a ready guest.

2 By every power, by heart and tongue,
By act and deed, thy praise be sung;
Inflame with perfect love each sense,
That others' souls may kindle thence.

3 O Father, that we ask be done,
Through Jesus Christ, thine only Son;
Who, with the Holy Ghost and thee,
Shall live and reign eternally.

SIXTH HOUR.

356   *"At noonday will I pray."*   [L. M.

O GOD of truth, O Lord of might,
Who, ordering time and change aright,
Sendest the early morning ray,
Kindling the glow of perfect day,

2 Extinguish thou each sinful fire,
And banish every ill desire:
And, keeping all the body whole,
Shed forth thy peace upon the soul.

3 O Father, that we ask be done,
Through Jesus Christ, thine only Son;
Who, with the Holy Ghost and thee,
Shall live and reign eternally.

NINTH HOUR.

357   *"The hour of prayer being the ninth hour."*   [L. M.

O GOD! creation's secret force,
Thyself unmoved, all motion's source,
Who, from the morn till evening's ray,
Through all its changes guid'st the day,

2 Grant us, when this short life is past,
The glorious evening that shall last;
That, by a holy death attained,
Eternal glory may be gained.

THE SEVEN HOURS.

3 O Father, that we ask be done,
   Through Jesus Christ, thine only Son;
   Who, with the Holy Ghost and thee,
   Shall live and reign eternally.

SUNSET.

358 *"I will meditate upon thee in the night watches."* [C. M.

AS now the sun's declining rays
   Toward the eve descend,
E'en so our years are sinking down
   To their appointed end.

2 Lord, on the cross thine arms were stretch'd,
   To draw thy people nigh;
O grant us then that cross to love,
   And in those arms to die.

3 To God the Father, God the Son,
   And God the Holy Ghost,
All glory be from saints on earth,
   And from the angel host.

NIGHT WATCH.

359 *"Thou shalt not be afraid for any terror by night."* [L. M.

BEFORE the ending of the day,
   Creator of the world, we pray,
That with thy wonted favour, thou
Wouldst be our guard and keeper now.

2 From all ill dreams defend our sight,
   From fears and terrors of the night;
   Withhold from us our ghostly foe,
   That spot of sin we may not know.

3 O Father, that we ask be done,
   Through Jesus Christ, thine only Son;
   Who, with the Holy Ghost and thee,
   Doth live and reign eternally.

VIII. THE HOLY SCRIPTURES.

360   *" Thy statutes have been my songs in the house*   [C. M.
of my pilgrimage."

FATHER of mercies! in thy word
   What endless glory shines!
For ever be thy name adored
   For these celestial lines.

2 Here the Redeemer's welcome voice
   Spreads heavenly peace around;
And life and everlasting joys
   Attend the blissful sound.

3 O may these heavenly pages be
   My ever dear delight;
And still new beauties may I see,
   And still increasing light.

4 Divine Instructor, gracious Lord,
   Be thou for ever near;
Teach me to love thy sacred word,
   And view my Saviour there.

361 *"O Lord, how manifold are thy works."* [L. M.

THE heavens declare thy glory, Lord,
    In every star thy wisdom shines;
But when our eyes behold thy word,
    We read thy name in fairer lines.

2 The rolling sun, the changing light,
    And nights and days thy power confess;
But the blest volume thou hast writ
    Reveals thy justice and thy grace.

3 Sun, moon, and stars convey thy praise
    Round the whole earth, and never stand
So when thy truth began its race,
    It touched and glanced on every land.

4 Nor will thy spreading Gospel rest,
    Till through the world thy truth has run;
Till Christ has all the nations blest,
    That see the light, or feel the sun.

5 Great Sun of Righteousness, arise;
    Bless the dark world with heavenly light;
Thy Gospel makes the simple wise,
    Thy laws are pure, thy judgments right.

6 Thy noblest wonders here we view,
    In souls renewed and sins forgiven:
Lord, cleanse my sins, my soul renew,
    And make thy word my guide to heaven.

362 *"Thy word is a lamp unto my feet, and a light unto my path."* [7s. 6s. Double.

O WORD of God incarnate,
  O wisdom from on high,
O truth unchanged, unchanging,
  O Light of our dark sky!
We praise thee for the radiance
  That from the hallow'd page,
A lantern to our footsteps,
  Shines on from age to age.

2 The Church from her dear Master
  Received the gift divine,
And still that light she lifteth
  O'er all the earth to shine.
It is the golden casket
  Where gems of truth are stored,
It is the heaven-drawn picture
  Of Christ the living Word.

3 It floateth like a banner
  Before God's host unfurl'd;
It shineth like a beacon
  Above the darkling world;
It is the chart and compass
  That o'er life's surging sea,
Mid mists, and rocks, and quicksands,
  Still guide, O Christ, to thee.

4 O make thy Church, dear Saviour,
  A lamp of burnish'd gold,
To bear before the nations
  Thy true light as of old;

O teach thy wandering pilgrims
  By this their path to trace,
Till, clouds and darkness ended,
  They see thee face to face.

363 *"The law of the Lord is an undefiled law, converting the soul."* [C. M.

From the xix. Psalm.

GOD'S perfect law converts the soul,
  Reclaims from false desires;
With sacred wisdom his sure word
  The ignorant inspires.

2 The statutes of the Lord are just,
  And bring sincere delight;
His pure commands, in search of truth,
  Assist the feeblest sight.

3 His perfect worship here is fix'd,
  On sure foundations laid;
His equal laws are in the scales
  Of truth and justice weigh'd;

4 Of more esteem than golden mines,
  Or gold refined with skill;
More sweet than honey, or the drops
  That from the comb distil.

5 My trusty counsellors they are,
  And friendly warning give:
Divine rewards attend on those
  Who by thy precepts live.

HOLY SCRIPTURES.

364 *"How excellent is thy loving kindness, O God."* [S. M.

BEHOLD, the morning sun
Begins his glorious way!
His beams through all the nations run,
And life and light convey.

2 But where the Gospel comes,
It spreads diviner light;
It calls dead sinners from their tombs,
And gives the blind their sight.

3 My gracious God, how plain
Are thy directions given!
O may I never read in vain,
But find the path to heaven.

4 I hear thy word with love,
And I would fain obey;
Send thy good Spirit from above,
To guide me, lest I stray.

365 *"Thy word is true from the beginning."* [C. M

A GLORY gilds the sacred page,
Majestic like the sun:
It gives a light to every age:
It gives, but borrows none.

2 The Hand that gave it still supplies
The gracious light and heat:
His truths upon the nations rise;
They rise, but never set.

3 Let everlasting thanks be thine,
   For such a bright display,
As makes a world of darkness shine
   With beams of heavenly day.

4 My soul rejoices to pursue
   The steps of him I love,
Till glory break upon my view
   In brighter worlds above.

366 *"Thy word is a lantern unto my feet, and a light* [C. M.
unto my paths."

From the cxix. Psalm.

THY word is to my feet a lamp,
   The way of truth to show;
A watch-light, to point out the path
   In which I ought to go.

2 I've vow'd—and from my covenant, Lord,
   Will never start aside—
That in thy righteous judgments I
   Will steadfastly abide.

3 Let still my sacrifice of praise
   With thee acceptance find;
And in thy righteous judgments, Lord,
   Instruct my willing mind.

4 Thy testimonies I have made
   My heritage and choice;
For they, when other comforts fail,
   My drooping heart rejoice.

5 My heart with early zeal began
 Thy statutes to obey;
And, till my course of life is done,
 Shall keep thine upright way.

367 *"The invisible things of him from the creation* [C. M
*of the world are clearly seen, being understood
by the things that are made."*

GREAT God, with wonder and with praise
 On all thy works I look;
But still thy wisdom, power, and grace,
 Shine brightest in thy book.

2 The stars that in their courses roll,
 Have much instruction given;
But thy good word informs my soul
 How I may soar to heaven.

3 The fields provide me food, and show
 The goodness of the Lord;
But fruits of life and glory grow
 In thy most holy word.

4 Here are my choicest treasures hid,
 Here my best comfort lies;
Here my desires are satisfied,
 And here my hopes arise.

5 Lord, make me understand thy law,
 Show what my faults have been;
And from thy Gospel let me draw
 Pardon for all my sin.

6 Here would I learn how Christ has died
 To save my soul from hell;

Not all the books on earth beside,
  Such heavenly wonders tell.

7 Then let me love my Bible more,
  And take a fresh delight,
By day to read these wonders o'er,
  And meditate by night.

368 *"Teach me, O Lord, the way of thy statutes, and* [C. M.
   I shall keep it unto the end."

From the cxix. Psalm.

INSTRUCT me in thy statutes, Lord,
  Thy righteous paths display;
And I from them, through all my life,
  Will never go astray.

2 If thou true wisdom from above
  Wilt graciously impart,
To keep thy perfect laws I will
  Devote my zealous heart.

3 Direct me in the sacred ways
  To which thy precepts lead;
Because my chief delight has been
  Thy righteous paths to tread.

4 Do thou to thy most just commands
  Incline my willing heart;
Let no desire of worldly wealth
  From thee my thoughts divert.

IX. REDEMPTION.

369 *"My heart shall rejoice in thy salvation."* [C. M. with Chorus.

SALVATION! O the joyful sound,
  Glad tidings to our ears;
A sovereign balm for every wound,
  A cordial for our fears.

2 Salvation! buried once in sin,
  At hell's dark door we lay;
But now we rise by grace divine,
  And see a heavenly day.

3 Salvation! let the echo fly
  The spacious earth around;
While all the armies of the sky
  Conspire to raise the sound.

4 Salvation! O thou bleeding Lamb,
  To thee the praise belongs:
Our hearts shall kindle at thy Name,
  Thy Name inspire our songs.

Chorus for the end of each verse.

Glory, honour, praise, and power,
  Be unto the Lamb forever!
Jesus Christ is our Redeemer!
  Alleluia, praise the Lord!

370 *"Every day will I give thanks unto thee, and praise thy name for ever and ever."* [8s. 7s.

SAVIOUR, source of every blessing,
  Tune my heart to grateful lays:
Streams of mercy, never ceasing,
  Call for ceaseless songs of praise.

2 Teach me some melodious measure,
   Sung by raptured saints above;
 Fill my soul with sacred pleasure,
   While I sing redeeming love.

3 Thou didst seek me when a stranger,
   Wandering from the fold of God;
 Thou to save my soul from danger,
   Didst redeem me with thy blood.

4 By thy hand restored, defended,
   Safe through life thus far I've come;
 Safe, O Lord, when life is ended,
   Bring me to my heavenly home.

371 *"The Son of God, who loved me, and gave himself for me."* [L. M.

ALL glorious God, what hymns of praise
  Shall our transported voices raise!
What ardent love and zeal are due,
While heaven stands open to our view!

2 Once we were fallen, and O how low!
  Just on the brink of endless woe:
  When Jesus, from the realms above,
  Borne on the wings of boundless love,

3 Scattered the shades of death and night,
  And spread around his heavenly light:
  By him what wondrous grace is shown
  To souls impoverish'd and undone!

4 He shows, beyond these mortal shores,
  A bright inheritance as ours;
  Where saints in light our coming wait
  To share their holy, happy state.

372 *"Greater love hath no man than this, that a man lay down his life for his friends."* [C.]

TO our Redeemer's glorious name
  Awake the sacred song;
O may his love (immortal flame!)
  Tune every heart and tongue.

2 His love, what mortal thought can reach,
  What mortal tongue display!
Imagination's utmost stretch
  In wonder dies away.

3 He left his radiant throne on high,
  Left the bright realms of bliss,
And came to earth to bleed and die:
  Was ever love like this?

4 Dear Lord, while we adoring pay
  Our humble thanks to thee,
May every heart with rapture say,
  "The Saviour died for me."

5 O may the sweet, the blissful theme,
  Fill every heart and tongue;
Till strangers love thy charming name,
  And join the sacred song.

373 *"There is none other name under heaven given among men, whereby we must be saved."* [7s.

SING, my soul, his wondrous love,
Who, from yon bright throne above,
Ever watchful o'er our race,
Still to man extends his grace.

2 Heaven and earth by him were made,
All is by his sceptre sway'd;
What are we that he should show
So much love to us below?

3 God, the merciful and good,
Bought us with the Saviour's blood;
And, to make our safety sure,
Guides us by his Spirit pure.

4 Sing, my soul, adore his name,
Let his glory be thy theme:
Praise him till he calls thee home,
Trust his love for all to come.

374 *"God hath given him a name which is above every name."* [8s. 6s.

O COULD I speak the matchless worth,
O could I sound the glories forth,
Which in my Saviour shine,
I'd soar, and touch the heavenly strings,
And vie with Gabriel, while he sings
In notes almost divine.

2 I'd sing the characters he bears,
   And all the forms of love he wears,
     Exalted on his throne:
In loftiest songs of sweetest praise,
I would, to everlasting days,
     Make all his glories known.

3 O the delightful day will come,
   When my dear Lord will bring me home,
     And I shall see his face;
Then, with my Saviour, Brother, Friend,
A blest eternity I'll spend,
     Triumphant in his grace.

375   *"Casting all your care upon him, for he*   [SIX 8s.
      careth for you."

PEACE, troubled soul, whose plaintive moan
   Hath taught each scene the note of woe;
Cease thy complaint, suppress thy groan,
   And let thy tears forget to flow:
Behold, the precious balm is found,
To lull thy pain and heal thy wound.

2 Come, freely come, by sin opprest,
   On Jesus cast thy weighty load;
In him thy refuge find, thy rest,
   Safe in the mercy of thy God:
Thy God's thy Saviour, glorious word;
O hear, believe, and bless the Lord.

376   *"By grace ye are saved through faith."*   [S. M.

GRACE! 'tis a charming sound,
  Harmonious to my ear;
Heaven with the echo shall resound,
  And all the earth shall hear.

2 Grace first contrived a way
  To save rebellious man,
And all the steps that grace display
  Which drew the wondrous plan.

3 Grace taught my wandering feet
  To tread the heavenly road;
And new supplies each hour I meet
  While pressing on to God.

4 Grace all the work shall crown
  Through everlasting days;
It lays in heaven the topmost stone,
  And well deserves the praise.

377   *"Blessed is he whose unrighteousness is forgiven, and whose sin is covered."*   [L. M.

From the xxxii. Psalm.

HE'S blest, whose sins have pardon gain'd,
  No more in judgment to appear,
Whose guilt remission has obtain'd,
  And whose repentance is sincere.

2 No sooner I my wound disclosed,
  The guilt that tortured me within,
But thy forgiveness interposed,
  And mercy's healing balm pour'd in.

3 Sorrows on sorrows multiplied,
    The harden'd sinner shall confound;
But them who in his truth confide,
    Blessings of mercy shall surround.

4 His saints that have perform'd his laws,
    Their life in triumph shall employ;
Let them, as they alone have cause,
    In grateful raptures shout for joy.

378 *"I have trodden the wine-press alone; and of*   [C. M.
the people there was none with me."

BEHOLD the Saviour of mankind
    Nail'd to the shameful tree;
How vast the love that him inclined
    To bleed and die for me!

2 Hark, how he groans! while nature shakes,
    And earth's strong pillars bend;
The temple's veil in sunder breaks,
    The solid marbles rend.

3 'Tis done! the precious ransom's paid;
    "Receive my soul!" he cries;
See where he bows his sacred head!
    He bows his head and dies.

4 But soon he'll break death's envious chain,
    And in full glory shine;

O Lamb of God, was ever pain,
Was ever love like thine!

379 *"The blood of Jesus Christ his Son cleanseth us* [L. M.
from all sin."

AH, not like erring man is God,
That men to answer him should dare;
Condemn'd, and into silence awed,
They helpless stand before his bar.

2 There must a Mediator plead,
Who, God and man, may both embrace;
With God for man to intercede,
And offer man the purchased grace.

3 And lo! the Son of God is slain
To be this Mediator crown'd:
In him, my soul, be cleansed from stain,
In him thy righteousness be found.

380 *"He healeth the broken in heart."* [C. M.

WHEN, wounded sore, the stricken soul
Lies bleeding and unbound,
One only hand, a piercèd hand,
Can heal the sinner's wound.

2 When sorrow swells the laden heart,
And tears of anguish flow,
One only heart, a broken heart,
Can feel the sinner's woe.

3 When penitence has wept in vain
    Over some foul, dark spot,
One only stream, a stream of blood,
    Can wash away the blot.

4 'Tis Jesus' blood that washes white,
    His hand that brings relief,
His heart that's touch'd with all our joys,
    And feeleth for our grief.

5 Lift up thy bleeding hand, O Lord!
    Unseal that cleansing tide:
We have no shelter from our sin
    But in thy wounded side.

381 *"Him that cometh unto me, I will in no wise* [8s. 7s. 4
            cast out."

COME, ye sinners, poor and needy,
    Weak and wounded, sick and sore:
Jesus ready stands to save you,
    And his heart with love runs o'er;
        He is able,
    He is willing: doubt no more.

2 Come, ye needy, come and welcome,
    God's free bounty glorify;
True belief and true repentance,
    Every grace that brings you nigh,
        Without money,
    Come to Jesus Christ and buy.

3 Come, ye weary, heavy-laden,
　　Lost and ruin'd by the fall,
　If you tarry till you're better,
　　You will never come at all:
　　　Not the righteous,
　　Sinners Jesus came to call.

4 Agonizing in the garden,
　　Your Redeemer prostrate lies;
　On the bloody tree behold him!
　　Hear him cry, before he dies,
　　　"It is finish'd!"
　　Sinners, will not this suffice?

5 Lo! th' incarnate God, ascending,
　　Pleads the merit of his blood;
　Venture on him—venture wholly,
　　Let no other trust intrude;
　　　None but Jesus
　　Can do helpless sinners good.

6 Saints and angels, join'd in concert,
　　Sing the praises of the Lamb;
　While the blissful courts of heaven
　　Sweetly echo with his name;
　　　Alleluia!
　　Sinners here may sing the same.

382　　"*How should a man be just with God!*"　　[S. M.

AH, how shall fallen man
　Be just before his God!
If he contend in righteousness,
　We sink beneath his rod.

2 If he our ways should mark,
  With strict inquiring eyes,
Could we for one of thousand faults
  A just excuse devise?

3 All-seeing, powerful God!
  Who can with thee contend?
Or who that tries the unequal strife,
  Shall prosper in the end?

4 The mountains, in thy wrath,
  Their ancient seats forsake:
The trembling earth deserts her place,
  Her rooted pillars shake.

5 Ah, how shall guilty man
  Contend with such a God?
None, none can meet him, and escape,
  But through the Saviour's blood.

383 *"There shall be a fountain opened for sin*   [C. M.
         and uncleanness."

THERE is a fountain fill'd with blood
  Drawn from Emmanuel's veins;
And sinners plunged beneath that flood
  Lose all their guilty stains.

2 The dying thief rejoiced to see
  That fountain in his day;
And there may I, as vile as he,
  Wash all my sins away.

3 Dear, dying Lamb, thy precious blood
   Shall never lose its power,
Till all the ransom'd Church of God
   Be saved to sin no more.

4 E'er since, by faith, I saw the stream
   Thy flowing wounds supply,
Redeeming love has been my theme,
   And shall be till I die.

5 Then in a nobler, sweeter song,
   I'll sing thy power to save,
When this poor, lisping, stammering tongue
   Lies silent in the grave.

384   *"Escape for thy life; look not behind thee,*   [P. M. *neither stay thou in all the plain; escape to the mountain, lest thou be consumed."*

THE voice of free grace
   Cries, Escape to the mountain;
For Adam's lost race
   Christ hath opened a fountain:
For sin and uncleanness
   And every transgression,
His blood flows most freely
   In streams of salvation.
      Alleluia to the Lamb
         Who hath bought us our pardon;
      We'll praise him again
         When we pass over Jordan.

REDEMPTION.

2 Ye souls that are wounded,
   To Jesus repair;
He calls you in mercy,
   And can you forbear?
Though your sins be as scarlet,
   Still flee to the mountain,
That blood can remove them
   Which streams from this fountain.
     Alleluia, etc.

3 O Jesus! ride onward,
   Triumphantly glorious;
O'er sin, death, and hell
   Thou'rt more than victorious;
Thy name is the theme
   Of the great congregation,
While angels and saints
   Raise the shout of salvation.
     Alleluia, etc.

4 With joy shall we stand
   When escaped to that shore;
With our harps in our hand
   We will praise him the more;
We'll range the sweet fields
   On the banks of the river,
And sing of salvation
   For ever and ever.
     Alleluia, etc.

385 *"Unite my heart to fear thy name."* [8s. 7s.

O TO grace how great a debtor
  Daily I'm constrained to be;
Let thy love, Lord, like a fetter,
  Bind my wand'ring heart to thee!

2 Prone to wander, Lord, I feel it;
  Prone to leave the God I love;
Here's my heart, O take and seal it,
  Seal it for thy courts above!

X. THE CHRISTIAN LIFE.

REPENTANCE.

386. *"If any man sin, we have an advocate with the Father."* [L. M.

O THOU that hear'st when sinners cry,
  Though all my crimes before thee lie,
Behold them not with angry look,
But blot their memory from thy book.

2 Create my nature pure within,
  And form my soul averse to sin:
Let thy good Spirit ne'er depart,
Nor hide thy presence from my heart.

3 I cannot live without thy light,
  Cast out and banish'd from thy sight:
  Thy holy joys, my God, restore,
  And guard me that I fall no more.

4 A broken heart, my God, my King,
  Is all the sacrifice I bring;
  The God of grace will ne'er despise
  A broken heart for sacrifice.

5 O may thy love inspire my tongue!
  Salvation shall be all my song:
  And all my powers shall join to bless
  The Lord, my strength and righteousness.

387   *"Take not thy Holy Spirit from me."*   [L. M.

STAY, thou long-suffering Spirit, stay,
  Though I have done thee such despite;
Nor cast the sinner quite away,
  Nor take thine everlasting flight.

2 Though I have most unfaithful been,
    And long in vain thy grace received;
  Ten thousand times thy goodness seen,
    Ten thousand times thy goodness grieved;

3 Yet O the mourning sinner spare,
    In honour of my great High-priest;
  Nor in thy righteous anger swear
    T' exclude me from thy people's rest.

4 My weary soul, O God, release;
    Uphold me with thy gracious hand;
  Guide me into thy perfect peace,
    And bring me to the promised land.

388   *"Him that cometh to me, I will in no wise cast out."*   [C. M

O JESUS, Saviour of the lost,
  My rock and hiding-place,
By storms of sin and sorrow toss'd,
  I seek thy sheltering grace.

2 Guilty, forgive me, Lord, I cry;
  Pursued by foes, I come;
A sinner, save me, or I die;
  An outcast, take me home.

3 Once safe in thine almighty arms,
  Let storms come on amain;
There danger never, never harms;
  There death itself is gain.

4 And when I stand before thy throne,
  And all thy glory see,
Still be my righteousness alone
  To hide myself in thee.

389   *"God be merciful to me, a sinner."*   [L. M

O THAT my load of sin were gone,
  O that I could at last submit
At Jesus' feet to lay it down,
  To lay my soul at Jesus' feet!

2 Rest for my soul I long to find;
  Saviour of all, if mine thou art,
Give me thy meek and lowly mind,
  And stamp thine image on my heart.

3 Break off the yoke of inbred sin,
    And fully set my spirit free;
I cannot rest till pure within,
    Till I am wholly lost in thee.

4 Fain would I learn of thee, my God;
    Thy light and easy burden prove,
The cross, all stain'd with hallow'd blood,
    The labour of thy dying love.

5 I would, but thou must give the power,
    My heart from every sin release;
Bring near, bring near the joyful hour,
    And fill me with thy perfect peace.

FAITH.

390   *"If God be for us, who can be against us."*   [C. M.

O LET triumphant faith dispel
    The fears of guilt and woe:
If God be for us, God the Lord,
    Who, who shall be our foe?

2 He who his only Son gave up
    To death, that we might live,
Shall he not all things freely grant
    That boundless love can give?

3 Who now his people shall accuse?
    'Tis God hath justified;
Who now his people shall condemn?
    The Lamb of God hath died.

4 And he who died hath risen again,
  Triumphant from the grave;
 At God's right hand for us he pleads,
  Omnipotent to save.

391 *"I will put thee in a clift of the rock."* [SIX 7s

 ROCK of Ages, cleft for me,
  Let me hide myself in thee;
 Let the water and the blood,
 From thy riven side which flow'd,
 Be of sin the double cure,
 Cleanse me from its guilt and power.

2 Not the labours of my hands
 Can fulfil thy law's demands;
 Could my zeal no respite know,
 Could my tears for ever flow,
 All for sin could not atone,
 Thou must save, and thou alone.

3 Nothing in my hand I bring;
 Simply to thy cross I cling;
 Naked, come to thee for dress;
 Helpless, look to thee for grace:
 Foul, I to the fountain fly;
 Wash me, Saviour, or I die.

4 While I draw this fleeting breath,
 When my eyelids close in death,
 When I soar through tracts unknown,
 See thee on thy judgment throne,
 Rock of Ages, cleft for me,
 Let me hide myself in thee.

392   *"To whom shall we go but unto thee."*   [8s. 6.

JUST as I am,—without one plea,
But that thy blood was shed for me,
And that thou bidd'st me come to thee,
    O Lamb of God, I come.

2 Just as I am,—and waiting not
To rid my soul of one dark blot,
To thee, whose blood can cleanse each spot,
    O Lamb of God, I come.

3 Just as I am,—though toss'd about
With many a conflict, many a doubt,
Fightings and fears within, without,
    O Lamb of God, I come.

4 Just as I am,—poor, wretched, blind—
Sight, riches, healing of the mind,
Yea, all I need, in thee to find,
    O Lamb of God, I come.

5 Just as I am,—thou wilt receive,
Wilt welcome, pardon, cleanse, relieve;
Because thy promise I believe,
    O Lamb of God, I come.

6 Just as I am,—thy love unknown
Has broken every barrier down;
Now to be thine, yea, thine alone,
    O Lamb of God, I come.

FAITH.

393   *"I flee unto thee to hide me."*   [7s. DOUBLE.

JESUS, lover of my soul,
  Let me to thy bosom fly,
While the nearer waters roll,
  While the tempest still is high:
Hide me, O my Saviour, hide,
  Till the storm of life be past;
Safe into the haven guide,
  O receive my soul at last.

2 Other refuge have I none,
  Hangs my helpless soul on thee;
Leave, ah! leave me not alone,
  Still support and comfort me:
All my trust on thee is stay'd;
  All my help from thee I bring;
Cover my defenceless head
  With the shadow of thy wing.

3 Plenteous grace with thee is found,
  Grace to cover all my sin;
Let the healing streams abound,
  Make and keep me pure within:
Thou of life the fountain art,
  Freely let me take of thee:
Spring thou up within my heart,
  Rise to all eternity.

394   *"Whom have I in heaven but thee?"*   [8s. 4

JESUS, my Saviour! look on me,
  For I am weary and opprest;
I come to cast myself on thee:
  Thou art my Rest.

2 Look down on me, for I am weak,
   I feel the toilsome journey's length;
Thine aid omnipotent I seek:
   Thou art my Strength.

3 I am bewilder'd on my way,
   Dark and tempestuous is the night;
O send thou forth some cheering ray:
   Thou art my Light.

4 When Satan flings his fiery darts,
   I look to thee; my terrors cease;
Thy cross a hiding-place imparts:
   Thou art my Peace.

5 Standing alone on Jordan's brink,
   In that tremendous latest strife,
Thou wilt not suffer me to sink:
   Thou art my Life.

6 Thou wilt my every want supply,
   E'en to the end, whate'er befall;
Through life, in death, eternally,
   Thou art my All.

395   *"Thy name is as ointment poured forth."*   [C. M.

HOW sweet the name of Jesus sounds
   In a believer's ear!
It soothes his sorrows, heals his wounds,
   And drives away his fear.

2 It makes the wounded spirit whole,
    And calms the troubled breast;
'Tis manna to the hungry soul,
    And to the weary rest.

3 Dear name, the rock on which I build,
    My shield and hiding-place,
My never-failing treasury, filled
    With boundless stores of grace.

4 Jesus! my Shepherd, Husband, Friend,
    My Prophet, Priest, and King,
My Lord, my life, my way, my end,—
    Accept the praise I bring.

5 Weak is the effort of my heart,
    And cold my warmest thought:
But when I see thee as thou art,
    I'll praise thee as I ought.

6 Till then I would thy love proclaim
    With every fleeting breath;
And may the music of thy name
    Refresh my soul in death.

---

396   *"The blood of Jesus Christ cleanseth us from all sin."*   C. M.

FOR ever here my rest shall be,
    Close to thy bleeding side;
This all my hope and all my plea,
    "For me the Saviour died."

2 My dying Saviour and my God,
    Fountain for guilt and sin!
Sprinkle me ever with thy blood,
    And cleanse and keep me clean.

3 Wash me, and make me thus thine own;
    Wash me, and mine thou art;
Wash me, but not my feet alone—
    My hands, my head, my heart.

4 The atonement of thy blood apply,
    Till faith to sight improve;
Till hope in full fruition die,
    And all my soul is love.

397   *"My hope, and my fortress, my castle."*   [P. M

A MOUNTAIN fastness is our God,
    On which our souls are planted:
And though the fierce foe rage abroad,
    Our hearts are nothing daunted.
        What though he beset,
        With weapon and net,
        Array'd in death-strife?
        In God are help and life:
He is our sword and armour.

2 By our own might we naught can do;
    To trust it were sure losing;
For us must fight the Right and True,
    The Man of God's own choosing.

FAITH. 355

>Dost ask for his name?
>Christ Jesus we claim;
>The Lord God of hosts;
>The only God: vain boasts
>Of others fall before him.

3 What though the troops of Satan fill'd
    The world with hostile forces?
E'en then our fears should all be still'd:
    In God are our resources.
>The world and its King
>No terrors can bring:
>Their threats are no worth:
>Their doom is now gone forth:
>A single word can quell them.

4 God's word through all shall have free sway,
    And ask no man's permission:
The Spirit and his gifts convey
    Strength to defy perdition.
>The body to kill,
>Wife, children, at will,
>The wicked have power:
>Yet lasts it but an hour!
>The kingdom's ours for ever!

5 To Father, Son and Holy Ghost,
    For ever be outpouring
One chorus from the heavenly host
    And saints on earth adoring!
>That chorus resound
>To earth's utmost bound,
>And spread from shore to shore,
>Like stormy ocean's roar,
>Through endless ages rolling.

THE CHRISTIAN LIFE.

398 *"I will keep thee in all places whither thou goest."* [118.

HOW firm a foundation, ye saints of the Lord,
Is laid for your faith in his excellent word!
What more can he say than to you he hath said,
You who unto Jesus for refuge have fled?

2 Fear not, I am with thee, O be not dismay'd,
I, I am thy God, and will still give thee aid;
I'll strengthen thee, help thee, and cause thee to stand,
Upheld by my righteous, omnipotent hand.

3 When through the deep waters I call thee to go,
The rivers of woe shall not thee overflow;
For I will be with thee, thy troubles to bless,
And sanctify to thee thy deepest distress.

4 When through fiery trials thy pathway shall lie,
My grace, all-sufficient, shall be thy supply;
The flame shall not hurt thee; I only design
Thy dross to consume, and thy gold to refine.

5 The soul that to Jesus hath fled for repose,
I will not, I will not desert to his foes;
That soul, though all hell shall endeavour to shake,
I'll never—no, never—no, never forsake.

PRAYER.

399 *"If any man sin, we have an advocate with the* [C. M.
Father, Jesus Christ, the righteous."

APPROACH, my soul, the mercy-seat,
Where Jesus answers prayer;
There humbly fall before his feet,
For none can perish there.

2 Thy promise is my only plea,
　　With this I venture nigh;
　Thou callest burden'd souls to thee,
　　And such, O Lord, am I.

3 Bow'd down beneath a load of sin,
　　By Satan sorely press'd,
　By war without, and fears within,
　　I come to thee for rest.

4 Be thou my shield and hiding-place;
　　That, shelter'd near thy side,
　I may my fierce accuser face,
　　And tell him thou hast died!

5 O wondrous love, to bleed and die,
　　To bear the cross and shame,
　That guilty sinners, such as I,
　　Might plead thy gracious name.

400　　*"Men ought always to pray, and not to faint."*　　[C. M

LORD, teach us how to pray aright,
　　With reverence and with fear:
Though dust and ashes in thy sight,
　　We may, we must draw near.

2 Give deep humility; the sense
　　Of godly sorrow give;
　A strong desiring confidence
　　To hear thy voice and live.

3 Patience, to watch, and wait, and weep,
   Though mercy long delay;
Courage, our fainting souls to keep,
   And trust thee, though thou slay.

4 Give these, and then thy will be done;
   Thus, strengthen'd with all might,
We, through thy Spirit and thy Son,
   Shall pray, and pray aright.

401   *"Ask, and it shall be given you."*   [7s.

COME, my soul, thy suit prepare;
Jesus loves to answer prayer;
He himself has bid thee pray,
Therefore will not say thee nay.

2 Thou art coming to a King,—
Large petitions with thee bring;
For his grace and power are such,
None can ever ask too much.

3 With my burden I begin:
Lord, remove this load of sin;
Let thy blood, for sinners spilt,
Set my conscience free from guilt.

4 Lord, I come to thee for rest,
Take possession of my breast;
There thy blood-bought right maintain,
And without a rival reign.

5 While I am a pilgrim here,
Let thy love my spirit cheer;
As my guide, my guard, my friend,
Lead me to my journey's end.

6 Show me what I have to do,
　Every hour my strength renew;
　Let me live a life of faith,
　Let me die thy people's death.

402 *"And he said, I will not let thee go, except thou bless me."* [C. M.

SHEPHERD divine, our wants relieve,
　In this our evil day:
To all thy tempted followers give
　The power to trust and pray.

2 Long as our fiery trials last,
　　Long as the cross we bear,
　O let our souls on thee be cast
　　In never-ceasing prayer.

3 The Spirit's interceding grace
　　Give us the faith to claim;
　To wrestle till we see thy face,
　　And know thy hidden name.

4 Till thou the Father's love impart,
　　Till thou thyself bestow,
　Be this the cry of every heart—
　　I will not let thee go:

5 I will not let thee go, unless
　　Thou tell thy name to me;
　With all thy great salvation bless,
　　And say,—I died for thee.

403 *"There I will meet with thee; and I will commune with thee from above the mercy seat."* [L. M.

FROM every stormy wind that blows,
From every swelling tide of woes,
There is a calm, a sure retreat;
'Tis found beneath the mercy-seat.

2 There is a place where Jesus sheds
The oil of gladness on our heads—
A place than all beside more sweet;
It is the blood-stained mercy-seat.

3 There is a spot where spirits blend,
Where friend holds fellowship with friend;
Though sunder'd far, by faith they meet
Around one common mercy-seat.

4 There, there, on eagles' wings we soar,
And time and sense seem all no more;
And heaven comes down, our souls to greet,
And glory crowns the mercy-seat.

404 *"Lord, teach us to pray."* [C. M.

PRAYER is the soul's sincere desire,
Utter'd or unexpress'd;
The motion of a hidden fire
That trembles in the breast.

2 Prayer is the burden of a sigh,
The falling of a tear;
The upward glancing of an eye
When none but God is near.

3 Prayer is the simplest form of speech
    That infant lips can try;
Prayer, the sublimest strains that reach
    The Majesty on high.

4 Prayer is the Christian's vital breath,
    The Christian's native air;
The watch-word at the gates of death,—
    He enters heaven with prayer.

5 Prayer is the contrite sinner's voice,
    Returning from his ways;
While angels in their songs rejoice,
    And cry, "Behold, he prays!"

6 In prayer, on earth, the saints are one;
    They're one in word and mind;
When with the Father and the Son
    Sweet fellowship they find.

7 O Thou, by whom we come to God,
    The Life, the Truth, the Way,
The path of prayer thyself hast trod;
    Lord, teach us how to pray.

8 To Father, Son, and Holy Ghost,
    The God whom we adore,
Be glory, as it was, is now,
    And shall be evermore.

PRAISE.

405 *"O be joyful in the Lord, all ye lands."*   [L. M.

ALL people that on earth do dwell,
  Sing to the Lord with cheerful voice:
Him serve with fear, his praise forth tell,
  Come ye before him and rejoice.

2 Know that the Lord is God indeed;
  Without our aid he did us make:
We are his flock, he doth us feed,
  And for his sheep he doth us take.

3 O enter then his gates with praise,
  Approach with joy his courts unto;
Praise, laud, and bless his name always,
  For it is seemly so to do.

4 For why? the Lord our God is good,
  His mercy is for ever sure;
His truth at all times firmly stood,
  And shall from age to age endure.

406 *"O sing unto the Lord a new song: let the congregation of saints praise him."*   [5s. 6s. 5s.

From the cxlix. Psalm.

O PRAISE ye the Lord,
  Prepare your glad voice
His praise in the great
  Assembly to sing:

In their great Creator
  Let Israel rejoice;
And children of Sion
  Be glad in their King.

2 Let them his great name
    Extol in their songs,
  With hearts well attuned
    His praises express;
  Who always takes pleasure
    To hear their glad tongues,
  And waits with salvation
    The humble to bless.

3 With glory adorned,
    His people shall sing
  To God, who their heads
    With safety doth shield;
  Such honour and triumph
    His favour shall bring:
  O therefore for ever
    All praise to him yield!

407 *"Thou, O God, art praised in Sion."*   [L. M.
         From the lxv. Psalm.

FOR thee, O God, our constant praise
  In Sion waits, thy chosen seat;
Our promised altars there we'll raise,
  And all our zealous vows complete.

2 Thou, who to every humble prayer
    Dost always bend thy listening ear,
To thee shall all mankind repair,
    And at thy gracious throne appear.

3 Our sins, though numberless, in vain
    To stop thy flowing mercy try;
Whilst thou o'erlook'st the guilty stain,
    And washest out the crimson dye.

4 Bless'd is the man who, near thee placed,
    Within thy sacred dwelling lives!
'Tis there abundantly we taste
    The vast delights thy temple gives.

408 *"O give thanks unto the Lord: for he is gracious,* [7s.
*   and his mercy endureth for ever."*

From the cvii. Psalm.

MAGNIFY Jehovah's name;
    For his mercies ever sure,
From eternity the same,
    To eternity endure.

2 Let his ransom'd flock rejoice,
    Gather'd out of every land,
As the people of his choice,
    Pluck'd from the destroyer's hand.

3 In the wilderness astray,
    In the lonely waste they roam,
Hungry, fainting by the way,
    Far from refuge, shelter, home:

4 To the Lord their God they cry;
　　He inclines a gracious ear,
　Sends deliverance from on high,
　　Rescues them from all their fear.

5 Them to pleasant lands he brings,
　　Where the vine and olive grow;
　Where from verdant hills, the springs
　　Through luxuriant valleys flow.

6 O that men would praise the Lord,
　　For his goodness to their race;
　For the wonders of his word,
　　And the riches of his grace!

409 *"Serve the Lord with gladness, and come before* [L. M.
his presence with a song."

From the c. Psalm.

BEFORE Jehovah's awful throne,
　Ye nations, bow with sacred joy;
Know that the Lord is God alone;
　He can create, and he destroy.

2 His sovereign power, without our aid,
　　Made us of clay, and form'd us men;
　And when like wandering sheep we stray'd,
　　He brought us to his fold again.

3 We are his people, we his care,
　　Our souls, and all our mortal frame;
　What lasting honours shall we rear,
　　Almighty Maker, to thy name?

4 We'll crowd thy gates with thankful songs,
   High as the heaven our voices raise;
And earth, with her ten thousand tongues,
   Shall fill thy courts with sounding praise.

5 Wide as the world is thy command,
   Vast as eternity thy love;
Firm as a rock thy truth must stand,
   When rolling years shall cease to move.

410 *"O Lord, thou art become exceeding glorious;* [L. M.
thou art clothed with majesty and honour."

From the civ. Psalm.

BLESS God, my soul; thou, Lord, alone
   Possessest empire without bounds,
With honour thou art crown'd, thy throne
   Eternal majesty surrounds.

2 With light thou dost thyself enrobe,
   And glory for a garment take;
Heaven's curtains stretch beyond the globe,
   The canopy of state to make.

3 God builds on liquid air, and forms
   His palace-chambers in the skies;
The clouds his chariots are, and storms
   The swift-wing'd steeds with which he flies.

4 As bright as flame, as swift as wind,
   His ministers heaven's palace fill;
They have their sundry tasks assign'd,
   All prompt to do their sovereign's will.

5 In praising God while he prolongs
   My breath, I will that breath employ;
And join devotion to my songs,
   Sincere, as in him is my joy.

411   *"O praise the Lord of heaven."*   [6s. 4s.
        From the cxlviii. Psalm.

YE boundless realms of joy,
   Exalt your Maker's fame;
His praise your song employ
   Above the starry frame:
     Your voices raise,
    Ye cherubim
    And seraphim,
     To sing his praise.

2 Thou moon, that rul'st the night
   And sun, that guid'st the day;
Ye glittering stars of light,
   To him your homage pay:
     His praise declare,
    Ye heavens above,
    And clouds that move
     In liquid air.

3 Let them adore the Lord,
   And praise his holy name,
By whose almighty word
   They all from nothing came;
     And all shall last
    From changes free;
    His firm decree
     Stands ever fast.

THE CHRISTIAN LIFE.

412   *"Let everything that hath breath praise the Lord."*   [L. M.

From the cl. Psalm.

O PRAISE the Lord in that blest place
    From whence his goodness largely flows;
Praise him in heaven, where he his face,
    Unveiled, in perfect glory shows.

2 Praise him for all the mighty acts
    Which he in our behalf has done;
His kindness this return exacts,
    With which our praise should equal run.

3 Let the shrill trumpet's warlike voice
    Make rocks and hills his praise rebound;
Praise him with harp's melodious noise,
    And gentle psaltery's silver sound.

4 Let them who joyful hymns compose,
    To cymbals set their songs of praise—
To well-tuned cymbals, and to those
    That loudly sound on solemn days.

5 Let all that vital breath enjoy,
    The breath he does to them afford,
In just returns of praise employ:
    Let every creature praise the Lord!

413   *"Praise the Lord, O my soul; and all that is within me, praise his holy name."*   [S. M.

From the ciii. Psalm.

O BLESS the Lord, my soul,
    His grace to thee proclaim;
And all that is within me, join
    To bless his holy name.

2 O bless the Lord, my soul,
    His mercies bear in mind;
Forget not all his benefits,
    Who is to thee so kind.

3 He pardons all thy sins,
    Prolongs thy feeble breath;
He healeth thine infirmities,
    And ransoms thee from death.

4 He feeds thee with his love,
    Upholds thee with his truth;
And, like the eagle's, he renews
    The vigour of thy youth.

5 Then bless the Lord, my soul,
    His grace, his love proclaim;
Let all that is within me, join
    To bless his holy name.

414 *"My heart is fixed, O God, my heart is fixed:* [L. M.
    I will sing and give praise."

From the lvii. Psalm.

O GOD, my heart is fix'd, 'tis bent,
    Its thankful tribute to present;
And, with my heart, my voice I'll raise
To thee, my God, in songs of praise.

2 Awake, my glory; harp and lute,
No longer let your strings be mute:
And I, my tuneful part to take,
Will with the early dawn awake.

3 Thy praises, Lord, I will resound
To all the listening nations round:
Thy mercy highest heaven transcends,
Thy truth beyond the clouds extends.

4 Be thou, O God, exalted high;
And as thy glory fills the sky,
So let it be on earth displayed,
Till thou art here, as there, obeyed.

415 *"I will alway give thanks unto the Lord."*   [C. M.
From the xxxiv. Psalm.

THROUGH all the changing scenes of life,
  In trouble and in joy,
The praises of my God shall still
  My heart and tongue employ.

2 Of his deliverance I will boast,
  Till all that are distressed
From my example comfort take,
  And charm their griefs to rest.

3 O magnify the Lord with me,
  With me exalt his name;
When in distress to him I call'd,
  He to my rescue came.

4 The angel of the Lord encamps
  Around the good and just;
Deliverance he affords to all
  Who on his succour trust.

5 O make but trial of his love,
   Experience will decide
How blest they are, and only they,
   Who in his truth confide.

6 Fear him, ye saints; and you will then
   Have nothing else to fear;
Make you his service your delight,
   Your wants shall be his care.

416 *"O give thanks unto the Lord: for he is gracious,* [L. M.
and his mercy endureth for ever."

From the cvi. Psalm.

O RENDER thanks to God above,
   The fountain of eternal love;
Whose mercy firm through ages past
Has stood, and shall for ever last.

2 Who can his mighty deeds express,
   Not only vast, but numberless?
What mortal eloquence can raise
His tribute of immortal praise?

3 Extend to me that favour, Lord,
   Thou to thy chosen dost afford;
When thou return'st to set them free,
Let thy salvation visit me.

4 Let Israel's God be ever bless'd,
   His name eternally confess'd;
Let all his saints, with full accord,
Sing loud Amens, Praise ye the Lord!

417 *"O Lord, our Lord, how excellent is thy name* [C. M.
in all the earth."
From the viii. Psalm.

I SING the almighty power of God,
  That made the mountains rise,
That spread the flowing seas abroad,
  And built the lofty skies.

2 I sing the wisdom that ordain'd
  The sun to rule the day;
The moon shines full at his command,
  And all the stars obey.

3 Lord, how thy wonders are display'd
  Where'er I turn my eye;
If I survey the ground I tread,
  Or gaze upon the sky,

4 There's not a plant nor flower below
  But makes thy glories known;
And clouds arise, and tempests blow
  By order from thy throne.

5 His hand is my perpetual guard;
  He keeps me with his eye:
Why should I, then, forget the Lord,
  Who is forever nigh?

418 *"The Lord is King; the earth may be glad* [L. M.
thereof."
From the xcvii. Psalm.

JEHOVAH reigns, let all the earth
  In his just government rejoice;
Let all the lands, with sacred mirth,
  In his applause unite their voice.

2 Darkness and clouds of awful shade
   His dazzling glory shroud in state;
Judgment and righteousness are made
   The habitation of his seat.

3 For thou, O God, art seated high,
   Above earth's potentates enthroned;
Thou, Lord, unrivalled in the sky,
   Supreme by all the gods art owned.

419   *"Let everything that hath breath praise the Lord."*   [8s. 6s.

From the cxlviii. Psalm.

BEGIN, my soul, th' exalted lay;
  Let each enraptured thought obey,
    And praise th' Almighty's name:
Let heaven and earth, and seas and skies,
In one melodious concert rise,
    To swell th' inspiring theme.

2 Ye angels, catch the thrilling sound,
While all the adoring thrones around
   His boundless mercy sing;
Let every listening saint above
Wake all the tuneful soul of love,
   And touch the sweetest string.

3 Whate'er this living world contains,
That wings the air or treads the plains,
   United praise bestow:
Ye tenants of the ocean wide,
Proclaim him through the mighty tide,
   And in the deeps below.

4 Let man, by nobler passions sway'd,
  The feeling heart, the judging head,
    In heavenly praise employ;
  Spread his tremendous name around,
  Till heav'n's broad arch rings back the sound,
    The general burst of joy.

420 *"As long as I have any being, I will sing praises unto my God."* [SIX 8s.

From the cxlvi. Psalm.

I'LL praise my Maker with my breath,
  And when my voice is lost in death,
    Praise shall employ my nobler powers:
  My days of praise shall ne'er be past
  While life, and thought, and being last,
    Or immortality endures.

2 Happy the man whose hopes rely
  On Israel's God: he made the sky,
    And earth, and seas, with all their train;
  He saves th' oppress'd, he feeds the poor;
  His truth for ever stands secure,
    And none shall find his promise vain.

421 *"The Lord is my strength, and my shield."* [C. M.

From the xxviii. Psalm.

ADORED for ever be the Lord;
  His praise I will resound,
From whom the cries of my distress
  A gracious answer found.

2 He is my strength and shield; my heart
 Has trusted in his name;
And now relieved, my heart, with joy,
 His praises shall proclaim.

3 The Lord, the everlasting God,
 Is my defence and rock,
The saving health, the saving strength,
 Of his anointed flock.

4 O save and bless thy people, Lord,
 Thy heritage preserve;
Feed, strengthen, and support their hearts,
 That they may never swerve.

422 *"The morning stars sang together, and all the sons of God shouted for joy."* [7s.

SONGS of praise the angels sang;
 Heaven with alleluias rang,
When Jehovah's work begun,
When he spake and it was done.

2 Songs of praise awoke the morn,
 When the Prince of Peace was born;
Songs of praise arose, when he
Captive led captivity.

3 Heaven and earth must pass away;
Songs of praise shall crown that day:
God will make new heavens and earth;
Songs of praise shall hail their birth.

4 And shall man alone be dumb
  Till that glorious kingdom come?
  No; the Church delights to raise
  Psalms, and hymns, and songs of praise.

5 Saints below, with heart and voice,
  Still in songs of praise rejoice;
  Learning here, by faith and love,
  Songs of praise to sing above.

6 Borne upon their latest breath,
  Songs of praise shall conquer death;
  Then, amidst eternal joy,
  Songs of praise their powers employ.

423 *"I will magnify thee, O God, my King."* [8s. 7s.

From the cxlv. Psalm.

GOD, my King, thy might confessing,
  Ever will I bless thy name;
Day by day thy throne addressing,
  Still will I thy praise proclaim.

2 Honour great our God befitteth;
    Who his majesty can reach?
  Age to age his works transmitteth,
    Age to age his power shall teach.

3 They shall talk of all thy glory,
    On thy might and greatness dwell,
  Speak of thy dread acts the story,
    And thy deeds of wonder tell.

4 Nor shall fail from memory's treasure,
     Works by love and mercy wrought—
  Works of love surpassing measure,
     Works of mercy passing thought.

5 Full of kindness and compassion,
     Slow to anger, vast in love,
  God is good to all creation;
     All his works his goodness prove.

6 All thy works, O Lord, shall bless thee,
     Thee shall all thy saints adore;
  King supreme shall they confess thee,
     And proclaim thy sovereign power.

424 *"He is Lord of lords and King of kings."* [C. M.

ALL hail the power of Jesus' name!
     Let angels prostrate fall;
  Bring forth the royal diadem,
     And crown him Lord of all.

2 Crown him, ye martyrs of our God,
     Who from his altar call;
  Extol the Stem of Jesse's rod,
     And crown him Lord of all.

3 Hail him, the Heir of David's line,
     Whom David, Lord did call;
  The God incarnate! Man divine!
     And crown him Lord of all!

4 Ye seed of Israel's chosen race,
　Ye ransomed of the fall,
Hail him who saves you by his grace,
　And crown him Lord of all.

5 Sinners, whose love can ne'er forget
　The wormwood and the gall,
Go, spread your trophies at his feet,
　And crown him Lord of all.

6 Let every kindred, every tribe,
　On this terrestrial ball,
To him all majesty ascribe,
　And crown him Lord of all.

425　　*"All thy works praise thee, O Lord."*　　[P. M.

THE strain upraise of joy and praise,　Alleluia!
　To the glory of their King
Shall the ransom'd people sing,　Alleluia!
And the choirs that dwell on high
Shall re-echo through the sky,　Alleluia!

They in the rest of Paradise who dwell
The blessèd ones with joy the chorus swell, Alleluia!
The planets beaming on their heavenly way,
The shining constellations, join and say,　Alleluia!

　Ye clouds that onward sweep,
　Ye winds on pinions light,
Ye thunders, echoing loud and deep,
　Ye lightnings, wildly bright,
In sweet consent unite your　　　　　Alleluia!

Ye floods and ocean billows,
   Ye storms and winter snow,
Ye days of cloudless beauty,
   Hoar frost and summer glow:
Ye groves that wave in spring,
   And glorious forests, sing,   Alleluia!

First let the birds, with painted plumage gay,
Exalt their great Creator's praise, and say, Alleluia!
Then let the beasts of earth, with varying strain,
Join in creation's hymn, and cry again,   Alleluia!

Here let the mountains thunder forth sonorous,
                                          Alleluia!
There let the valleys sing in gentler chorus,
                                          Alleluia!
Thou jubilant abyss of ocean, cry,   Alleluia!
Ye tracts of earth and continents, reply, Alleluia!

To God, who all creation made,
The frequent hymn be duly paid: Alleluia!
This is the strain, the eternal strain, the Lord
   Almighty loves: Alleluia!
This is the song, the heavenly song, that Christ, the
   King, approves: Alleluia!
Wherefore we sing, both heart and voice awaking,
                                          Alleluia!
And children's voices echo, answer making,
                                          Alleluia!

   Now from all men be outpour'd
   Alleluia to the Lord;
   With Alleluia evermore
   The Son and Spirit we adore.
   Praise be done to the Three in One,
      Alleluia! Alleluia! Alleluia!   Amen.

426 *"My cup runneth over."* [C. M.

WHEN all thy mercies, O my God
   My rising soul surveys,
Transported with the view, I'm lost
   In wonder, love, and praise.

2 O how shall words with equal warmth
   The gratitude declare
That glows within my ravish'd heart?
   But thou canst read it there.

3 Ten thousand thousand precious gifts
   My daily thanks employ;
Nor is the least a cheerful heart,
   That tastes those gifts with joy.

4 Through every period of my life
   Thy goodness I'll pursue;
And after death, in distant worlds,
   The glorious theme renew.

5 When nature fails, and day and night
   Divide thy works no more,
My ever grateful heart, O Lord,
   Thy mercy shall adore.

6 Through all eternity, to thee
   A joyful song I'll raise;
But oh! eternity's too short
   To utter all thy praise.

427

"The Lord is King."   [L. M.

From the xciii. Psalm.

WITH glory clad, with strength arrayed,
  The Lord that o'er all nature reigns
The world's foundation strongly laid,
  And the vast fabric still sustains.

2 How surely stablish'd is thy throne!
  Which shall no change or period see;
For thou, O Lord, and thou alone,
  Art God from all eternity.

3 The floods, O Lord, lift up their voice,
  And toss the troubled waves on high;
But God above can still their noise,
  And make the angry sea comply.

4 Thy promise, Lord, is ever sure,
  And they that in thy house would dwell,
That happy station to secure,
  Must still in holiness excel.

428

"Holy, Holy, Holy."   [6s. 4s.

COME, thou Almighty King,
  Help us thy name to sing,
    Help us to praise!
Father all glorious,
O'er all victorious,
Come and reign over us,
    Ancient of days.

2 Come, thou incarnate Word,
   Gird on thy mighty sword;
     Our prayer attend;
   Come, and thy people bless;
   Come, give thy word success;
   Spirit of holiness,
     On us descend!

3 Come, holy Comforter,
   Thy sacred witness bear,
     In this glad hour:
   Thou, who almighty art,
   Now rule in every heart,
   And ne'er from us depart,
     Spirit of power.

4 To thee, great One in Three,
   The highest praises be,
     Hence evermore;
   Thy sovereign majesty
   May we in glory see,
   And to eternity
     Love and adore.

429   "*Praise the Lord, O my soul.*"   [L. M.

AWAKE, my soul, to joyful lays,
   And sing thy great Redeemer's praise:
He justly claims a song from thee;
His loving-kindness, O how free!

2 He saw me ruin'd in the fall,
  Yet loved me, notwithstanding all;
  He saved me from my lost estate;
  His loving-kindness, O how great!

3 Though numerous hosts of mighty foes,
  Though earth and hell my way oppose,
  He safely leads my soul along;
  His loving-kindness, O how strong!

4 When trouble, like a gloomy cloud,
  Has gather'd thick, and thunder'd loud,
  He near my soul has always stood;
  His loving-kindness, O how good!

5 Often I feel my sinful heart
  Prone from my Saviour to depart,
  But though I oft have him forgot,
  His loving-kindness changes not.

6 Soon shall I pass the gloomy vale,
  Soon all my mortal powers must fail;
  O may my last expiring breath
  His loving-kindness sing in death!

430 *"And again they said, Alleluia."* [8s. 7s. Six Lines

ALLELUIA! song of gladness,
  Voice of everlasting joy:
Alleluia! sound the sweetest
  Heard among the choirs on high,
Hymning in God's blissful mansion
  Day and night incessantly.

2 Alleluia! Church victorious,
   Thou may'st lift the joyful strain:
Alleluia! songs of triumph
   Well befit the ransomed train.
Faint and feeble are our praises
   While in exile we remain.

3 Alleluia! songs of gladness
   Suit not always souls forlorn,
Alleluia! sounds of sadness
   'Midst our joyful strains are borne;
For in this dark world of sorrow
   We with tears our sins must mourn.

4 Praises with our prayers uniting,
   Hear us, blessed Trinity;
Bring us to thy blissful presence,
   There the Paschal Lamb to see,
Then to thee our alleluia
   Singing everlastingly.

431 *"One cried unto another, and said, Holy, holy, holy."* [8s. 7s. Double.

ROUND the Lord in glory seated
   Cherubim and seraphim
Fill'd his temple, and repeated
   Each to each the alternate hymn.
"Lord, thy glory fills the heaven,
   Earth is with thy fulness stored;
Unto thee be glory given,
   Holy, holy, holy Lord."

2 Heaven is still with glory ringing,
    Earth takes up the angels' cry,
"Holy, holy, holy," singing,
    "Lord of hosts, the Lord most High."
With his seraph train before him,
    With his holy Church below,
Thus conspire we to adore him,
    Bid we thus our anthem flow:

3 "Lord, thy glory fills the heaven,
    Earth is with thy fulness stored;
Unto thee be glory given,
    Holy, holy, holy Lord."
Thus thy glorious name confessing,
    We adopt thy angels' cry,
"Holy, holy, holy," blessing
    Thee, the Lord of hosts most High.

432   *"And all her streets shall say, Alleluia."*   [P. M

SING Alleluia forth in duteous praise,
O citizens of heaven; and sweetly raise
    An endless Alleluia.

2 Ye next, who stand before the Eternal Light,
In hymning choirs re-echo to the height
    An endless Alleluia.

3 The holy city shall take up your strain,
And with glad songs resounding wake again
    An endless Alleluia.

4 In blissful antiphons ye thus rejoice
To render to the Lord with thankful voice
    An endless Alleluia.

5 Ye who have gained at length your palms in bliss,
Victorious ones, your chant shall still be this,
An endless Alleluia.

6 There, in one grand acclaim, for ever ring
The strains which tell the honour of your King,
An endless Alleluia.

7 This is the rest for weary ones brought back,
This is the food and drink which none shall lack,
An endless Alleluia.

8 While thee, by whom were all things made, we praise
For ever, and tell out in sweetest lays
An endless Alleluia.

9 Almighty Christ, to thee our voices sing
Glory for evermore; to thee we bring
An endless Alleluia.

433 *"Of him and through him and to him are all things: to whom be glory for ever. Amen."* [8s. 7s.

ANGEL bands, in strains sweet sounding,
Anthems to the Saviour raise:
Host of heaven, his throne surrounding,
Hymn the great Creator's praise.

2 Radiant orb of day, adore him,
Praise him, thou who rul'st the night;
Heaven of heavens, O bow before him,
Laud him, all ye worlds of light.

3 Praise him, wild and restless ocean,
   Praise him, monsters of the deep;
   Praise him in your rude commotion,
   Storms that at his mandate sweep.

4 Hills and mountains, heavenward towering
   Fires that in their bosom glow;
   Clouds around their cliffs dark lowering,
   Torrents down their steeps that flow;

5 Verdant fields and valleys blooming,
   Insect myriads, own his care;
   Wild beasts through the forest roaming,
   Warbling tenants of the air,

6 Kings and rulers, shout his glory,
   People, join the loud acclaim,
   Maidens, youth, and fathers hoary,
   Infants, lisp his holy name.

7 Every kindred, tongue, and nation,
   Him who gave you life adore;
   Earth and heaven, and all creation,
   Praise his name for evermore.

SELF-CONSECRATION.

434   *"Put on the whole armour of God."*   [D S. M

JESUS, my strength, my hope,
   On thee I cast my care,
With humble confidence look up,
   And know thou hear'st my prayer:

  Give me on thee to wait,
   Till I can all things do—
 On thee, almighty to create,
   Almighty to renew.

2 Give me a sober mind,
  A self-renouncing will,
That tramples down and casts behind
  The baits of pleasing ill:
  A soul inured to pain,
  To hardship, grief, and loss,
Ready to take up and sustain
  The consecrated cross.

3 Give me a godly fear,
  A quick, discerning eye,
That looks to thee when sin is near,
  And sees the tempter fly;
  A spirit still prepared,
  And arm'd with jealous care,
For ever standing on its guard,
  And watching unto prayer.

4 Give me a true regard,
  A single, steady aim,
Unmoved by threatening or reward,
  To thee and thy great name;
  Give me a heart to pray,
  To pray and never cease,
Never to murmur at thy stay,
  Or wish my sufferings less.

5 I rest upon thy word,
  The promise is for me;
My succour and salvation, Lord,
  Shall surely come from thee;
But let me still abide,
  Nor from my hope remove,
Till thou my patient spirit guide
  Into thy perfect love.

435   *"Enoch walked with God."*   [C. ♫

O FOR a closer walk with God,
  A calm and heavenly frame;
A light to shine upon the road
  That leads me to the Lamb.

2 Return, O holy Dove, return,
  Sweet messenger of rest;
I hate the sins that made thee mourn,
  And drove thee from my breast.

3 The dearest idol I have known,
  Whate'er that idol be,
Help me to tear it from thy throne,
  And worship only thee.

4 So shall my walk be close with God,
  Calm and serene my frame;
So purer light shall mark the road
  That leads me to the Lamb.

TRUST.

436 *"They that put their trust in the Lord shall be even as the Mount Sion, which may not be removed, but standeth fast for ever."* [C. M.

From the cxxv. Psalm.

WHO place on Sion's God their **trust**,
 Like Sion's rock shall stand;
Like her immovable be fix'd
 By his almighty hand.

2 Look how the hills on every side
 Jerusalem enclose;
So stands the Lord around his saints,
 To guard them from their foes.

437 *"I will love thee, O Lord, my strength."* [L. M.

From the xviii. Psalm.

NO change of time shall ever shock
 My firm affection, Lord, to thee;
For thou hast always been my rock,
 A fortress and defence to me.

2 Thou my deliverer art, my God;
 My trust is in thy mighty power:
Thou art my shield from foes abroad,
 At home my safeguard and my tower.

3 To thee I will address my prayer,
 To whom all praise we justly owe;
So shall I, by thy watchful care,
 Be guarded safe from every foe.

TRUST.

438 *"The Lord is my shepherd; therefore can I lack nothing."* [C. M.

From the xxiii. Psalm.

THE Lord himself, the mighty Lord,
  Vouchsafes to be my guide;
The shepherd, by whose constant care
  My wants are all supplied.

2 In tender grass he makes me feed,
  And gently there repose;
Then leads me to cool shades, and where
  Refreshing water flows.

3 He does my wandering soul reclaim,
  And, to his endless praise,
Instruct with humble zeal to walk
  In his most righteous ways.

4 I pass the gloomy vale of death,
  From fear and danger free;
For there his aiding rod and staff
  Defend and comfort me.

5 Since God doth thus his wondrous love
  Through all my life extend,
That life to him I will devote,
  And in his temple spend.

439 *"My soul truly waiteth still upon God."* [L. M.

From the lxii. Psalm

MY soul, for help on God rely,
  On him alone thy trust repose
My rock and health will strength supply
  To bear the shock of all my foes.

2 God does his saving health dispense,
 And flowing blessings daily send;
He is my fortress and defence,
 On him my soul shall still depend.

3 In him, ye people, always trust;
 Before his throne pour out your hearts:
For God, the merciful and just,
 His timely aid to us imparts.

440 *"The Lord shall give his people the blessing of* [C. M.
 peace."

FATHER, whate'er of earthly bliss
 Thy sovereign will denies,
Accepted at thy throne of grace
 Let this petition rise.

2 Give me a calm and thankful heart,
 From every murmur free;
The blessings of thy grace impart,
 And let me live to thee.

3 Let the sweet hope that thou art mine
 My path of life attend:
Thy presence through my journey shine
 And crown my journey's end.

441 *"My peace I give unto you."* [C. M

WHILE thee I seek, protecting Power,
 Be my vain wishes stilled;
And may this consecrated hour
 With better hopes be filled.

TRUST.

2 Thy love the power of thought bestowed,
   To thee my thoughts would soar:
Thy mercy o'er my life has flowed,
   That mercy I adore.

3 In each event of life, how clear
   Thy ruling hand I see:
Each blessing to my soul more dear,
   Because conferred by thee.

4 In every joy that crowns my days,
   In every pain I bear,
My heart shall find delight in praise,
   Or seek relief in prayer.

5 When gladness wings my favoured hour,
   Thy love my thoughts shall fill;
Resigned when storms of sorrow lower,
   My soul shall meet thy will.

6 My lifted eye, without a tear,
   The gathering storms shall see;
My steadfast heart shall know no fear,
   That heart will rest on thee.

442   *"I will rejoice in the Lord."*   [8s. 6s.

ALTHOUGH the vine its fruit deny,
   The budding fig tree droop and die,
No oil the olive yield;
Yet will I trust me in my God,
Yea, bend rejoicing to his rod,
   And by his grace be heal'd.

2 Though fields, in verdure once array'd,
By whirlwinds desolate be laid,
  Or parch'd by scorching beam;
Still in the Lord shall be my trust,
My joy; for, though his frown is just,
  His mercy is supreme.

3 Though from the folds the flock decay,
Though herds lie famish'd o'er the lea,
  And round the empty stall;
My soul above the wreck shall rise,
Its better joys are in the skies;
  There God is all in all.

4 In God my strength, howe'er distrest,
I yet will hope, and calmly rest,
  Nay, triumph in his love:
My lingering soul, my tardy feet,
Free as the hind he makes, and fleet,
  To speed my course above.

443 *"I have prayed for thee, that thy faith fail not."* [6s. 5s.
Double

IN the hour of trial,
  Jesus, plead for me;
Lest by base denial
  I depart from thee;
When thou see'st me waver,
  With a look recall,
Nor for fear or favour
  Suffer me to fall.

2 With forbidden pleasures
    Would this vain world charm
Or its sordid treasures
    Spread to work me harm;
Bring to my remembrance
    Sad Gethsemane,
Or, in darker semblance,
    Cross-crown'd Calvary.

3 Should thy mercy send me
    Sorrow, toil, and woe;
Or should pain attend me
    On my path below;
Grant that I may never
    Fail thy hand to see;
Grant that I may ever
    Cast my care on thee.

4 When my last hour cometh,
    Fraught with strife and pain,
When my dust returneth
    To the dust again;
On thy truth relying,
    Through that mortal strife,
Jesus, take me, dying,
    To eternal life.

444   *"My meditation of him shall be sweet."*   [L. M.

IS there a lone and dreary hour,
   When worldly pleasures lose their power?
My Father! let me turn to thee,
And set each thought of darkness free.

2 Is there an hour of peace and joy,
When hope is all my soul's employ?
My Saviour! still my hopes will roam,
Until they rest with thee, their home.

3 Is there a time of racking grief,
Which scorns the prospect of relief?
O Spirit! break the cheerless gloom,
And bid my heart its calm resume.

4 The noontide blaze, the midnight scene,
The dawn, or twilight's sweet serene,
The glow of life, the dying hour,
Shall own, O God! thy grace and power.

445 *"The Lord is my portion, saith my soul."* [7s

'TIS my happiness below
   Not to live without the cross;
But the Saviour's power to know,
   Sanctifying every loss.

2 Trials must and will befall;
   But with humble faith to see
Love inscribed upon them all—
   This is happiness to me.

3 Did I meet no trials here,
   No chastisement by the way,
Might I not with reason fear
   I should be a castaway?

4 Trials make the promise sweet;
  Trials give new life to prayer;
Bring me to my Saviour's feet,
  Lay me low and keep me there.

446 *"I cried unto God with my voice, and he gave* [L. M.
ear unto me."

GOD of my life, to thee I call;
  Afflicted at thy feet I fall:
When the great water-floods prevail,
Leave not my trembling heart to fail.

2 Friend of the friendless and the faint,
Where should I lodge my deep complaint?—
Where but with thee, whose open door
Invites the helpless and the poor?

3 Did ever mourner plead with thee,
And thou refuse that mourner's plea?
Does not the word still fix'd remain?
That none shall seek thy face in vain?

4 That were a grief I could not bear,
Didst thou not hear and answer prayer:
But a prayer-hearing, answering God
Supports me under every load.

5 Poor though I am, despised, forgot,
Yet God, my God, forgets me not:
And he is safe, and must succeed,
For whom the Lord vouchsafes to plead.

HOPE.

447   *"Our conversation is in heaven."*   [7s. 6s. Double.

RISE, my soul, and stretch thy wings,
   Thy better portion trace;
Rise from transitory things,
   Towards heaven, thy destined place:
Sun and moon and stars decay,
   Time shall soon this earth remove,
Rise, my soul, and haste away
   To seats prepared above.

2 Cease, my soul, O cease to mourn,
   Press onward to the prize;
Soon thy Saviour will return,
   To take thee to the skies:
There is everlasting peace,
   Rest, enduring rest, in heaven;
There will sorrow ever cease,
   And crowns of joy be given.

448   *"It is good for me to put my trust in the Lord God."*   [L. M.

From the lxxiii. Psalm.

THY presence, Lord, hath me supplied,
   Thou my right hand support dost give;
Thou first shalt with thy counsel guide,
   And then to glory me receive.

2 Whom then in heaven, but thee alone,
   Have I, whose favour I require?
Throughout the spacious earth there's none,
   Compared with thee, that I desire.

3 My trembling flesh and aching heart
   May often fail to succour me;
But God shall inward strength impart,
   And my eternal portion be.

449   *"If any man serve me, let him follow me."*

CHILDREN of the heavenly King,
   As we journey, sweetly sing;
Sing our Saviour's worthy praise,
Glorious in his works and ways.

2 We are travelling home to God,
   In the way the fathers trod:
They are happy now, and we
Soon their happiness shall see.

3 Banish'd once, by sin betray'd,
   Christ our advocate was made;
Pardon'd now, no more we roam,
Christ conducts us to our home.

4 Lord, obediently we go,
   Gladly leaving all below;
Only thou our leader be,
And we still will follow thee.

450   *"They desire a better country, that is, an heavenly."*   [L. M

AS, when the weary traveller gains
    The height of some commanding hill,
His heart revives, if o'er the plains
    He sees his home, though distant still;

2 Thus, when the Christian pilgrim views
    By faith his mansion in the skies,
The sight his fainting strength renews,
    And wings his speed to reach the prize.

3 The thought of heaven his spirit cheers;
    No more he grieves for troubles past;
Nor any future trial fears,
    So he may safe arrive at last.

4 Jesus, on thee our hopes we stay,
    To lead us on to thine abode;
Assured thy love will far o'erpay
    The hardest labours of the road.

451   *"Like as the hart desireth the water-brooks, so longeth my soul after thee, O God."*   [C. M.

From the xlii. Psalm.

AS pants the hart for cooling streams,
    When heated in the chase;
So longs my soul, O God, for thee,
    And thy refreshing grace.

2 For thee, my God, the living God,
   My thirsty soul doth pine;
 O when shall I behold thy face,
   Thou Majesty divine?

3 Why restless, why cast down, my soul?
   Trust God; who will employ
 His aid for thee, and change these sighs
   To thankful hymns of joy.

4 God of my strength, how long shall I
   Like one forgotten, mourn,
 Forlorn, forsaken, and exposed
   To my oppressor's scorn?

5 My heart is pierced, as with a sword,
   While thus my foes upbraid:
 "Vain boaster, where is now thy God?
   And where his promised aid?"

6 Why restless, why cast down, my soul?
   Hope still; and thou shalt sing
 The praise of him who is thy God,
   Thy health's eternal spring.

452 *"My soul is athirst for God, yea, even for the living God."* [SIX 8s.

AS, panting in the sultry beam,
   The hart desires the cooling stream,
So to thy presence, Lord, I flee,
So longs my soul, O God, for thee;
Athirst to taste thy living grace,
And see thy glory face to face.

2 But rising griefs distress my soul,
  And tears on tears successive roll;
  For many an evil voice is near
  To chide my woe and mock my fear;
  And silent memory weeps alone
  O'er hours of peace and gladness flown.

3 For I have walk'd the happy round
  That 'circles Sion's holy ground,
  And glădly swell'd the choral lays
  That hymn'd my great Redeemer's praise,
  What time the hallow'd arches rung
  Responsive to the solemn song.

4 Ah, why, by passing clouds opprest,
  Should vexing thoughts distract thy breast?
  Turn, turn to him, in every pain,
  Whom suppliants never sought in vain;
  Thy strength, in joy's ecstatic day,
  Thy hope, when joy has pass'd away.

453 *"Let not your heart be troubled: in my Father's house are many mansions: I go to prepare a place for you."* [C. M.

WHEN I can read my title clear
    To mansions in the skies,
  I bid farewell to every fear,
    And wipe my weeping eyes.

2 Should earth against my soul engage,
    And fiery darts be hurl'd,
  Then I can smile at Satan's rage,
    And face a frowning world.

3 Let cares like a wild deluge come,
   And storms of sorrow fall,
May I but safely reach my home,
   My God, my heaven, my all.

4 There shall I bathe my weary soul
   In seas of heavenly rest,
And not a wave of trouble roll
   Across my peaceful breast.

LOVE.

454   "*My song shall be alway of the loving-kindness of the Lord.*"   [8s. 7s. Double.]

LORD, with glowing heart I'd praise thee
   For the bliss thy love bestows,
For the pardoning grace that saves me,
   And the peace that from it flows:
Help, O God, my weak endeavour;
   This dull soul to rapture raise:
Thou must light the flame, or never
   Can my love be warm'd to praise.

2 Praise, my soul, the God that sought thee,
   Wretched wanderer, far astray;
Found thee lost, and kindly brought thee
   From the paths of death away;
Praise, with love's devoutest feeling,
   Him who saw thy guilt-born fear,
And, the light of hope revealing,
   Bade the blood-stain'd cross appear.

3 Lord, this bosom's ardent feeling
    Vainly would my lips express:
Low before thy footstool kneeling,
    Deign thy suppliant's prayer to bless:
Let thy grace, my soul's chief treasure,
    Love's pure flame within me raise;
And, since words can never measure,
    Let my life show forth thy praise.

455 *"That Christ may dwell in your hearts by faith."* [C. M.

JESUS, the very thought of thee
    With sweetness fills the breast;
But sweeter far thy face to see,
    And in thy presence rest.

2 No voice can sing, no heart can frame,
    Nor can the memory find,
A sweeter sound than Jesus' name,
    The Saviour of mankind.

3 O hope of every contrite heart,
    O joy of all the meek,
To those who fall, how kind thou art!
    How good to those who seek!

4 But what to those who find? Ah! this
    Nor tongue nor pen can show;
The love of Jesus, what it is
    None but his loved ones know.

5 Jesus, our only joy be thou,
    As thou our prize wilt be;
In thee be all our glory now,
    And through eternity.

456   *"The love of God which is in Christ Jesus our Lord."*   [8s. 7s. Double.

LOVE divine, all love excelling,
   Joy of heaven, to earth come down!
Fix in us thy humble dwelling,
   All thy faithful mercies crown.
Jesus, thou art all compassion,
   Pure, unbounded love thou art;
Visit us with thy salvation,
   Enter every trembling heart.

2 Breathe, O breathe thy loving Spirit
   Into every troubled breast!
Let us all in thee inherit,
   Let us find thy promised rest;
Take away the love of sinning,
   Alpha and Omega be,—
End of faith, as its beginning,
   Set our hearts at liberty.

3 Come, Almighty to deliver,
   Let us all thy grace receive;
Suddenly return, and never,
   Never more thy temples leave.
Thee we would be always blessing;
   Serve thee as thy hosts above;
Pray, and praise thee without ceasing;
   Glory in thy perfect love.

4 Finish then thy new creation,
   Pure and spotless let us be:
Let us see thy great salvation,
   Perfectly restored in thee.

THE CHRISTIAN LIFE.

Changed from glory into glory,
    Till in heaven we take our place:
Till we cast our crowns before thee,
    Lost in wonder, love, and praise.

457   *"I will love thee, O Lord my strength."*   [P. M.

I LOVE my God, but with no love of mine,
    For I have none to give;
I love thee, Lord, but all the love is thine,
    For by thy life I live;
I am as nothing, and rejoice to be
Emptied, and lost, and swallow'd up in thee.

2 Thou, Lord, alone art all thy children need,
    And there is none beside;
From thee the streams of blessedness proceed,
    In thee the blest abide:
Fountain of life and all-abounding grace,
Our source, our centre, and our dwelling-place.

458   *"Lovest thou me?"*   [C. M.

MY God, I love thee—not because
    I hope for heaven thereby:
Nor yet because if I love not
    I must for ever die.

2 But, O my Jesus, thou didst me
    Upon the cross embrace;
For me didst bear the nails and spear,
    And manifold disgrace,

3 And griefs and torments numberless,
    And sweat of agony,
E'en death itself; and all for me
    Who was thine enemy.

4 Then why, O blessed Jesus Christ,
    Should I not love thee well?
Not for the hope of winning heaven,
    Nor of escaping hell;

5 Not with the hope of gaining aught;
    Not seeking a reward;
But as thyself hast lovèd me,
    O ever-loving Lord!

6 E'en so I love thee, and will love,
    And in thy praise will sing;
Solely because thou art my God,
    And my eternal King.

459   *"My soul followeth hard after thee."*   [L. M.

THOU, whom my soul admires above
    All earthly joy and earthly love,
Tell me, dear Shepherd, let me know,
Where do thy sweetest pastures grow?

2 Where is the shadow of that rock
That from the sun defends thy flock?
Fain would I feed among thy sheep,
Among them rest, among them sleep.

3 Why should thy bride appear like one
That turns aside to paths unknown?
My constant feet would never rove,
Would never seek another love.

460 *"Thus saith the high and lofty One that inhab-* [C. M.
*iteth eternity, whose name is Holy: I dwell
in the high and holy place, with him also
that is of a contrite and humble spirit."*

MY God, how wonderful thou art,
    Thy majesty how bright,
How beautiful thy mercy-seat,
    In depths of burning light!

2 How dread are thine eternal years,
    O everlasting Lord;
By prostrate spirits day and night
    Incessantly adored!

3 How wonderful, how beautiful,
    The sight of thee must be,
Thine endless wisdom, boundless power,
    And awful purity!

4 O how I fear thee, living God,
    With deepest, tenderest fears,
And worship thee with trembling hope,
    And penitential tears!

5 Yet I may love thee too, O Lord,
    Almighty as thou art,
For thou hast stooped to ask of me
    The love of my poor heart.

461   *"I will love thee, O Lord my strength."*   [Six 8s.

THEE will I love, my strength, my tower,
    Thee will I love, my joy, my crown;
Thee will I love with all my power,
    In all my works, and thee alone:
Thee will I love, till sacred fire
Fill my whole soul with pure desire.

2 I thank thee, uncreated Sun,
    That thy bright beams on me have shined:
I thank thee, who hast overthrown
    My foes, and healed my wounded mind;
I thank thee, whose enlivening voice
Bids my freed heart in thee rejoice.

3 Uphold me in the doubtful race,
    Nor suffer me again to stray;
Strengthen my feet, with steady pace
    Still to press forward in thy way;
That all my powers, with all their might,
In thy sole glory may unite.

4 Thee will I love, my joy, my crown;
    Thee will I love, my Lord, my God!
Thee will I love, beneath thy frown
    Or smile, thy sceptre or thy rod;
What though my flesh and heart decay?
Thee shall I love in endless day.

JOY.

162 *"Serve the Lord with gladness: come before his presence with thanksgiving."* [S. M.

COME, ye that love the Lord,
    And let your joys be known;
Join in a song with sweet accord,
    And thus surround the throne.

2 Let those refuse to sing
    That never knew our God,
But children of the heavenly King
    May speak their joys abroad.

3 The God of heaven is ours,
    Our Father and our love;
His care shall guard life's fleeting hours,
    Then waft our souls above.

4 There shall we see his face,
    And never, never sin;
There, from the rivers of his grace,
    Drink endless pleasures in.

5 Yes, and before we rise
    To that immortal state,
The thoughts of such amazing bliss
    Should constant joys create.

6 Children of grace have found
    Glory begun below:
Celestial fruits on earthly ground
    From faith and hope may grow.

7 The hill of Sion yields
    A thousand sacred sweets,
Before we reach the heavenly fields,
    Or walk the golden streets.

8 Then let our songs abound,
    And every tear be dry;
We're trav'ling through Immanuel's ground,
    To fairer worlds on high.

463   *"They sing the song of Moses the servant of God,*   [S. M.
      and the song of the Lamb."

AWAKE, and sing the song
    Of Moses and the Lamb;
Wake every heart and every tongue,
    To praise the Saviour's name.

2 Sing of his dying love;
    Sing of his rising power;
Sing how he intercedes above
    For those whose sins he bore.

3 Sing on your heavenly way,
    Ye ransom'd sinners, sing;
Sing on, rejoicing every day
    In Christ the eternal King.

4 Soon shall ye hear him say,
    "Ye blessèd children, come!"
Soon will he call you hence away,
    And take his wanderers home.

464   *"The Lord is my Shepherd."*   [P. M.

THE King of love my Shepherd is,
    Whose goodness faileth never;
I nothing lack if I am his,
    And he is mine for ever.

2 Where streams of living water flow
  My ransom'd soul he leadeth,
And, where the verdant pastures grow,
  With food celestial feedeth.

3 Perverse and foolish, oft I stray'd,
  But yet in love he sought me,
And on his shoulder gently laid,
  And home, rejoicing, brought me.

4 In death's dark vale I fear no ill
  With thee, dear Lord, beside me;
Thy rod and staff my comfort still,
  Thy cross before to guide me.

5 Thou spreadst a table in my sight,
  Thy unction grace bestoweth,
And O the transport of delight
  With which my cup o'erfloweth!

6 And so, through all the length of days,
  Thy goodness faileth never;
Good Shepherd, may I sing thy praise
  Within thy house for ever!

HUMILITY.

465 *"My peace I give unto you."* [SIX 7s.

QUIET, Lord, my froward heart;
  Make me teachable and mild,
Upright, simple, free from art;
  Make me as a little child;
From distrust and envy free,
Pleased with all that pleases thee.

2 What thou shalt to-day provide,
   Let me as a child receive;
What to-morrow may betide,
   Calmly to thy wisdom leave;
'Tis enough that thou wilt care;
Why should I the burden bear?

3 As a little child relies
   On a care beyond his own,
Knows he's neither strong nor wise,
   Fears to stir a step alone,
Let me thus with thee abide,
As my Father, Guard, and Guide.

466 *"Father, I will that they whom thou hast given me* [7s.
    be with me where I am."

From the cxxxi. Psalm.

LORD, for ever at thy side
   Let my place and portion be:
Strip me of the robe of pride,
   Clothe me with humility.

2 Meekly may my soul receive
   All thy Spirit hath reveal'd;
Thou hast spoken—I believe,
   Though the oracle be seal'd.

3 Humble as a little child,
   Weanèd from the mother's breast,
But no subtleties beguiled,
   On thy faithful word I rest.

    4 Israel! now and evermore
        In the Lord Jehovah trust;
    Him, in all his ways, adore,
        Wise, and wonderful, and just.

PEACE.

467   *"A new heart will I give you, and a new spirit*   [C. M.
        will I put within you."

O FOR a heart to praise my God,
    A heart from sin set free!
A heart that's sprinkled with the blood
    So freely shed for me;

2 A heart resigned, submissive, meek,
    My dear Redeemer's throne;
Where only Christ is heard to speak,
    Where Jesus reigns alone;

3 An humble, lowly, contrite heart,
    Believing, true, and clean;
Which neither life nor death can part
    From him that dwells within.

4 A heart in every thought renewed,
    And full of love divine,
Perfect, and right, and pure, and good—
    A copy, Lord, of thine!

5 Thy nature, gracious Lord, impart;
    Come quickly from above;
Write thy new name upon my heart,
    Thy new, best name of Love.

468 *"They desire a better country, that is, an heavenly."* [C. M.

THERE is a fold whence none can stray,
   And pastures ever green,
Where sultry sun, or stormy day,
   Or night, is never seen.

2 Far up the everlasting hills,
   In God's own light, it lies;
His smile its vast dimension fills
   With joy that never dies.

3 One narrow vale, one darksome wave,
   Divides that land from this;
I have a Shepherd pledged to save,
   And bear me home to bliss.

4 Soon at his feet my soul will lie,
   In life's last struggling breath;
But I shall only seem to die,
   I shall not taste of death.

5 Far from this guilty world, to be
   Exempt from toil and strife;
To spend eternity with thee,—
   My Saviour, this is life!

COURAGE.

469 *"He shall give his angels charge over thee."* [8s. 7s.
From the xci. Psalm.

GOD shall charge his angel legions
   Watch and ward o'er thee to keep;
Though thou walk through hostile regions,
   Though in desert wilds thou sleep.

2 On the lion vainly roaring,
    On his young, thy foot shall tread;
  And, the dragon's den exploring,
    Thou shalt bruise the serpent's head.

3 Since, with pure and firm affection,
    Thou on God hast set thy love,
  With the wings of his protection
    He will shield thee from above.

4 Thou shalt call on him in trouble,
    He will hearken, he will save;
  Here for grief reward thee double,
    Crown with life beyond the grave.

470 *"Be strong in the Lord, and in the power of his might."* [S. M

My soul, be on thy guard;
  Ten thousand foes arise;
The hosts of sin are pressing hard
  To draw thee from the skies.

2 O watch, and fight, and pray;
    The battle ne'er give o'er;
  Renew it boldly every day,
    And help divine implore.

3 Ne'er think the victory won,
    Nor lay thine armour down:
  Thy arduous work will not be done
    Till thou obtain thy crown.

4 Fight on, my soul, till death
　　Shall bring thee to thy God;
　He'll take thee at thy parting breath,
　　Up to his blest abode.

471　　　"*Fight the good fight.*"　　　[C. M

AM I a soldier of the cross,
　　A follower of the Lamb?
　And shall I fear to own his cause,
　　Or blush to speak his name?

2 Must I be carried to the skies
　　On flowery beds of ease,
　While others fought to win the prize,
　　And sailed through bloody seas?

3 Are there no foes for me to face?
　　Must I not stem the flood?
　Is this vile world a friend to grace,
　　To help me on to God?

4 Sure I must fight if I would reign;
　　Increase my courage, Lord;
　I'll bear the cross, endure the pain,
　　Supported by thy word.

5 Thy saints, in all this glorious war,
　　Shall conquer, though they die;
　They view the triumph from afar,
　　And seize it with their eye.

6 When that illustrious day shall rise,
　　And all thy armies shine
　In robes of victory through the skies,
　　The glory shall be thine.

472 *"Be of good cheer: it is I: be not afraid."* [P. M.

BREAST the wave, Christian,
   When it is strongest;
Watch for day, Christian,
   When the night's longest;
Onward and onward still
   Be thine endeavour;
The rest that remaineth
   Will be for ever.

2 Fight the fight, Christian,
   Jesus is o'er thee;
Run the race, Christian,
   Heaven is before thee;
He who hath promisèd
   Faltereth never;
He who hath loved so well,
   Loveth for ever.

3 Lift thine eye, Christian,
   Just as it closeth;
Raise thy heart, Christian,
   Ere it reposeth;
Thee from the love of Christ
   Nothing shall sever;
And, when thy work is done,
   Praise him for ever.

473 *"Let us run with patience the race that is set before us."* [L. M.

AWAKE, our souls! away our fears,
   Let every trembling thought be gone;
Awake, and run the heavenly race,
   And put a cheerful courage on.

2 True, 'tis a straight and thorny road,
  And mortal spirits tire and faint;
  But they forget the mighty God,
  Who feeds the strength of every saint.

3 The mighty God, whose matchless power
  Is ever new, and ever young;
  And firm endures, while endless years
  Their everlasting circles run.

4 From thee, the overflowing spring,
  Our souls shall drink a full supply;
  While such as trust their native strength,
  Shall melt away, and droop, and die.

5 Swift as an eagle cuts the air,
  We'll mount aloft to thine abode;
  On wings of love our souls shall fly,
  Nor tire amidst the heavenly road.

ACTION.

474 *"Let us labour to enter into that rest."* [S. M.

A CHARGE to keep I have,
  A God to glorify;
A never-dying soul to save,
  And fit it for the sky:

2 From youth to hoary age,
  My calling to fulfil:
  O may it all my powers engage
  To do my Master's will.

3 Arm me with jealous care,
  As in thy sight to live,
And O thy servant, Lord, prepare
  A strict account to give.

4 Help me to watch and pray,
  And on thyself rely:
Assured if I my trust betray,
  I shall for ever die.

475 *"They that wait upon the Lord shall renew their strength."* [C. M.

SUPREME in wisdom as in power,
  The Rock of Ages stands;
Thou canst not search his mind, nor trace
  The working of his hands.

2 He gives the conquest to the weak,
  Supports the fainting heart;
And courage in the evil hour
  His heavenly aids impart.

3 Mere human energy shall faint,
  And youthful vigour cease;
But those who wait upon the Lord,
  In strength shall still increase.

4 They, with unwearied step, shall tread
  The path of life divine;
With growing ardour onward move,
  With growing brightness shine.

5 On eagles' wings they mount, they soar
    On wings of faith and love;
  Till, past the sphere of earth and sin,
    They rise to heaven above.

476 *"I press toward the mark for the prize of the*   [C. M
       high calling of God."

AWAKE, my soul, stretch every nerve,
  And press with vigour on;
A heavenly race demands thy zeal,
  And an immortal crown.

2 A cloud of witnesses around
    Hold thee in full survey;
  Forget the steps already trod,
    And onward urge thy way.

3 'Tis God's all-animating voice
    That calls thee from on high,
  'Tis his own hand presents the prize
    To thine uplifted eye.

4 Then wake, my soul, stretch every nerve,
    And press with vigour on;
  A heavenly race demands thy zeal,
    And an immortal crown.

477 *" Speak unto the children of Israel, that they*   [7s.
             go forward."

OFT in danger, oft in woe,
  Onward, Christians, onward go:
Fight the fight, maintain the strife,
Strengthen'd with the bread of life.

2 Onward, Christians, onward go,
　Join the war, and face the foe:
　Will ye flee in danger's hour?
　Know ye not your Captain's power?

3 Let your drooping hearts be glad:
　March in heavenly armour clad:
　Fight, nor think the battle long,
　Victory soon shall tune your song.

4 Let not sorrow dim your eye,
　Soon shall every tear be dry;
　Let not fears your course impede,
　Great your strength, if great your need.

5 Onward then in battle move,
　More than conquerors ye shall prove;
　Though opposed by many a foe,
　Christian soldiers, onward go.

478 *"These confessed that they were strangers and pilgrims on the earth."* [F. M.

SINCE I've known a Saviour's name,
　And sin's strong fetters broke,
Careful without care I am,
　Nor feel my easy yoke:
Joyful now my faith to show,
　I find his service my reward,
All the work I do below
　Is light, for such a Lord.

2 To the desert or the cell
　Let others blindly fly,

ACTION.

    In this evil world I dwell,
        Nor fear its enmity;
    Here I find a house of prayer,
        To which I inwardly retire;
    Walking unconcerned in care,
        And unconsumed in fire.

3 O that all the world might know
       Of living, Lord, to thee,
   Find their heaven begun below,
       And here thy goodness see;
   Walk in all the works prepared
       By thee to exercise their grace,
   Till they gain their full reward,
       And see thee face to face!

479   *"Work out your own salvation with fear and*   [S. M.
        trembling."

HEIRS of unending life,
    While yet we sojourn here,
O let us our salvation work
    With trembling and with fear.

2 God will support our hearts
    With might before unknown;
The work to be performed is ours,
    The strength is all his own.

3 'Tis he that works to will,
    'Tis he that works to do;
His is the power by which we act,
    His be the glory too!

XI. THE JUDGMENT.

480   *"He hath covered me with the robe of righteousness."*   [L. M.

JESUS, thy blood and righteousness
My beauty are, my glorious dress,
'Midst flaming worlds, in these array'd,
With joy shall I lift up my head.

2 Bold shall I stand in thy great day,
For who aught to my charge shall lay?
Fully absolved through these I am,
From sin and fear, from guilt and shame.

3 When from the dust of death I rise
To claim my mansion in the skies,
E'en then this shall be all my plea—
Jesus hath lived, hath died for me.

4 Thou God of power, thou God of love,
Let the whole world thy mercy prove;
Now let thy word o'er all prevail;
Now take the spoils of death and hell.

481   *"All that are in the graves shall hear his voice, and shall come forth."*   [8s. 7s. 4.

DAY of judgment, day of wonders!
Hark! the trumpet's awful sound,

Louder than a thousand thunders,
  Shakes the vast creation round!
    How the summons
  Will the sinner's heart confound!

2 See the Judge our nature wearing,
  Clothed in majesty divine!
You who long for his appearing,
  Then shall say, This God is mine:
    Gracious Saviour,
  Own me in that day for thine!

3 At his call the dead awaken,
  Rise to life from earth and sea:
All the powers of nature, shaken
  By his looks, prepare to flee:
    Careless sinner!
  What will then become of thee?

4 But to those who have confessèd,
  Loved, and served the Lord below,
He will say, Come near, ye blessèd,
  Take the kingdom I bestow:
    You for ever
  Shall my love and glory know.

---

482   *"Yet once more I shake not the earth only, but also heaven."*   [S. M.

HOW will my heart endure
  The terrors of that day,
When earth and heaven before his face
  Astonish'd shrink away?

2 But ere the trumpet shakes
   The mansions of the dead,
Hark! from the Gospel's cheering sound
   What joyful tidings spread.

3 Ye sinners, seek his grace,
   Whose wrath ye cannot bear;
Fly to the shelter of his cross,
   And find salvation there.

4 So shall that curse remove,
   By which the Saviour bled;
And the last awful day shall pour
   His blessings on your head.

483 *"The Lord grant him that he may find mercy* [P. M.
     of the Lord in that day."

DAY of wrath! that day of mourning!
   See fulfill'd the prophets' warning,
Heaven and earth in ashes burning!

2 O what fear man's bosom rendeth,
   When from heaven the Judge descendeth,
On whose sentence all dependeth!

3 Lo! the trumpet's wondrous swelling
   Peals through each sepulchral dwelling,
All before the throne compelling.

4 Death is struck, and nature quaking,
   All creation is awaking,
To its Judge an answer making.

5 Lo! the book exactly worded,
Wherein all hath been recorded:
Thence shall justice be awarded.

6 When the Judge his seat attaineth,
And each hidden deed arraigneth,
Nothing unavenged remaineth.

7 When shall I, frail man, be pleading?
Who for me be interceding,
When the just are mercy needing?

8 King of Majesty tremendous,
Who dost free salvation send us,
Fount of pity! then befriend us!

9 Think, kind Jesus, my salvation
Cost thy wondrous incarnation;
Leave me not to reprobation!

10 Faint and weary thou hast sought me,
On the cross of suffering bought me.
Shall such grace in vain be brought me?

11 Righteous Judge! for sin's pollution
Grant thy gift of absolution,
Ere that day of retribution.

12 Guilty, now I pour my moaning,
All my shame with anguish owning;
Spare, O God, thy suppliant groaning!

13 Thou the harlot gav'st remission,
Heard'st the dying thief's petition;
Hopeless else were my condition.

14 Worthless are my prayers and sighing,
  Yet, good Lord, in grace complying,
  Rescue me from fires undying!

15 With thy favoured sheep O place me!
  Nor among the goats abase me;
  But to thy right hand upraise me.

16 While the wicked are confounded,
  Doomed to flames of woe unbounded,
  Call me, with thy saints surrounded.

17 Bow my heart in meek submission,
  Strewn with ashes of contrition;
  Help me in my lost condition.

18 Day of sorrows, day of weeping,
  When, in dust no longer sleeping,
  Man awakes in thy dread keeping!

19 To the rest thou didst prepare him
  By thy Cross, O Christ, upbear him
  Spare, O God, in mercy spare him.

484 *"The time of the dead is come, that they should be judged."* [8s. 7s. 8s

GREAT God, what do I see and hear!
  The end of things created!
The Judge of mankind doth appear
  On clouds of glory seated!
The trumpet sounds; the graves restore
The dead which they contained before;
  Prepare, my soul, to meet him!

2 The dead in Christ shall first arise
   At the last trumpet's sounding,
Caught up to meet him in the skies,
   With joy their Lord surrounding:
No gloomy fears their souls dismay,
His presence sheds eternal day
   On those prepared to meet him.

3 But sinners, fill'd with guilty fears,
   Behold his wrath prevailing;
For they shall rise, and find their tears
   And sighs are unavailing:
The day of grace is past and gone;
Trembling, they stand before the throne,
   All unprepared to meet him.

4 Great God, what do I see and hear!
   The end of things created!
The Judge of mankind doth appear,
   On clouds of glory seated:
Low at his cross I view the day
When heaven and earth shall pass away,
   And thus prepare to meet him.

XII. HEAVEN.

485   *"The night is far spent, the day is at hand."*   [P. M.

HARK! hark, my soul! Angelic songs are swelling
   O'er earth's green fields and ocean's wave-beat shore:

How sweet the truth those blessèd strains are telling
Of that new life when sin shall be no more!
>Angels of Jesus,
>>Angels of light,
>Singing to welcome
>>The pilgrims of the night.

2 Onward we go, for still we hear them singing,
"Come, weary souls, for Jesus bids you come;"
And through the dark, its echoes sweetly ringing,
The music of the Gospel leads us home.
>Angels of Jesus,
>>Angels of light,
>Singing to welcome
>>The pilgrims of the night.

3 Far, far away, like bells at evening pealing,
The voice of Jesus sounds o'er land and sea,
And laden souls by thousands meekly stealing,
Kind Shepherd, turn their weary steps to thee.
>Angels of Jesus,
>>Angels of light,
>Singing to welcome
>>The pilgrims of the night.

4 Rest comes at length, though life be long and dreary,
The day must dawn, and darksome night be past;
All journeys end in welcome to the weary,
And heaven, the heart's true home, will come at last.
>Angels of Jesus,
>>Angels of light,
>Singing to welcome
>>The pilgrims of the night.

5 Angels, sing on! your faithful watches keeping;
  Sing us sweet fragments of the songs above;
  Till morning's joy shall end the night of weeping,
  And life's long shadows break in cloudless love.
        Angels of Jesus,
          Angels of light,
          Singing to welcome
            The pilgrims of the night.

486   *"Leaving us an example that ye should follow*   [C. M.
              his steps."

CHRIST leads me through no darker rooms
   Than he went through before;
And he that in God's kingdom comes
   Must enter by this door.

2 Come, Lord, when grace hath made me meet
     Thy blessèd face to see;
   For if thy work on earth be sweet,
     What must thy glory be!

3 Then I shall end my sad complaints,
     And weary, sinful days,
   And join with the triumphant saints
     To sing Jehovah's praise!

4 My knowledge of that life is small;
     The eye of faith is dim;
   But 'tis enough that Christ knows all,
     And I shall be with him!

487 *"While we look not at the things which are seen,* [C. M.
but at the things which are not seen."

HOW long shall earth's alluring toys
  Detain our hearts and eyes,
Regardless of immortal joys,
  And strangers to the skies?

2 These transient scenes will soon decay,
  They fade upon the sight;
And quickly will their brightest day
  Be lost in endless night.

3 Their brightest day, alas! how vain!
  With conscious sighs we own;
While clouds of sorrow, care, and pain
  O'ershade the smiling noon.

4 O, could our thoughts and wishes fly
  Above these gloomy shades,
To those bright worlds beyond the sky,
  Which sorrow ne'er invades!

5 There, joys unseen by mortal eyes,
  Or reason's feeble ray,
In ever-blooming prospects rise,
  Unconscious of decay.

6 Lord, send a beam of light divine
  To guide our upward aim:
With one reviving touch of thine
  Our languid hearts inflame.

7 Then shall, on faith's sublimest wing,
  Our ardent wishes rise,
To those bright scenes where pleasures spring
  Immortal in the skies.

488 "*They desire a better country, that is, an heavenly.*" [C. M.

THERE is a land of pure delight,
　　Where saints immortal reign;
Eternal day excludes the night,
　　And pleasures banish pain.

2 There everlasting spring abides,
　　And never-fading flowers;
Death, like a narrow sea, divides
　　This heavenly land from ours.

3 Bright fields beyond the swelling flood
　　Stand dress'd in living green;
So to the Jews fair Canaan stood,
　　While Jordan roll'd between.

4 But timorous mortals start and shrink
　　To cross the narrow sea;
And linger, trembling on the brink,
　　And fear to launch away.

5 O could we make our doubts remove,
　　Those gloomy doubts that rise,
And see the Canaan that we love,
　　With faith's illumin'd eyes;

6 Could we but climb where Moses stood,
　　And view the landscape o'er,
Not Jordan's stream, nor death's cold flood,
　　Should fright us from the shore.

489   *"And so shall we ever be with the Lord."*   [S. M.

FOR ever with the Lord!
   Amen, so let it be!
Life from the dead is in that word;
   'Tis immortality.

2 Here in the body pent,
   Absent from him I roam,
Yet nightly pitch my moving tent
   A day's march nearer home.

3 My Father's house on high,
   Home of my soul, how near
At times to faith's far-seeing eye
   Thy golden gates appear!

4 Ah, then my spirit faints
   To reach the land I love,
The bright inheritance of saints,
   Jerusalem above.

5 Yet clouds will intervene,
   And all my prospect flies;
Like Noah's dove, I flit between
   Rough seas and stormy skies.

6 Anon the clouds depart,
   The winds and waters cease,
And sweetly o'er my gladdened heart
   Expands the bow of peace.

490   *"Work your work betimes, and in his time he*   [7s. 6s
          will give you your reward."   Double

THE world is very evil,
    The times are waxing late,
Be sober and keep vigil,
    The Judge is at the gate;
The Judge who comes in mercy,
    The Judge who comes with might,
Who comes to end the evil,
    Who comes to crown the right.

2 Arise, arise, good Christian,
    Let right to wrong succeed;
Let penitential sorrow
    To heavenly gladness lead,
To light that has no evening,
    That knows nor moon nor sun,
The light so new and golden,
    The light that is but one.

3 O Home of fadeless splendour,
    Of flowers that fear no thorn,
Where they shall dwell as children
    Who here as exiles mourn;
'Midst power that knows no limit,
    Where wisdom has no bound,
The beatific vision
    Shall glad the saints around.

4 O happy, holy portion,
    Refection for the blest,
True vision of true beauty,
    True cure of the distrest:

Strive, man, to win that glory;
　Toil, man, to gain that light;
Send hope before to grasp it,
　Till hope be lost in sight.

5 O sweet and blessèd country,
　The home of God's elect!
O sweet and blessèd country
　That eager hearts expect!
Jesus, in mercy bring us
　To that dear land of rest;
Who art, with God the Father,
　And Spirit, ever blest.

491 *"Here have we no continuing city, but we seek one to come."* [7s. 6s. Double.

BRIEF life is here our portion,
　Brief sorrow, short-lived care;
The life that knows no ending,
　The tearless life is there.
O happy retribution!
　Short toil, eternal rest;
For mortals and for sinners
　A mansion with the blest.

2 And now we fight the battle,
　But then shall wear the crown
Of full and everlasting
　And passionless renown.
But he whom now we trust in
　Shall then be seen and known;
And they that know and see him
　Shall have him for their own.

3 The morning shall awaken,
   The shadows shall decay,
And each true-hearted servant
   Shall shine as doth the day.
There God, our King and Portion,
   In fulness of his grace,
Shall we behold for ever,
   And worship face to face.

4 O sweet and blessèd country,
   The home of God's elect!
O sweet and blessèd country,
   That eager hearts expect!
Jesus, in mercy bring us
   To that dear land of rest;
Who art, with God the Father,
   And Spirit, ever blest.

492 *"He that overcometh shall inherit all things."* [7s. 6s. Double.

FOR thee, O dear, dear country,
   Mine eyes their vigils keep;
For very love, beholding
   Thy happy name, they weep.
The mention of thy glory
   Is unction to the breast,
And medicine in sickness,
   And love, and life, and rest.

2 O one, O only mansion;
   O Paradise of joy!
Where tears are ever banished,
   And smiles have no alloy;

The Lamb is all thy splendour,
   The Crucified thy praise;
His laud and benediction
   Thy ransomed people raise.

3 With jasper glow thy bulwarks,
   Thy streets with emeralds blaze;
The sardius and the topaz
   Unite in thee their rays;
Thine ageless walls are bonded
   With amethyst unpriced;
The saints build up its fabric,
   And the corner-stone is Christ.

4 Thou hast no shore, fair ocean!
   Thou hast no time, bright day!
Dear fountain of refreshment
   To pilgrims far away!
Upon the Rock of Ages
   They raise thy holy tower;
Thine is the victor's laurel,
   And thine the golden dower.

5 O sweet and blessèd country,
   The home of God's elect!
O sweet and blessèd country,
   That eager hearts expect!
Jesus, in mercy bring us
   To that dear land of rest;
Who art, with God the Father,
   And Spirit, ever blest.

493 *"And he shewed me that great city, the holy Jerusalem, descending out of heaven from God, having the glory of God."* [7s. 6s. Double

JERUSALEM, the golden!
  With milk and honey blest;
Beneath thy contemplation
  Sink heart and voice opprest.
I know not, O I know not
  What joys await us there;
What radiancy of glory,
  What bliss beyond compare.

2 They stand, those halls of Zion,
  All jubilant with song,
And bright with many an angel,
  And all the martyr throng.
The Prince is ever in them,
  The daylight is serene;
The pastures of the blessèd
  Are decked in glorious sheen.

3 There is the throne of David;
  And there, from care released,
The shout of them that triumph,
  The song of them that feast.
And they, who with their Leader,
  Have conquered in the fight,
For ever and for ever
  Are clad in robes of white.

4 O sweet and blessèd country,
  The home of God's elect!
O sweet and blessèd country,
  That eager hearts expect!

Jesus, in mercy bring us
  To that dear land of rest;
Who art, with God the Father,
  And Spirit, ever blest.

494 *"What are these, which are arrayed in white robes."* [7s. DOUBLE

WHO are these in bright array,
  This innumerable throng,
Round the altar, night and day,
  Tuning their triumphant song?—
"Worthy is the Lamb, once slain,
  Blessing, honour, glory, power,
Wisdom, riches, to obtain,
  New dominion every hour."

2 These through fiery trials trod;
  These from great affliction came;
Now before the throne of God,
  Seal'd with his eternal name:
Clad in raiment pure and white,
  Victor-palms in every hand,
Through their great Redeemer's might,
  More than conquerors they stand.

3 Hunger, thirst, disease unknown,
  On immortal fruits they feed;
Them the Lamb amidst the throne,
  Shall to living fountains lead:
Joy and gladness banish sighs;
  Perfect love dispels their fears;
And for ever from their eyes,
  God shall wipe away their tears,

495 *"And the city had no need of the sun, neither of the moon to shine in it: for the glory of the Lord did lighten it, and the Lamb is the light thereof."* [C. M.

O MOTHER dear, Jerusalem!
   When shall I come to thee?
When shall my sorrows have an end?
   Thy joys when shall I see?

2 O happy harbour of God's saints!
   O sweet and pleasant soil!
In thee no sorrow can be found,
   Nor grief, nor care, nor toil.

3 No murky cloud o'ershadows thee,
   Nor gloom, nor darksome night;
But every soul shines as the sun;
   For God himself gives light.

4 O my sweet home, Jerusalem!
   Thy joys when shall I see?
The King that sitteth on thy throne
   In his felicity?

5 Thy gardens and thy goodly walks
   Continually are green,
Where grow such sweet and pleasant flowers
   As nowhere else are seen.

6 Right through thy streets, with pleasing sound,
   The living waters flow,
And on the banks, on either side,
   The trees of life do grow.

7 Those trees each month yield ripen'd fruit;
   For ever more they spring,
And all the nations of the earth
   To thee their honours bring.

8 O mother dear, Jerusalem!
   When shall I come to thee?
When shall my sorrows have an end?
   Thy joys when shall I see?

496   *"That great city, the holy Jerusalem."*   [C. M.

JERUSALEM, my happy home,
   Name ever dear to me,
When shall my labours have an end
   In joy, and peace, and thee?

2 When shall these eyes thy heaven-built walls
   And pearly gates behold?
Thy bulwarks, with salvation strong,
   And streets of shining gold?

3 There happier bowers than Eden's bloom,
   Nor sin nor sorrow know:
Blest seats! through rude and stormy scenes
   I onward press to you.

4 Why should I shrink from pain and woe,
   Or feel at death dismay?
I've Canaan's goodly land in view,
   And realms of endless day.

5 Apostles, martyrs, prophets, there
   Around my Saviour stand:
And soon my friends in Christ below
   Will join the glorious band.

6 Jerusalem, my happy home,
   My soul still pants for thee;
Then shall my labours have an end,
   When I thy joys shall see.

497 *"Eye hath not seen, nor ear heard, neither have* [P. M.
*entered into the heart of man the things which
God hath prepared for them that love him."*

JERUSALEM! high tower thy glorious walls,
   Would God I were in thee!
Desire of thee my longing heart enthrals,
   Desire at home to be:
Wide from the world outleaping,
   O'er hill and vale and plain,
My soul's strong wing is sweeping,
   Thy portals to attain.

2 O gladsome day, and yet more gladsome hour!
   When shall that hour have come,
When my rejoicing soul its own free power
   May use in going home?
Itself to Jesus giving,
   In trust to his own hand,
To dwell among the living,
   In that blest Fatherland.

3 A moment's time, the twinkling of an eye,
    Shall be enough to soar,
  In buoyant exultation, through the sky,
    And reach the heavenly shore.
  Elijah's chariot bringing
    The homeward traveller there;
  Glad troops of angels winging
    It onward through the air.

4 Great fastness thou of honour! thee I greet!
    Throw wide thy gracious gate,
  An entrance free to give these longing feet;
    At last released, though late,
  From wretchedness and sinning,
    And life's long, weary way;
  And now, of God's gift, winning
    Eternity's bright day.

5 What throng is this, what noble troop, that pours,
    Arrayed in beauteous guise,
  Out through the glorious city's open doors,
    To greet my wondering eyes?
  The hosts of Christ's elected,
    The jewels that he bears
  In his own crown, selected
    To wipe away my tears.

6 Of prophets great, and patriarchs high, a band
    That once has borne the cross,
  With all the company that won that land,
    By counting gain for loss,
  Now float in freedom's lightness,
    From tyrants' chains set free;
  And shine like suns in brightness,
    Arrayed to welcome me.

7 One more at last arrived they welcome there,
    To beauteous Paradise,
Where sense can scarce its full fruition bear,
    Or tongue for praise suffice;
Glad alleluias ringing
    With rapturous rebound,
And rich hosannas singing
    Eternity's long round.

8 Unnumber'd choirs before the Lamb's high throne
    There shout the jubilee,
With loud resounding peal and sweetest tone,
    In blissful ecstacy:
A hundred thousand voices
    Take up the wondrous song;
Eternity rejoices
    God's praises to prolong.

XIII. MISCELLANEOUS.

498 *"Thy mercy, O Lord, reacheth unto the heavens,* [L. M.
and thy faithfulness unto the clouds."

From the xxxvi. Psalm.

O LORD, thy mercy, my sure hope,
    The highest orb of heaven transcends;
Thy sacred truth's unmeasured scope
    Beyond the spreading sky extends.

2 Thy justice like the hills remains,
    Unfathom'd depths thy judgments are;
Thy providence the world sustains,
    The whole creation is thy care.

3 Since of thy goodness all partake,
    With what assurance should the just
Thy sheltering wings their refuge make,
    And saints to thy protection trust!

4 Such guests shall to thy courts be led,
    To banquet on thy love's repast;
And drink, as from a fountain's head,
    Of joys that shall for ever last.

5 With thee the springs of life remain,
    Thy presence is eternal day;
O let thy saints thy favour gain,
    To upright hearts thy truth display.

499   *"Praise the Lord, O my soul: and all that is*   [L. M.
      within me, praise his holy name."

    From the ciii. Psalm.

MY soul, inspired with sacred love,
    God's holy name for ever bless;
Of all his favours mindful prove,
    And still thy grateful thanks express.

2 'Tis he that all thy sins forgives,
    And after sickness makes thee sound;
From danger he thy life retrieves,
    By him with grace and mercy crown'd.

3 The Lord abounds with tender love
    And unexampled acts of grace;
  His waken'd wrath doth slowly move,
    His willing mercy flies apace.

4 God will not always harshly chide,
    But with his anger quickly part;
  And loves his punishment to guide
    More by his love than our desert.

5 As far as 'tis from east to west,
    So far has he our sins removed;
  Who, with a father's tender breast,
    Has such as fear him always loved.

500 *"He bowed the heavens, and came down, and it was dark under his feet."* [C. M

From the xviii. Psalm.

THE Lord descended from above,
    And bowed the heavens most high,
  And underneath his feet he cast
    The darkness of the sky.

2 On cherub and on cherubim,
    Full royally he rode,
  And on the wings of mighty winds,
    Came flying all abroad.

3 He sat serene upon the floods,
    Their fury to restrain;
  And he, as sovereign Lord and King,
    For evermore shall reign.

501 *"Jesus said unto him, I am the way, the truth, and the life."* [C. M.

THOU art the Way, to thee alone
  From sin and death we flee;
And he who would the Father seek,
  Must seek him, Lord, by thee.

2 Thou art the Truth, thy word alone
  True wisdom can impart;
Thou only canst inform the mind
  And purify the heart.

3 Thou art the Life, the rending tomb
  Proclaims thy conquering arm,
And those who put their trust in thee
  Nor death nor hell shall harm.

4 Thou art the Way, the Truth, the Life;
  Grant us that way to know,
That truth to keep, that life to win,
  Whose joys eternal flow.

502 *"Thy footsteps are not known."* [C. M.

GOD moves in a mysterious way
  His wonders to perform;
He plants his footsteps in the sea,
  And rides upon the storm.

2 Deep in unfathomable mines,
  With never-failing skill,
He treasures up his bright designs,
  And works his sovereign will.

3 Ye fearful saints, fresh courage take;
  The clouds ye so much dread
Are big with mercy, and shall break
  In blessings on your head.

4 Judge not the Lord by feeble sense,
  But trust him for his grace:
Behind a frowning providence
  He hides a smiling face.

5 His purposes will ripen fast,
  Unfolding every hour:
The bud may have a bitter taste,
  But sweet will be the flower.

6 Blind unbelief is sure to err,
  And scan his work in vain;
God is his own interpreter,
  And he will make it plain.

503   *"Blessed is the people, O Lord, that can rejoice*   [L. M.
          in thee."

From the lxxxix. Psalm.

HAPPY, thrice happy they, who hear
  Thy sacred trumpet's joyful sound;
Who may at festivals appear,
  With thy most glorious presence crown'd;

2 For in thy strength they shall advance,
    Whose conquests from thy favour spring:
  The Lord of hosts is our defence,
    And Israel's God our Israel's King.

504   *"The Lord is my Shepherd: therefore can I*   [Six 8s.
lack nothing."

THE Lord my pasture shall prepare,
And feed me with a shepherd's care;
His presence shall my wants supply,
And guard me with a watchful eye;
My noonday walks he shall attend,
And all my midnight hours defend.

2 When in the sultry glebe I faint,
Or on the thirsty mountain pant,
To fertile vales and dewy meads
My weary, wandering steps he leads,
Where peaceful rivers, soft and slow,
Amid the verdant landscape flow.

3 Though in the paths of death I tread,
With gloomy horrors overspread,
My steadfast heart shall fear no ill,
For thou, O Lord, art with me still;
Thy friendly crook shall give me aid,
And guide me through the dreadful shade.

505   *"These confessed that they were strangers and*   [8s. 7s. 4.
pilgrims on the earth."

GUIDE me, O thou great Jehovah,
Pilgrim through this barren land;
I am weak, but thou art mighty;
Hold me with thy powerful hand:
Bread of heaven,
Feed me now and evermore.

2 Open now the crystal fountain,
 Whence the healing streams do flow;
Let the fiery cloudy pillar
 Lead me all my journey through:
  Strong deliverer,
 Be thou still my strength and shield.

3 When I tread the verge of Jordan,
 Bid my anxious fears subside,
Death of death and hell's destruction,
 Land me safe on Canaan's side:
  Songs of praises
 I will ever give to thee.

506 *"The ark of the covenant went before them."* [8s. 7s. 4.

LEAD us, heavenly Father, lead us
 O'er the world's tempestuous sea;
Guard us, guide us, keep us, feed us,
 For we have no help but thee:
  Yet possessing
  Every blessing,
 If our God our Father be.

2 Saviour, breathe forgiveness o'er us;
 All our weakness thou dost know;
Thou didst tread this earth before us,
 Thou didst feel its keenest woe;
  Lone and dreary,
  Faint and weary,
 Through the desert thou didst go.

3 Spirit of our God, descending,
    Fill our hearts with heavenly joy;
Love with every passion blending,
    Pleasure that can never cloy:
        Thus provided,
        Pardon'd, guided,
Nothing can our peace destroy.

507   *"A people near unto him."*   [P. M

NEARER, my God, to thee,
    Nearer to thee,
E'en though it be a cross
    That raiseth me;
Still all my song shall be,
Nearer, my God, to thee,
    Nearer to thee!

2 Though like a wanderer,
    Weary and lone,
Darkness comes over me,
    My rest a stone;
Yet in my dreams I'd be
Nearer, my God, to thee,
    Nearer to thee!

3 There let my way appear
    Steps unto heaven;
All that thou sendest me
    In mercy given;
Angels to beckon me
Nearer, my God, to thee,
    Nearer to thee!

4 Then, with my waking thoughts
　　Bright with thy praise,
　Out of my stony griefs
　　Altars I'll raise;
So by my woes to be
Nearer, my God, to thee,
　　Nearer to thee!

5 Or, if on joyful wing,
　　Cleaving the sky,
　Sun, moon, and stars forgot,
　　Upward I fly,
Still all my song shall be
Nearer, my God, to thee,
　　Nearer to thee!

508   *"The heavens declare the glory of God."*   [L. M. Double.

THE spacious firmament on high,
　With all the blue ethereal sky,
And spangled heavens, a shining frame,
Their great Original proclaim.
The unwearied sun, from day to day,
Does his Creator's power display,
And publishes to every land
The work of an Almighty Hand.

2 Soon as the evening shades prevail,
　The moon takes up the wondrous tale,
And nightly to the listening earth
Repeats the story of her birth;

Whilst all the stars that round her burn,
And all the planets in their turn,
Confirm the tidings as they roll,
And spread the truth from pole to pole.

3 What though in solemn silence all
Move round this dark terrestrial ball;
What though no real voice nor sound
Amidst their radiant orbs be found;
In reason's ear they all rejoice,
And utter forth a glorious voice;
For ever singing, as they shine,
" The Hand that made us is divine."

509 *" Having a desire to depart, and to be with Christ,* [P. M. *which is far better."*

O PARADISE, O Paradise,
  Who doth not crave for rest,
Who would not seek the happy land
  Where they that loved are blest?
    Where loyal hearts and true
    Stand ever in the light,
All rapture through and through,
  In God's most holy sight.

2 O Paradise, O Paradise,
  The world is growing old;
Who would not be at rest and free
  Where love is never cold?
    Where loyal hearts and true, etc.

3 O Paradise, O Paradise,
 'Tis weary waiting here;
I long to be where Jesus is,
 To feel, to see him near;
  Where loyal hearts and true, etc.

4 O Paradise, O Paradise,
 I want to sin no more,
I want to be as pure on earth
 As on thy spotless shore;
  Where loyal hearts and true, etc.

5 O Paradise, O Paradise,
 I greatly long to see
The special place my dearest Lord
 In love prepares for me;
  Where loyal hearts and true, etc.

6 Lord Jesus, King of Paradise,
 O keep me in thy love,
And guide me to that happy land
 Of perfect rest above;
  Where loyal hearts and true,
   Stand ever in the light,
  All rapture through and through,
   In God's most holy sight.

510 "*In thee, O Lord, have I put my trust; let me* [C. M.
 never be put to confusion."
  From the lxxi. Psalm.

IN thee I put my steadfast trust,
 Defend me, Lord, from shame:
Incline thine ear, and save my soul,
 For righteous is thy name.

2 Be thou my strong abiding-place,
  To which I may resort:
Thy promise, Lord, is my defence,
  Thou art my rock and fort.

3 My steadfast and unchanging hope
  Shall on thy power depend;
And I in grateful songs of praise
  My time to come will spend.

4 While God vouchsafes me his support,
  I'll in his strength go on;
All other righteousness disclaim,
  And mention his alone.

5 Therefore, with psaltery and harp,
  Thy truth, O Lord, I'll praise;
To thee, the God of Jacob's race,
  My voice in anthems raise.

511 *"Behold we come unto thee: for thou art the Lord our God."* [8s. 7s. 8s.

ALMIGHTY God! I call to thee,
  By sore temptation shaken;
Incline thy gracious ear to me,
  And leave me not forsaken;
For who that feels the power within
Of past remorse and present sin,
  Can stand, O Lord, before thee?

2 On thee alone my stay I place,
  All human help rejecting;
Relying on thy sovereign grace,
  Thy sovereign aid expecting,

I rest upon thy sacred word,
That thou'lt repel him not, O Lord,
Who to thy mercy fleeth.

3 And though I travail all the night,
And travail all the morrow,
My trust is in Jehovah's might,
My triumph in my sorrow;
Forgetting not that thou of old
Didst Israel, though weak, uphold;
When weakest then most loving!

4 What though my sinfulness be great,
Redeeming love is greater;
What though all hell should lie in wait,
Supreme is my Creator;
And he my rock and fortress is,
And when most helpless, most I'm his,
My strength and my Redeemer.

512 *"In the day-time he also led them with a cloud,* [P. M.
*and all the night through with the light of
fire."*

LEAD, kindly Light, amid the encircling gloom,
Lead thou me on;
The night is dark, and I am far from home,
Lead thou me on.
Keep thou my feet; I do not ask to see
The distant scene; one step enough for me.

2 I was not ever thus, nor pray'd that thou
    Shouldst lead me on;
I loved to choose and see my path; but now
    Lead thou me on.
I loved the garish day; and, spite of fears,
Pride ruled my will: remember not past years.

3 So long thy power has blest me, sure it still
    Will lead me on
O'er moor and fen, o'er crag and torrent, till
    The night is gone,
And with the morn those angel faces smile,
Which I have loved long since, and lost awhile.

513   *"Let us labour to enter into that rest."*   [S. M.

O WHERE shall rest be found,
    Rest for the weary soul?
'Twere vain the ocean's depths to sound,
    Or pierce to either pole.

2 The world can never give
    The bliss for which we sigh:
'Tis not the whole of life to live,
    Nor all of death to die.

3 Beyond this vale of tears
    There is a life above,
Unmeasured by the flight of years;
    And all that life is love.

4 There is a death whose pang
    Outlasts the fleeting breath;
O what eternal horrors hang
    Around the second death!

5 Lord God of truth and grace,
   Teach us that death to shun,
Lest we be banished from thy face,
   And evermore undone.

514 *"If any man serve me, let him follow me; and* [P. M.
where I am, there shall also my servant be."

ART thou weary, art thou languid,
   Art thou sore distress'd?
"Come to me," saith One, "and coming,
   Be at rest."

2 Hath he marks to lead me to him,
   If he be my Guide?
"In his feet and hands are wound-prints,
   And his side."

3 Is there diadem, as Monarch,
   That his brow adorns?
"Yea, a crown, in very surety,
   But of thorns."

4 If I find him, if I follow,
   What his guerdon here?
"Many a sorrow, many a labour,
   Many a tear."

5 If I still hold closely to him,
   What hath he at last?
"Sorrow vanquish'd, labour ended,
   Jordan pass'd."

MISCELLANEOUS.

6 If I ask him to receive me,
    Will he say me nay?
"Not till earth, and not till heaven
    Pass away."

7 Finding, following, keeping, struggling,
    Is he sure to bless?
"Saints, apostles, prophets, martyrs,
    Answer, Yes."

515   *"Whom have I in heaven but thee?"*   [Six 8s.

THOU hidden love of God, whose height,
    Whose depth unfathom'd no man knows:
I see from far thy beauteous light,
    Inly I sigh for thy repose:
My heart is pain'd, nor can it be
At rest till it find rest in thee.

2 Is there a thing beneath the sun
    That strives with thee my heart to share?
Ah! tear it thence, and reign alone,
    The Lord of every motion there.
Then shall my heart from earth be free,
When it hath found repose in thee.

3 O hide this self from me, that I
    No more, but Christ in me, may live;
My vile affections crucify,
    Nor let one darling lust survive;
In all things nothing may I see,
Nothing desire, or seek, but thee.

4 Each moment draw from earth away
  My heart, that lowly waits thy call:
Speak to my inmost soul, and say,
  I am thy love, thy God, thy all:
To feel thy power, to hear thy voice,
To taste thy love, be all my choice.

516   *"O Lord, how manifold are thy works."*   [C. M.

THE Lord our God is clothed with might,
  The winds obey his will;
He speaks, and, in his heavenly height,
  The rolling sun stands still.

2 Rebel, ye waves, and o'er the land
    With threatening aspect roar;
  The Lord uplifts his awful hand,
    And chains you to the shore.

3 Howl, winds of night, your force combine;
    Without his high behest,
  Ye shall not, in the mountain pine,
    Disturb the sparrow's nest.

4 His voice sublime is heard afar,
    In distant peals it dies;
  He yokes the whirlwind to his car,
    And sweeps the howling skies.

Ye nations, bend, in reverence bend;
  Ye monarchs, wait his nod,
And bid the choral song ascend
  To celebrate your God.

517 "*O Lord, our Governor, how excellent is thy name in all the world.*" [C. M.

From the viii. Psalm.

O THOU to whom all creatures bow
   Within this earthly frame,
Through all the world how great art thou!
   How glorious is thy name!

2 In heaven thy wondrous acts are sung,
   Nor fully reckon'd there;
And yet thou mak'st the infant tongue
   Thy boundless praise declare.

3 When heaven, thy beauteous work on high,
   Employs my wondering sight;
The moon, that nightly rules the sky,
   With stars of feebler light;

4 O what is man, that, Lord, thou lov'st
   To keep him in thy mind?
Or what his offspring, that thou prov'st
   To them so wondrous kind?

5 O thou to whom all creatures bow
   Within this earthly frame,
Through all the world how great art thou!
   How glorious is thy name!

518 "*Be strong, and he shall establish your heart, all ye that put your trust in the Lord.*" [S. M.

From the xxxi. Psalm.

MY hope, my steadfast trust,
   I on thy help repose;
That thou, my God, art good and just,
   My soul with comfort knows.

MISCELLANEOUS.

2 Whate'er events betide,
 Thy wisdom times them all;
Then, Lord, thy servant safely hid
 From those that seek his fall.

3 The brightness of thy face
 To me, O Lord, disclose;
And as thy mercies still increase,
 Preserve me from my foes.

4 How great thy mercies are
 To such as fear thy name,
Which thou, for those that trust thy
 Dost to the world proclaim!

5 O all ye saints, the Lord
 With eager love pursue;
Who to the just will help afford,
 And give the proud their due.

6 Ye that on God rely,
 Courageously proceed;
For he will still your hearts supply
 With strength in time of need.

519 *"O Lord, my God, thou art very great; thou art clothed with honour and majesty."*

O WORSHIP the King,
 All glorious above;
O gratefully sing
 His power and his love;
Our Shield and Defender,
 The Ancient of days,
Pavilion'd in splendour,
 And girded with praise.

2 O tell of his might,
   O sing of his grace,
Whose robe is the light;
   Whose canopy, space;
His chariots of wrath
   Deep thunder-clouds form,
And dark is his path
   On the wings of the storm.

3 The earth, with its store
   Of wonders untold,
Almighty, thy power
   Hath founded of old—
Hath stablished it fast
   By a changeless decree,
And round it hath cast,
   Like a mantle, the sea.

4 Thy bountiful care
   What tongue can recite?
It breathes in the air,
   It shines in the light;
It streams from the hills;
   It descends to the plain,
And sweetly distils
   In the dew and the rain.

5 Frail children of dust,
   And feeble as frail,
In thee do we trust,
   Nor find thee to fail;
Thy mercies, how tender,
   How firm to the end,
Our Maker, Defender,
   Redeemer, and Friend!

6 O measureless might,
 Ineffable Love!
While angels delight
 To hymn thee above,
The ransomed creation,
 Though feeble their lays,
With true adoration
 Shall lisp to thy praise.

520 *"My soul thirsteth for thee, my flesh also longeth* [S. M
*after thee; in a barren and dry land where no
water is."*

FAR from my heavenly home;
 Far from my Father's breast,
Fainting I cry, blest Spirit, come,
 And speed me to my rest.

2 My spirit homeward turns,
 And fain would thither flee;
My heart, O Sion, droops and yearns,
 When I remember thee.

3 To thee, to thee I press,
 A dark and toilsome road;
When shall I pass the wilderness,
 And reach the saints' abode?

4 God of my life, be near:
 On thee my hopes I cast:
O guide me through the desert here,
 And bring me home at last.

521   *"Lovest thou me?"*   [7s.

HARK! my soul, it is the Lord;
'Tis thy Saviour, hear his word;
Jesus speaks, and speaks to thee—
Say, poor sinner, lovest thou me?

2 I delivered thee when bound,
And when wounded healed thy wound;
Sought thee wandering, set thee right,
Turned thy darkness into light.

3 Can a woman's tender care
Cease toward the child she bare?
Yes, she may forgetful be,
Yet will I remember thee.

4 Mine is an unchanging love,
Higher than the heights above,
Deeper than the depths beneath,
Free and faithful, strong as death.

5 Thou shalt see my glory soon,
When the work of grace is done;
Partner of my throne shalt be;
Say, poor sinner, lovest thou me?

6 Lord, it is my chief complaint,
That my love is weak and faint;
Yet I love thee and adore;
O for grace to love thee more!

MISCELLANEOUS.

522   *"The strength of my salvation."*   [L. M.

MY hope, my all, my Saviour thou!
To thee, lo! now my soul I bow;
I feel the bliss thy wounds impart,
I find thee, Saviour, in my heart.

2 Be thou my strength, be thou my way,
Protect me thro' my life's short day;
In all my acts may wisdom guide
And keep me, Saviour, near thy side.

3 Correct, reprove, and comfort me;
As I have need, my Saviour be;
And if I should from thee depart,
Then clasp me, Saviour, to thy heart.

4 In fierce temptation's darkest hour
Save me from sin and Satan's power;
Tear every idol from thy throne,
And reign, my Saviour, reign alone.

523   *"My times are in thy hand."*   [7s.

SOVEREIGN ruler of the skies,
Ever gracious, ever wise,
All our times are in thy hand,
All events at thy command.

2 He that form'd us in the womb,
He shall guide us to the tomb;
All our ways shall ever be
Order'd by his wise decree.

3 Times of sickness, times of health,
    Blighting want and cheerful wealth,
    All our pleasures, all our pains,
    Come, and end, as God ordains.

4 May we always own thy hand,
    Still to thee surrender'd stand,
    Know that thou art God alone,
    We and ours are all thy own!

524 *"As the waters fail from the sea, and the flood* [S. M.
*decayeth and drieth up; so man lieth down,
and riseth not: till the heavens be no more,
they shall not awake, nor be raised out of
their sleep."*

THE mighty flood that rolls
    Its torrents to the main,
Can ne'er recall its waters lost
    From that abyss again;

2 So days, and years, and time,
    Descending down to night,
Can thenceforth never more return
    Back to the sphere of light:

3 And man, when in the grave,
    Can never quit its gloom,
Until th' eternal morn shall wake
    The slumber of the tomb.

4 O may I find in death
    A hiding-place with God,
Secure from woe and sin, till call'd
    To share his blest abode.

5 Cheer'd by this hope, I wait,
    Through toil, and care, and grief,
Till my appointed course is run,
    And death shall bring relief.

525   *"Strive to enter in at the straight gate."*   [7s

SEEK, my soul, the narrow gate,
    Enter ere it be too late;
Many ask to enter there
    When too late to offer prayer.

2 God from mercy's seat shall rise,
    And forever bar the skies:
Then, though sinners cry without,
    He will say, "I know you not."

3 Mournfully will they exclaim:
    "Lord, we have professed thy Name;
We have ate with thee, and heard
    Heavenly teaching in thy word."

4 Vain, alas, will be their plea,
    Workers of iniquity;
Sad their everlasting lot;
    Christ will say, "I know you not."

526   *"Thanks be to God, which giveth us the victory,* [6s. 11s.
    through our Lord Jesus Christ."

THY bitter anguish o'er,
    To this dark tomb they bore
Thee, Life of life—thee, Lord of all creation!

The hollow, rocky cave,
Must serve thee for a grave,
Who wast thyself the rock of our salvation!

2 O Prince of Life! I know
That when I too lie low,
Thou wilt at last my soul from death awaken:
Wherefore I will not shrink
From the grave's awful brink;
The heart that trusts in thee shall ne'er be shaken.

3 To me the darksome tomb
Is but a narrow room,
Where I may rest in peace, from sorrow free.
Thy death shall give me power
To cry in that dark hour,
O Death! O Grave! where is your victory?

4 My Jesus, day by day
Help me to watch and pray
Beside the tomb wherein, my heart, thou'rt laid.
Thy bitter death shall be
My constant memory,
My guide at last into death's awful shade.

527 *"And now abideth faith, hope, charity, these three:* [7s.
but the greatest of these is charity."

GRACIOUS Spirit, Holy Ghost,
Taught by thee we covet most
Of thy gifts at Pentecost
Holy, heavenly Love.

2 Love is kind, and suffers long,
 Love is meek, and thinks no wrong,
 Love than death itself more strong;
  Therefore, give us Love.

3 Prophecy will fade away,
 Melting in the light of day;
 Love will ever with us stay;
  Therefore, give us Love.

4 Faith will vanish into sight;
 Hope be emptied in delight;
 Love in heaven will shine more bright;
  Therefore, give us Love.

5 Faith and Hope and Love we see
 Joining hand in hand agree;
 But the greatest of the three,
  And the best, is Love.

6 From the overshadowing
 Of thy gold and silver wing,
 Shed on us, who to thee sing,
  Holy, heavenly Love.

528 *"He that cometh to me shall never hunger, and* [8s. 6s
 he that believeth in me shall never thirst."

I HEARD the voice of Jesus say,
  "Come unto me and rest;
 Lay down, thou weary one, lay down
  Thy head upon my breast:"

I came to Jesus as I was,
　　Weary, and worn, and sad;
I found in him a resting-place,
　　And he has made me glad.

2 I heard the voice of Jesus say,
　　"Behold I freely give
The living water, thirsty one,
　　Stoop down, and drink, and live:"
I came to Jesus, and I drank
　　Of that life-giving stream;
My thirst was quenched, my soul revived,
　　And now I live in him.

3 I heard the voice of Jesus say,
　　"I am this dark world's Light;
Look unto me, thy morn shall rise,
　　And all thy day be bright:"
I looked to Jesus, and I found
　　In him my Star, my Sun;
And in that Light of life I'll walk
　　Till traveling days are done.

529 *"Praise the Lord, O my soul; and all that is within me praise his Holy Name."* [8s. 7s.

PRAISE, my soul, the King of heaven;
　　To his feet thy tribute bring,
Ransomed, healed, restored, forgiven,
　　Evermore his praises sing,
　　　Alleluia! Alleluia!
　　Praise the everlasting King.

2 Praise him for his grace and favour
    To our fathers in distress;
Praise him still the same as ever,
    Slow to chide, and swift to bless;
      Alleluia! Alleluia!
    Glorious in his faithfulness.

3 Father-like he tends and spares us,
    Well our feeble frame he knows;
In his hands he gently bears us,
    Rescues us from all our foes;
      Alleluia! Alleluia!
    Widely yet his mercy flows.

4 Angels in the height adore him!
    Ye behold him face to face;
Saints triumphant bow before him!
    Gathered in from every race.
      Alleluia! Alleluia!
    Praise with us the God of grace.

530 *"These confessed that they were strangers and pilgrims on the earth."* [8s. 7s.

GUIDE me, O thou great Jehovah,
    Pilgrim through this barren land,
I am weak, but thou art mighty;
    Hold me with thy powerful hand.

2 Open now the crystal fountains
    Whence the living waters flow;
Let the fiery, cloudy pillar
    Lead me all my journey through.

3 Feed me with the heavenly manna
   In this barren wilderness;
Be my sword, and shield, and banner;
   Be the Lord my righteousness.

4 When I tread the verge of Jordan,
   Bid my anxious fears subside;
Death of death, and hell's destruction,
   Land me safe on Canaan's side.

531   *"I will put thee in a clift of the rock."*   [SIX 7s

ROCK of Ages, cleft for me,
   Let me hide myself in thee;
Let the water and the blood,
From thy side, a healing flood,
Be of sin the double cure,
Save from wrath, and make me pure.

2 Should my tears forever flow,
Should my zeal no languor know,
This for sin could not atone,
Thou must save, and thou alone;
In my hand no price I bring,
Simply to thy cross I cling.

3 While I draw this fleeting breath,
When mine eyelids close in death,
When I rise to worlds unknown,
And behold thee on thy throne,
Rock of Ages, cleft for me,
Let me hide myself in thee.

532   *"I flee unto thee to hide me."*   [7s. Double.

JESUS, Saviour of my soul,
  Let me to thy bosom fly,
While the waves of trouble roll,
  While the tempest still is high:
Hide me, O my Saviour, hide,
  Till the storm of life is past;
Safe into the haven guide;
  Oh, receive my soul at last.

2 Other refuge have I none,
  Hangs my helpless soul on thee:
Leave, ah, leave me not alone,
  Still support and comfort me:
All my trust on thee is stay'd,
  All my hope from thee I bring;
Cover my defenceless head
  With the shadow of thy wing.

GLORIA PATRI.

L. M.

PRAISE God from Whom all blessings flow:
  Praise Him all creatures here below;
Praise Him above, ye heavenly host;
Praise Father, Son, and Holy Ghost.   Amen.

L. M.

TO Father, Son, and Holy Ghost,
  The God Whom earth and heaven adore,
Be glory, as it was of old,
  Is now, and shall be evermore.   'Amen.

C. M.

TO Father, Son, and Holy Ghost,
  The God Whom we adore,
Be glory, as it was, is now,
  And shall be evermore.   Amen.

D. C. M.

TO praise the Father, and the Son,
  And Spirit all-divine,—
The One in Three, and Three in One
  Let saints and angels join;—
Glory to Thee, bless'd Three in One,
  The God Whom we adore,
As was, and is, and shall be done,
  When time shall be no more.   Amen.

GLORIA PATRI.

S. M.

TO God the Father, Son,
 And Spirit, glory be,
As 'twas, and is, and shall be so
 To all eternity. Amen.

D. S. M.

PRAISE as in ages past,
 Praise as in glory now,
Praise while eternity shall last,
 To Thee, O God, we vow;
Whom all the heavenly host
 And saints on earth adore;
To Father, Son, and Holy Ghost
 Be glory evermore. Amen.

8s. 6s.

TO Father, Son, and Holy Ghost,
 The God Whom heaven's triumphant host
And saints on earth adore,
Be glory as in ages past,
As now it is, and so shall last
 When time shall be no more. Amen.

Six 8s.

TO God the Father, God the Son,
 And God the Spirit, Three in One,
Be glory in the highest given,
By all in earth, and all in heaven,
As was through ages heretofore,
Is now, and shall be evermore. Amen.

Six 8s.

TO Father, Son, and Holy Ghost,
  The God Whom heaven's triumphant host
And suffering saints on earth adore,
Be glory as in ages past,
As now it is, and so shall last
  When time itself shall be no more. Amen.

8s. 7s. 8s.

TO Father, Son, and Spirit bless'd,
  Supreme o'er earth and heaven.
Eternal Three in One confess'd,
  Be highest glory given,
As was through ages heretofore,
Is now, and shall be evermore,
  By all in earth and heaven. Amen.

7s.

HOLY Father, Holy Son,
  Holy Spirit, Three in One!
Glory, as of old, to Thee,
Now, and evermore shall be! Amen.

Six 7s.

PRAISE the Name of God most high,
  Praise Him, all below the sky,
Praise Him, all ye heavenly host,
Father, Son, and Holy Ghost;
As through countless ages past,
Evermore His praise shall last. Amen.

GLORIA PATRI.

7s. DOUBLE.

HOLY Father, fount of light,
  God of wisdom, goodness, might;
Holy Son, Who cam'st to dwell,
  God with us, Emmanuel;
Holy Spirit, heavenly Dove,
  God of comfort, peace, and love;
Evermore be Thou adored,
  Holy, Holy, Holy Lord.   Amen.

N. B.—For metre Ten 7s. begin this doxology by prefixing the last two lines, thus:—

    Holy, Holy, Holy Lord,
    Evermore be Thou adored,
    Holy Father, etc.

8s. 7s.

PRAISE the Father, earth and heaven,
  Praise the Son, the Spirit praise,
As it was, and is, be given
  Glory through eternal days.   Amen.

8s. 7s. DOUBLE.

LET the voice of all creation,
  Earth and heaven's triumphant host,
Praise the God of our salvation,
  Father, Son, and Holy Ghost.
See the heavenly elders casting
  Golden crowns before His throne:
Alleluias everlasting
  Be to Him, and Him alone.   Amen.

GLORIA PATRI.

8s. 7s. 4.

GREAT Jehovah! we adore Thee,
  God the Father, God the Son,
God the Spirit, join'd in glory
  On the same eternal throne:
    Endless praises
  To Jehovah, Three in One.   Amen.

8s. 7s. 7s.

TO the Father, throned in heaven,
  To the Saviour, Christ, His Son,
To the Spirit, praise be given,
  Everlasting Three in One:
As of old, the Trinity
Still is worshipped, still shall be.   Amen.

10s.

TO God the Father, and to God the Son,
  To God the Holy Spirit, Three in One,
Be praise from all on earth and all in heaven,
As was, and is, and ever shall be given.   Amen.

5s. 6s. 5.

BY angels in heaven
  Of every degree,
And saints upon earth,
  All praise be address'd,
To God in Three Persons,
  One God ever bless'd;
As it has been, now is,
  And always shall be.   **Amen.**

GLORIA PATRI.

6s.

TO Father, and to Son,
   And Holy Ghost, to Thee,
Eternal Three in One,
   Eternal glory be. Amen.

6s. DOUBLE.

TO Father and to Son,
   And, Holy Ghost, to Thee,
Eternal Three in One,
   Eternal glory be;
As hath been, and is now,
   And shall be evermore:
Before Thy throne we bow,
   And Thee our God adore. Amen.

7s. 6s. DOUBLE.

O FATHER ever glorious,
   O everlasting Son,
O Spirit all victorious,
   Thrice Holy Three in One,—
Great God of our salvation,
   Whom earth and heaven adore,
Praise, glory, adoration,
   Be Thine for evermore. Amen.

6s. 4s.

TO Father and to Son
   And Spirit, Three in One,
   All praise be given,
As hath been heretofore
And shall be evermore:
Let all His Name adore
   In earth and heaven. Amen.

8s. 6s. 4.

TO Father, Son, and Spirit, praise
   From earth and heaven ascend:
The loftiest notes that saints can raise
   World without end. Amen.

7s. 5.

HOLY Father, Holy Son,
   Holy Spirit, Three in One,
Alleluias round Thy throne
   Rise eternally. Amen.

6s. 4s. or 6s. 8s.

TO God the Father, Son,
   And Spirit, ever bless'd,
Eternal Three in One,
   All worship be address'd,
     As heretofore
      It was, is now,
     And shall be so
For evermore. Amen.

6s. 5s.

GLORY to the Father,
   Glory to the Son,
And to Thee, blest Spirit,
   Whilst all ages run. Amen.

8s. 4s.

FATHER, Son, and Holy Spirit,
   Thou One in Three,
Praise to Thine eternal merit,
   All praise to Thee:

GLORIA PATRI.

From the morning of creation,
From the tribes of every nation,
Glory, power, and adoration,
   Thine ever be. Amen.

8s. 6.

O HOLY Father, Holy Son,
   And Holy Spirit, Three in One,
As was, and is, and shall be done,
   Glory to Thee, O Lord. Amen.

8s. 7s.

LAUD and honour to the Father,
   Laud and honour to the Son,
Laud and honour to the Spirit,
   Ever Three and ever One,
Consubstantial, Co-eternal,
   While unending ages run. Amen.

8s.

ALL praise to the Father, the Son,
   And Spirit, thrice holy and bless'd,
Th' eternal, supreme Three in One,
   Was, is, and shall still be address'd. Amen.

11s.

O FATHER Almighty, to Thee be address'd,
   With Christ and the Spirit, One God ever bless'd,
All glory and worship from earth and from heaven,
As was, and is now, and shall ever be given. Amen.

GLORIA PATRI.

COME, let us adore Him; come, bow at His feet;
 O give Him the glory, the praise that is meet;
Let joyful hosannas unceasing arise,
And join the full chorus that gladdens the skies.
Amen.

INDEX OF FIRST LINES.

	HYMN.
A charge to keep I have	474
A few more years shall roll	28
A glory gilds the sacred page	365
A mountain fastness is our God	397
Abide with me; fast falls the eventide	335
According to thy gracious word	211
Adored for ever be the Lord	421
Again the Lord of life and light	156
Ah, how shall fallen man	382
Ah, not like erring man is God	379
All glorious God, what hymns of praise	371
All glory, laud, and honour	72
All hail the power of Jesus' name	424
All is o'er, the pain, the sorrow	92
All people that on earth do dwell	405
Alleluia, song of gladness	430
Almighty Father, bless the word	166
Almighty God, I call to thee	511
Almighty Lord, before thy throne	311
Although the vine its fruit deny	442
Am I a soldier of the cross	471
And are we now brought near to God	206
Angel bands, in strains sweet sounding	433
Angels, from the realms of glory	24

INDEX OF FIRST LINES.

	HYMN.
Angels, roll the rock away	101
Another six days' work is done	153
Approach, my soul, the mercy seat	399
Arise, my soul, with rapture rise	328
Arm of the Lord, awake, awake	287
Arm these thy soldiers, mighty Lord	242
Art thou weary, art thou languid	514
As by the light of opening day	246
As now the sun's declining rays	358
As o'er the past my memory strays	61
As, panting in the sultry beam	452
As pants the hart for cooling streams	451
As pants the wearied hart for cooling springs	155
As the sweet flower that scents the morn	262
As, when the weary traveller gains	450
As with gladness men of old	45
Asleep in Jesus, blessèd sleep	260
At the Lamb's high feast we sing	100
Awake, and sing the song	463
Awake, my soul, and with the sun	332
Awake, my soul, stretch every nerve	476
Awake, my soul, to joyful lays	429
Awake, our souls! away our fears	473
Awake, ye saints, awake	148
Before Jehovah's awful throne	409
Before the ending of the day	359
Before the Lord we bow	307
Begin, my soul, the exalted lay	419
Behold a humble train	180
Behold the glories of the Lamb	123
Behold the Lamb of God	80

INDEX OF FIRST LINES.

	HYMN.
Behold the morning sun	364
Behold the Saviour of mankind	378
Be still, my heart, these anxious cares	249
Bless God, my soul; thou, Lord, alone	410
Blest be the tie that binds	315
Blest day of God! most calm, most bright	149
Bound upon the accursèd tree	82
Bread of heaven, on thee we feed	209
Bread of the world, in mercy broken	207
Breast the wave, Christian	472
Brief life is here our portion	491
Brightest and best of the sons of the morning	37
By cool Siloam's shady rill	224
Calm on the listening ear of night	26
Children of the heavenly King	449
Christ is made the sure foundation	282
Christ is our corner-stone	279
Christ leads me through no darker rooms	486
Christ the Lord is risen again	106
Christ the Lord is risen to-day	98
Christ, whose glory fills the skies	331
Christian! dost thou see them	68
Christians, awake, salute the happy morn	21
Come, gracious Spirit, heavenly Dove	131
Come hither, ye faithful	25
Come, Holy Ghost, Creator, come	127
Come, Holy Ghost, eternal God	274
Come, Holy Ghost, our souls inspire	137
Come, Holy Ghost, with God the Son	355
Come, Holy Spirit, come	135
Come, Holy Spirit, heavenly Dove	128

INDEX OF FIRST LINES

	HYMN.
Come let us join our cheerful songs	208
Come, let us join our friends above	188
Come, my soul, thou must be waking	330
Come, my soul, thy suit prepare	401
Come pure hearts, in sweetest measures	272
Come, quickly come, dread Judge of all	9
Come see the place where Jesus lay	102
Come, thou Almighty King	428
Come ye that love the Lord	462
Come, ye sinners, poor and needy	381
Come, ye thankful people, come	306
Creator Spirit, by whose aid	129
Crown him with many crowns	116
Dawn purples all the East with light	354
Day of judgment, day of wonders	481
Day of wrath! that day of mourning	483
Deign this union to approve	247
Draw, Holy Ghost, thy seven-fold veil	240
Dread Jehovah, God of nations	310
Dismiss us with thy blessing, Lord	167
Disown'd of heaven, by man oppress'd	294
Eternal Father! strong to save	267
Far from my heavenly home	520
Far from my thoughts, vain world, begone	161
Father of all, whose love profound	142
Father of mercies, bow thine ear	271
Father of mercies! in thy word	360
Father, whate'er of earthly bliss	440
Fierce was the wild billow	265
For all the saints who from their labours rest	187

INDEX OF FIRST LINES.

	HYMN.
For ever here my rest shall be	396
For ever with the Lord	489
For the Apostles' glorious company	186
For thee, O dear, dear country	492
For thee, O God, our constant praise	407
Forth from the dark and stormy sky	201
Forth in thy name, O Lord, I go	318
Forty days and forty nights	49
Fountain of good, to own thy love	296
From all that dwell below the skies	289
From all thy saints in warfare, etc	175
From every stormy wind that blows	403
From Greenland's icy mountains	283
Glorious things of thee are spoken	190
Glory be to Jesus	74
Glory to the Father give	220
Glory to thee, my God, this night	333
Glory to thee, O Lord	179
Go forth, ye heralds, in my name	273
Go to dark Gethsemane	86
God bless our native land	309
God is our refuge in distress	194
God moves in a mysterious way	502
God, my King, thy might confessing	423
God of my life, O Lord most high	94
God of my life, to thee I call	446
God of our fathers, by whose hand	326
God shall charge his angel legions	469
God that madest earth and heaven	344
God's perfect law converts the soul	363
God's temple crowns the holy mount	193

INDEX OF FIRST LINES.

HYMN.

Grace! 'tis a charming sound	376
Gracious Spirit, Holy Ghost	527
Great God, this sacred day of thine	151
Great God, to thee my evening song	343
Great God, what do I see and hear	484
Great God, with wonder and with praise	367
Great is our guilt, our fears are great	174
Guide me, O thou great Jehovah (Pr. Bk. ver. 530)	505
Hail, thou long-expected Jesus	16
Hail, thou once despisèd Jesus	76
Hail to the Lord's Anointed	34
Happy, thrice happy they, who hear	503
Hark! hark, my soul! Angelic songs are swelling	485
Hark! my soul, it is the Lord	521
Hark! the glad sound! the Saviour comes	15
Hark! the herald angels sing	17
Hark! the song of jubilee	42
Hark! the sound of holy voices	189
Hark! the voice of love and mercy	88
Hark! what mean those holy voices	20
Hasten, sinner! to be wise	58
Hasten the time appointed	296
Have mercy, Lord, on me	60
He is risen! he is risen!	107
He that has God his guardian made	319
Head of the hosts in glory	198
Hear what the voice from heaven declares	259
Heirs of unending life	479
He's blest, whose sins have pardon gained	377
He's come, let every knee be bent	125
High on the bending willows hung	295

INDEX OF FIRST LINES.

	HYMN.
His mercy and his truth	243
Holy Father, great Creator	145
Holy, holy, holy Lord	140
Holy, holy, holy Lord	144
Holy, holy, holy! Lord God Almighty	138
Hosanna to the living Lord	4
How beauteous are their feet	44
How bless'd are they who always keep	221
How bright these glorious spirits shine	177
How firm a foundation, ye saints of the Lord	398
How long shall earth's alluring toys	487
How oft alas! this wretched heart	56
How sweet the name of Jesus sounds	395
How vast must their advantage be	185
How will my heart endure	482
How wondrous and great	35
I heard the voice of Jesus say	528
I love my God, but with no love of mine	457
I love thy kingdom, Lord	191
I sing the almighty power of God	417
I think when I read that sweet story of old	226
I would not live alway; I ask not to stay	93
I'll praise my Maker with my breath	420
I'll wash my hands in innocence	278
In loud exalted strains	152
In mercy, not in wrath	50
In the hour of trial	443
In the vineyard of our Father	227
In thee I put my steadfast trust	510
In token that thou shalt not fear	214
Inspirer and Hearer of prayer	339

INDEX OF FIRST LINES.

	HYMN.
Instruct me in thy statutes, Lord	368
Is there a lone and dreary hour	444
It came upon the midnight clear	22
It is not death to die	97
Jehovah reigns, let all the earth	418
Jerusalem! high tow'r thy glorious walls	497
Jerusalem, my happy home	496
Jerusalem, the golden	493
Jesus, meek and gentle	225
Jesus, the very thought of thee	455
Jesus, and shall it ever be	218
Jesus Christ is risen to-day	99
Jesus, I my cross have taken	236
Jesus lives: no longer now	104
Jesus, lover of my soul	393
Jesus, my strength, my hope	434
Jesus, my Saviour, look on me	394
Jesus! Name of wondrous love	33
Jesus, Saviour of my soul	532
Jesus shall reign where'er the sun	284
Jesus, tender Shepherd, hear me	352
Jesus, thy blood and righteousness	480
Joy fills the dwelling of the just	112
Joy to the world! the Lord is come	40
Just as I am,—without one plea	392
Lead, kindly Light, amid the encircling gloom	512
Lead us, heavenly Father, lead us	506
Let me with light and truth be bless'd	162
Lift up your heads, eternal gates	121
Lift your glad voices in triumph on high	108

	HYMN.
Light of those whose dreary dwelling	39
Like Noah's weary dove	195
Lo, he comes, with clouds descending	1
Lo! hills and mountains shall bring forth	38
Lo! what a cloud of witnesses	183
Look, ye saints; the sight is glorious	115
Lord, as to thy dear cross we flee	251
Lord, dismiss us with thy blessing	165
Lord, for ever at thy side	466
Lord, for the just thou dost prepare	269
Lord God, the Holy Ghost	130
Lord God, we worship thee	308
Lord! in the morning thou shalt hear	154
Lord, in this thy mercy's day	63
Lord, in thy name thy servants plead	172
Lord, lead the way the Saviour went	300
Lord, let me know my term of days	258
Lord of the harvest, hear	170
Lord of the worlds above	157
Lord, pour thy spirit from on high	270
Lord, shall thy children come to thee	241
Lord, spare and save our sinful race	173
Lord, teach us how to pray aright	400
Lord, when this holy morning broke	351
Lord, when we bend before thy throne	69
Lord, with glowing heart I'd praise thee	454
Love divine, all love excelling	456
Magnify Jehovah's name	408
May God accept our vow	244
May the grace of Christ our Saviour	168
My faith looks up to thee	237

INDEX OF FIRST LINES.

	HYMN.
My God, accept my heart this day	234
My God, and is thy table spread	205
My God, how endless is thy love	324
My God, how wonderful thou art	460
My God, I love thee not because	458
My God, my Father, while I stray	256
My God, permit me not to be	57
My God! thy covenant of love	217
My grateful soul shall bless the Lord	95
My hope, my all, my Saviour thou	522
My hope, my steadfast trust	518
My opening eyes with rapture see	158
My Saviour hanging on the tree	75
My sins, my sins, my Saviour	64
My soul be on thy guard	470
My soul, for help on God rely	439
My soul, inspired with sacred love	499
My soul with patience waits	55
Nearer, my God, to thee	507
New every morning is the love	329
No change of time shall ever shock	437
Not for the dead in Christ we weep	261
Not to the terrors of the Lord	184
Now from the altar of our hearts	347
Now may he who from the dead	164
Now may the God of grace and power	313
Now thank we all our God	303
O all ye people, clap your hands	120
O bless the Lord, my soul	413
O come, all ye faithful	19

INDEX OF FIRST LINES.

	HYMN.
O come and mourn with me awhile	89
O come, loud anthems let us sing	301
O come, O come, Emmanuel	13
O could I speak the matchless worth	374
O day of rest and gladness	160
O for a closer walk with God	435
O for a heart to praise my God	467
O God! creation's secret force	357
O God, my gracious God, to thee	320
O God, my heart is fix'd, 'tis bent	414
O God of hosts, the mighty Lord	245
O God of love, O King of peace	312
O God of truth, O Lord of might	356
O God, our help in ages past	29
O gracious God, in whom I live	66
O happy day, that stays my choice	235
O happy is the man who hears	222
O holy, holy, holy Lord	139
O in the morn of life, when youth	215
O Jesus, thou art standing	10
O Jesus, Saviour of the lost	388
O let triumphant faith dispel	390
O Lord of hosts, whose glory fills	276
O Lord, the Holy Innocents	178
O Lord, thy mercy, my sure hope	498
O mother dear, Jerusalem	495
O Paradise, O Paradise	509
O praise the Lord in that blest place	412
O praise ye the Lord	406
O render thanks to God above	416
O sacred Head, now wounded	87
O Spirit of the living God	125

INDEX OF FIRST LINES.

                                                                                 HYMN

O that my load of sin were gone	389
O thou, from whom all goodness flows	65
O thou that hear'st when sinners cry	386
O thou to whom all creatures bow	517
O thou to whose all-searching sight	62
O thou who didst prepare	268
O to grace how great a debtor	385
O 'twas a joyful sound to hear	281
O where shall rest be found	513
O with due reverence let us all	280
O Wisdom! spreading mightily,	
O Root of Jesse! Ensign thou,	
O Israel's Sceptre! David's Key, Advent	14
O Day-Spring and Eternal Light, Anthems,	
O King! Desire of nations! come,	
O Lawgiver! Emmanuel! King,	
O Word of God Incarnate	362
O worship the King	519
O write upon my memory, Lord	228
O'er mountain-tops the mount of God	41
O'er the gloomy hills of darkness	288
Oft in danger, oft in woe	477
On Jordan's bank the Baptist's cry	12
On Sion and on Lebanon	286
One sole baptismal sign	197
Once in royal David's city	233
Once more, O Lord, thy sign shall be	8
Once more the solemn season calls	48
Once the angel started back	111
Onward, Christian soldiers	232
Our blest Redeemer, ere he breathed	132
Our Lord is risen from the dead	117

INDEX OF FIRST LINES.

HYMN.

Pain and toil are over now	91
Peace, troubled soul, whose plaintive moan	375
Pleasant are thy courts above	200
Praise, my soul, the King of heaven	529
Praise, O praise our God and King	305
Praise to God, immortal praise	302
Praise to God who reigns above	182
Praise we the Lord this day	181
Prayer is the soul's sincere desire	404
Quiet, Lord, my froward heart	465
Rejoice, rejoice, believers	5
Resting from his work to-day	90
Rich are the joys which cannot die	297
Ride on! ride on in majesty	73
Rise, crown'd with light, imperial Salem, rise	36
Rise, my soul, and stretch thy wings	447
Rock of Ages, cleft for me (Pr. Book ver. 531)	391
Round the Lord in glory seated	431
Ruler of Israel, Lord of might, Advent Anthem.	14
Safely through another week	350
Salvation doth to God belong	304
Salvation! O the joyful sound	369
Saviour, again to thy dear name we raise	169
Saviour, like a shepherd lead us	229
Saviour, source of every blessing	370
Saviour, when in dust to thee	53
Saviour, when night involves the skies	325
Saviour, who thy flock art feeding	213
See the destined day arise	81
Seek, my soul, the narrow gate	525

INDEX OF FIRST LINES.

	HYMN.
Shepherd divine, our wants relieve	402
Shepherd of souls, refresh and bless	210
Shout the glad tidings, exultingly sing	23
Since I've known a Saviour's name	478
Sing Alleluia forth in duteous praise	432
Sing, my soul, his wondrous love	373
Sinner, rouse thee from thy sleep	59
Sinners! turn, why will ye die	54
Softly now the light of day	340
Soldiers of Christ, arise	216
Songs of praise the angels sang	422
Sons of men, behold from far	47
Souls in heathen darkness lying	292
Sovereign ruler of the skies	523
Sow in the morn thy seed	298
Spirit of mercy, truth, and love	133
Stand up, my soul, shake off thy fears	124
Star of peace, to wanderers weary	264
Stay, thou long-suffering Spirit, stay	387
Sun of my soul, thou Saviour dear	336
Supreme in wisdom as in power	475
Sweet is the work, my God, my King	150
Sweet Saviour, bless us ere we go	338
Sweet the moments, rich in blessing	84
Tender Shepherd, thou hast still'd	263
That day of wrath, that dreadful day	3
The ancient law departs	32
The atoning work is done	118
The Church's one foundation	202
The day is gently sinking to a close	349
The day is past and gone	334

INDEX OF FIRST LINES. 499

	HYMN.
The day is past and over	341
The day of praise is done	346
The day of resurrection	105
The gentle Saviour calls	212
The Head, that once was crowned with thorns	114
The God of Abraham praise	141
The God of life, whose constant care	30
The heavens declare thy glory, Lord	361
The King of love my Shepherd is	464
The Lord descended from above	500
The Lord hath spoke, the mighty God	11
The Lord himself, the mighty Lord	438
The Lord my pasture shall prepare	504
The Lord our God is clothed with might	516
The Lord, the only God, is great	196
The Lord unto my Lord thus spake	6
The Lord will come; the earth shall quake	2
The mighty flood that rolls	524
The rising God forsakes the tomb	119
The royal banners forward go	79
The servants of Jehovah's will	122
The shadows of the evening hours	337
The Son of God goes forth to war	176
The spacious firmament on high	508
The Spirit in our hearts	134
The strain upraise of joy and praise	425
The strife is o'er, the battle done	103
The sun is sinking fast	345
The voice of free grace	384
The voice that breathed o'er Eden	248
The wingèd herald of the day	353
The world is very evil	490

INDEX OF FIRST LINES.

	HYMN.
Thee will I love, my strength, my tower	461
There is a blessèd home	317
There is a fold whence none can stray	468
There is a fountain fill'd with blood	383
There is a green hill far away	231
There is a land of pure delight	488
Thine for ever:—God of love	238
This is the day of light	159
This life's a dream, an empty show	96
This stone to thee in faith we lay	275
Thou art gone up on high	113
Thou art my hiding-place, O Lord	253
Thou art the Way, to thee alone	501
Thou, God, all glory, honour, power	203
Thou hidden love of God, whose height	515
Thou, Lord, by strictest search hast known	52
Thou, whom my soul admires above	459
Thou, whose almighty word	146
Through all the changing scenes of life	415
Through the day thy love has spared us	342
Thus God declares his sovereign will	110
Thy bitter anguish o'er	526
Thy chastening wrath, O Lord, restrain	51
Thy kingdom come, O God	7
Thy presence, Lord, hath me supplied	448
Thy way, not mine, O Lord	254
Thy word is to my feet a lamp	366
Time hastens on: ye longing saints	348
'Tis finished: so the Saviour cried	85
'Tis my happiness below	445
To bless thy chosen race	285
To hail thy rising, Sun of life	27

INDEX OF FIRST LINES. 501

	HYMN.
To him who for our sins was slain	109
To Jesus, our exalted Lord	204
To our Redeemer's glorious name	372
To Sion's hill I lift my eyes	316
To thy temple I repair	163
To-morrow, Lord, is thine	327
Triumphant Sion! lift thy head	192
Up to the hills I lift mine eyes	321
Watchman! tell us of the night	43
We build with fruitless cost, unless	322
We give immortal praise	143
We give thee but thine own	299
We sing the praise of him who died	78
Weary of earth, and laden with my sin	67
Weary of wandering from my God	70
Welcome, sweet day of rest	147
What a strange and wondrous story	223
Whate'er my God ordains is right	257
When all thy mercies, O my God	426
When gathering clouds around I view	250
When God of old came down from heaven	136
When his salvation bringing	219
When I can read my title clear	453
When I can trust my all with God	323
When I survey the wondrous cross	83
When Jesus left his Father's throne	230
When, Lord, to this our western land	293
When, marshall'd on the nightly plain	46
When musing sorrow weeps the past	255
When our heads are bowed with woe	252

INDEX OF FIRST LINES.

HYMN.

When streaming from the eastern skies 314
When through the torn sail the wild tempest, etc. . 266
When wounded sore, the stricken soul 380
While shepherds watch'd their flocks by night 18
While thee I seek, protecting Power 441
While with ceaseless course the sun 31
Who are these in bright array 494
Who is this that comes from Edom 77
Who place on Sion's God their trust 436
With broken heart and contrite sigh 71
With glory clad, with strength arrayed 427
With joy shall I behold the day 199
With one consent let all the earth 277
Witness, ye men and angels, now 239

Ye boundless realms of joy 411
Ye Christian heralds, go, proclaim 290
Ye servants of the Lord 171

THE NEW YORK PUBLIC LIBRARY
REFERENCE DEPARTMENT

This book is under no circumstances to be taken from the Building

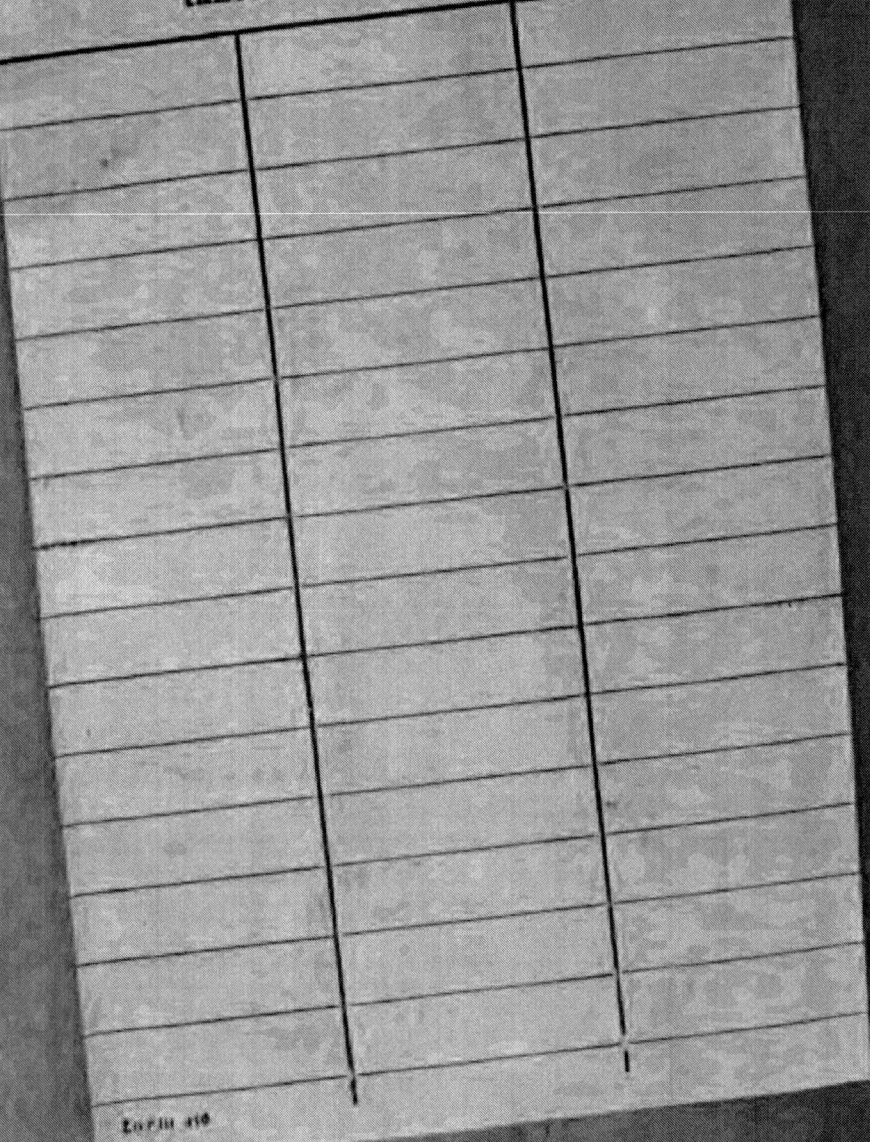